ABOUT FACE

ABOUT

How I Stumbled onto
Japan's Social Revolution

FACE

CLAYTON NAFF

KODANSHA INTERNATIONAL
New York • Tokyo • London

Kodansha America, Inc.
114 Fifth Avenue, New York, New York 10011, U.S.A.

Kodansha International Ltd.
17-14 Otowa 1-chome, Bunkyo-ku, Tokyo 112, Japan

Published in 1994 by Kodansha America, Inc.

Printed in the United States of America

94 95 96 97 98 99 7 6 5 4 3 2 1

Library of Congress Cataloging-in-Publication Data
Naff, Clayton, 1956–
    About face : how I stumbled onto Japan's social revolution / by
Clayton Naff.
        p.   cm.
    Includes bibliographical references and index.
    ISBN 1-56836-041-X
    1. Japan—Civilization—1945–   2. Japan—Social conditions—
1945–   3. Japan—Social life and customs—20th century. I. Title.
DS822.5.N24   1994
952.04—dc20   94-17188

Book design and composition by Graphic Composition, Inc.,
Athens, Georgia
The text of this book was set in Trump Mediaeval.

The jacket was printed by Phoenix Color Corporation,
Hagerstown, Maryland

Printed and bound by R. R. Donnelley and Sons,
Harrisonburg, Virginia

CONTENTS

ACKNOWLEDGMENTS, vi

AUTHOR'S NOTE, i x

1: HAPPY NEW YEAR, MICKEY MOUSE 1

2: ANYBODY HOME? 35

3: OF HUMAN CAPITALISM AND ITS CORPSES, 101

4: FOLLOW THE FLOATING WORLD, 167

5: THE DEAD TREE GIVES NO SHELTER, 229

6: OUT OF THE CAGE, 283

NOTES, 309

INDEX, 3 33

ACKNOWLEDGMENTS

This book could not have been written without the generous help of many people. Among them are:

Economist F. Gerard Adams of the University of Pennsylvania, who made a painstaking review of the manuscript and offered many helpful suggestions for its improvement.

Minato Asakawa of Kodansha America, who not only published this book, with its many thorny observations about his country, but who urged me to make it "unconventional."

Dr. Glenn Boris, associate clinical professor at the Texas Tech School of Medicine, who put his experience as a physician in Japan to good use in giving a critical reading of the manuscript.

David Butts, Tokyo bureau chief for *Bloomberg Business News*, my old friend and mentor who took me on at UPI and later helped me complete my research between assignments at BBN.

Professor Robert Danly, former director of the Center for Japanese Studies at the University of Michigan, who gave me a perch at that renowned center from which to research and write.

Jonathan Dolger and Carol-Ann Dearnaley, my agents, whose enthusiasm kept the manuscript alive even after many rejections.

James Fallows of the *Atlantic Monthly*, long an inspiration to me, who offered encouragement despite our somewhat differing viewpoints, and who took the time to read the manuscript.

Professor Norma Field of the University of Chicago, who read an early draft of my first few chapters and cheered me on.

Professors Carolyn Haynes and Susan Napier of the University of Texas at Austin, who read the manuscript and gave me a chance to try some of it out on their students.

Senator Daniel Inouye of Hawaii and his staff assistant Heidi Umbhau, who read the manuscript.

Professor Chalmers Johnson of the University of California, San Diego, who gave generously of his time and wisdom while I was a reporter, and who later read the manuscript.

Dr. Alixa Naff of the Smithsonian Institution, who kept a hawklike eye on news of Japan in Washington for me, and whose auntlike example kept me hard at work.

Dr. Erdman B. Palmore of Duke University, who brought his expertise as a social gerontologist to bear on my chapter concerning birth, aging, and death.

Professor Yung-mei Tsai, director of Asian Pacific Rim Studies at Texas Tech University, who provided me valuable insights and the continuing security of a research post.

Philip Turner, my editor at Kodansha America, who had the courage to champion this work when the notion of a troubled Japan was unfashionable, and who ably and diligently tended it to fruition.

Professor Merry White of Harvard and Boston universities, who made time to read the manuscript and offered incisive criticisms.

Dewey Wallace, now retired in Mexico, who served as a one-man volunteer clipping service for me.

After all the help I have received, any remaining mistakes are entirely my own.

Additional thanks are due to my many Japanese friends and colleagues, whom I choose not to name out of respect for their privacy. A terrible trait of writers is that they turn life into a commodity. I hope it will be believed that the idea of a book followed from my experience with my family and friends, and not the other way around.

Thanks also to my parents, for reading the first draft and sticking by me even though, unworthy son that I am, I rejected their advice to get a real job.

Thanks to Ichio and Tatsuko, for nurturing and inspiring me in a land far from my home, and to Tatsuko again, for allowing this highly personal project to go ahead.

And finally yet foremost, thanks to Rumiko and Maya, for patience, help, and courage.

AUTHOR'S NOTE

Busy readers—and who is otherwise?—seldom bother with introductions anymore, so I'll say this right here: My book has a quirky structure. It alternates personal glimpses of my Japanese family and friends with a bird's-eye view of Japanese society. This will no doubt please some and irritate others. But to those who find the structure objectionable, who may even suspect me of self-indulgence, I offer this defense: Japan is an exceedingly complex and dynamic society. Too often, attempts to write about "the Japanese" end in caricature. By the same token, no single family or circle of friends is entirely representative. The two strands of this book, then, are woven together in hopes of creating a tapestry both vivid and broad.

In the interests of truth, I must note that many of the people and some of the places and institutions mentioned in this book appear under pseudonyms meant to shield their privacy. In my anecdotes, I have also made a few minor alterations in some circumstances, either for privacy or brevity. I have not, however, knowingly distorted anyone's words or deeds.

1

HAPPY NEW YEAR, MICKEY MOUSE

We were doing our best to appear as if nothing could please us more than the candied minnows, pickled octopus tentacles, chestnut paste, and other New Year's treats laid out before us. Then the abbot arrived. Scrambling up from the tatami mats, we bowed with the usual awkwardness of Westerners whose legs have long since gone to sleep. The abbot waved off the formalities and growled something at his wife.

Midnight was approaching. It was time to go.

The abrupt end of our meal was a great relief to me. It was not so much that I disliked candied minnows—they were certainly preferable to dried squid eyeballs, another Japanese delicacy. But we had been served an identical feast just hours before at our inn. The Japanese New Year's meal is not calculated to leave you peckish. With its yams, chestnut paste, and rice, it has what you might call staying power.

All the same, we five Americans—an expert in Japanese art, a chef, a potter, a nurse, and a journalist (that was me)—had cause to be grateful. We were the only foreigners privileged to witness the ancient New Year's

ceremony that year at the Sanryū temple. A tax dispute
with the city over tourist revenues had led all the Buddhist temples in the ancient Japanese capital of Kyoto to
close their doors to the public. Only the shrines of Japan's native Shinto religion would be open to revelers
that night. But our friend the potter taught English to
the Buddhist abbot's eight-year-old son. As guests of the
English teacher, we had been welcomed with great
honor and led directly to the banquet table.[1]

The abbot rustled impatiently, like a magnificent but-
terfly in his embroidered silk robes of purple, silver, and
gold. He might have stepped out of the mists of the
twelfth century, when his temple was founded, if only
he hadn't been wearing that watch. Wasn't it a Rolex?
Whatever the make, it must have been shockproof: He
tapped it sharply and swept out of the room, leaving his
chipmunk-cheeked son to guide us through the temple
grounds.

Clearly, it would not do to be late for our encounter
with the gods. Bowing our thanks to the abbot's wife,
we set off behind the boy to watch the temple's monks
ring in the New Year. It was a chilly night. Long, thin
clouds wriggled across the sky. From Sanryū's mountainside perch, I glimpsed a torchlight procession in the city
below. The crisp air was filled with the scent of pine,
citrus, and incense. We approached a cluster of temple
buildings with intricately carved rafters and roofs
bowed like the wings of eagles. Smoke wafted from a
brazier; water gurgled from a dragon's head fountain;
and standing upright around huge, waxy cakes of rice
topped with oranges were an honor guard of bamboo
stakes. Each was as thick as a muscular arm at its base
and rose to a point as fine as a quill.

Ahead I could hear the clopping of clogs on the
temple's stony pathways. Imitating our young guide, we

paused to ladle water over our hands and draw smoke from the brazier across our bodies. Purified in this way, we huddled around a sort of gazebo where the abbot and his monks were preparing to honor the New Year. A low, hypnotic chant arose. Entranced, I started to sway and echo their words under my breath. Someone put an elbow in my ribs.

Standing on those ancient temple grounds in the cold Kyoto air as the stars rolled on toward midnight, I felt the unfathomable power of the Japanese spirit. It seemed to rise up out of the ground and invest those around me with the unity, the discipline, and the serene determination that had made its nation great.

At a sign from the abbot, two monks drew back a harness-hung log, cried "Yosh!" and heaved it toward a bell as big as a man. A melancholy peal rolled down the mountain. The sixty-first year of Showa—1986 to us— had arrived. How was I, or anyone else, to know that just a few years later the Japanese spirit would be wasting away into the vapor above?

THE DANCER AND THE DANCE

Japan made its astonishing uphill charge from isolated feudalism to ultramodernity in a little more than a century, a mere blink of history's eye. Nothing seemed to hinder it for long—not defeat in World War II, not the oil shocks of the seventies, not the exchange rate crisis of the eighties. At the fiftieth anniversary of the attack on Pearl Harbor, Karel van Wolferen, the influential Dutch journalist, writing in the *New York Times* under the headline "An Economic Pearl Harbor?" said of Japan: "This unstoppable and politically rudderless entity will pass the U.S. as the world's largest economy early in the next decade. . . ."[2]

Then suddenly, everything seemed to fall apart. Barely a year later, a spate of books and articles proclaimed Japan's impending demise.[3] By 1993 the *Washington Post* was ready to declare: "Japan Inc. on the Blink."[4]

At one moment, then, the press was hooting about Japan's desperate labor shortage, and the next it was hollering about unprecedented layoffs in Japanese companies. The mantle of economic superstar was stripped from Japan's shoulders and handed to China—yes, backward, communist China. Now it was China, with its capitalist partners Hong Kong and Taiwan, that was destined to outstrip the United States by the turn of the century.

Meanwhile, in the summer of 1993, the Japanese people did what the experts had said they would never do: After thirty-eight years under one-party rule, they voted out their corrupt, venal leaders. A reformist coalition took over the reins of government. Immediately, the press served up a highly conflicted picture: The *Wall Street Journal* proclaimed it "the great Tokyo earthquake," while others, including the maverick Japanese businessman and commentator Kenichi Ohmae, insisted that little had changed, that indeed the backstage wirepullers were stronger than ever.

What was going on? Could it really be that Japan, a rocky island nation no bigger than California, had ever been poised to displace America as the world's industrial and financial leader? Had that been a bad dream or had Japan met its comeuppance? Could Japan the galloping nightmare change overnight into the also-ran of Asia, and if so, couldn't it return to form just as quickly?

Westerners could be forgiven if they felt confused about these questions. As a member of the foreign press in Japan during the years it crested and fell, I share the blame for creating such a confused picture. The fundamental problem, I will argue in this book, lies in the inability of many journalists—and even some scholars—to distinguish between Japan and the Japanese.

Japan, like the ground she lies on, is riddled with faults and prone to sudden, tectonic shifts. If you keep your eye only on Japan the bureaucratic-industrial complex, you may find it a mysterious, threatening, and unpredictable entity. And contrary to what Japanese officials always insist is a lack of understanding, the better you become acquainted with official Japan, the more you are apt to fear and loathe it.

The Japanese, by contrast, are an immensely likable, highly civilized people. More to the point, Japan today teems with critics, dissidents, dropouts, and most important, great masses of people yearning, preparing, and struggling for change. They are like the hot magma that flows silently underground until suddenly it bursts through the surface and forever reshapes the landscape. Shunji the banker comes to mind. Once he spent fourteen hours a day at his office; now he leaves work every day at 5:30 to pick up his infant son from the nursery and care for him until his wife gets home from her job at seven.

To believe this matters, you must discard the notion that the Japanese are a faceless, lumpen mass directed entirely by the nimble fingers of bureaucrats and business leaders. You must look past the crude mislabeling of the Japanese as "economic animals."

That may not be easy. The very idea of Japanese populism has long attracted sneers. In the heat of the eighties, for example, William J. Holstein, a *Business Week* editor, wrote this in a book about trade conflicts with Japan: "Despite the frustration that Japanese readily demonstrate to foreigners, in many ways the stronger—but silent—force is their acceptance of the inherent limits that being Japanese imposes on them."[5]

Not anymore. In the pages that follow, I hope to show how ordinary Japanese have begun to slip their bonds and why a grassroots revolution now under way will utterly undo the Japan we have known.

It is a most timely revolution, for Japan, despite its recent economic setbacks, has become the silent leader of what may soon emerge as the most formidable economic bloc in the world. Throughout Asia, Japan's postwar miracle has inspired—and financed—a brand of highly successful authoritarian capitalism. This has led some to argue that that Asians would rather grow rich than free. But by the end of this book, I hope to have demonstrated that no amount of wealth can suppress a natural human desire for the freedom and dignity of the individual. Quite the contrary.

SANTA ON A HOG

I arrived in Japan on Christmas Eve, a few days before the bullet train whisked me off to Kyoto. Tokyo dazzled me from the start. I had lived in cities all my life—New York, London, and Cairo among them—but never had I seen anything like Tokyo. It is vast beyond imagining: To travel from one end to the other by train takes almost as long as to go from New York to Washington. But what really sets it apart is the almost surreal coexistence of past and future. Tokyo has no present.

My first night there I saw sights so fantastic that I began to wonder whether the city's hyperfast redevelopment hadn't left its residents a little off balance.

Jet lag and excitement made sleep impossible. About

midnight I gave up trying and stepped out of my $40-a-night cubicle and onto the throbbing streets of Tokyo. Outside, it was cool and damp, like a winter's evening in San Francisco. Ambling aimlessly, dropping imaginary bread crumbs to ensure my return, I wandered along a narrow street. My way was illuminated by paper lanterns hanging over the doors of tiny wooden shacks where elderly women served grilled chicken and beer to the grizzled old men who squeezed inside. I passed a street vendor hawking roasted sweet potatoes from a ramshackle wooden cart. A mournful song, strangely like the muezzin's call to the faithful, wafted from a tape recorder on the cart. That electronic touch made it all seem slightly unreal, like a Disneyland version of old Edo, as the capital was once known.

Suddenly, the alley opened up onto a huge, glittering intersection. Stunned, I paused in astonishment. It was as if I had stumbled through a door to Tomorrowland. Overhead, cars and trucks crawled on a highway in the air. Huge neon displays exploded like fireworks on every tall building. Taped messages cannonaded from loudspeakers on all sides.

"Step right up, step right up. Bargain sale in progress!" Or: "A car is now emerging from the garage. Please be careful."

Off in the distance, skyscrapers reached for the clouds, defying the fatal logic of the quaking earth.[6] *All around me packs of young Japanese women promenaded in razor-edged, wasp-waisted jackets with epaulets and glinting brass buttons over miniskirts and knitted leg warmers. Some tottered on high heels that made their long, dark hair swing wide of their narrow hips as they walked. Others, with hair bobbed and curled like flappers, clopped along in high-fashion calfskin boots. Gig-*

gling, squealing, shrieking, thrusting glossy fingertips over neon-painted lips, they swarmed about in twos, threes, dozens.

Clearly they were the ones out for a good time. The businessmen, ties askew, still in the suits they had worn to work, looked more like casualties than revelers as they stumbled homeward after a night of hard drinking. A small, red-faced man was vomiting wretchedly at the curbside not far from me. Two policemen emerged from their sidewalk police box to save him from pitching headlong into traffic.

The noise—of traffic, wild laughter, hoarse cries, and somewhere, a loudspeaker—was deafening. As I stood there gawking I heard someone behind me gunning a motorcycle engine. Drugged with fatigue and wonder, I turned in slow motion. Now, set the tale in New York or L. A., and maybe you would hear three sharp pops and I would slide to the ground with a high-caliber slug in my chest.

But this was Tokyo and it was Christmas Eve. There was no drug-crazed killer brandishing a semiautomatic on a Harley Hog. It was Santa.

He came roaring past me, his white beard and red suit flapping in the wind, and screeched to a stop about twenty feet ahead, where three fancy-dress, high-heeled women stood smoking. As I stared with bulging eyes, the helmet came off and the illusion popped like a soap bubble. I could see now that he was a thin, long-limbed young man with dark hair greased in a pompadour. He pulled down his beard, lit a cigarette, and cocked his head in what was unmistakably calculated to be a James Dean–like manner.

It was all too much. I hurried back to my hotel, trying to suppress an insane cackle.

WA THE HELL

While Japan was on the rise, everyone wanted to discover the secret of its success. Some responses were thoughtful and penetrating.[7] But many self-anointed experts proposed ridiculously simplistic answers to the Japan question. The title of one book, by the prolific and often astute Japan-watcher Boye Lafayette de Mente, sums up the slickness of the genre: *Japan's Secret Weapon: The Kata Factor* (subtitled *The Cultural Programming That Made the Japanese a Superior People*).[8] *Kata*, more often called *yarikata*, refers to the Japanese belief that there is one and only one way to do each task. Women who ride a bicycle, for instance, should not just hop on and ride away. The proper yarikata is to put the left foot on the left pedal and then push off several times with the right foot, so that the bike is rolling along at a nice clip, before swinging the right leg onto the other pedal. This preposterous method often results in near collisions. All the same, it is faithfully practiced by millions of Japanese housewives.

In short, *yarikata*, "the way of doing," is little more than conformity put into practice. As a cultural precept it makes for superb assembly-line workers. But conformism leads to serious problems where individual initiative is needed. This is increasingly the case in Japan. So frustrating is the traditional Japanese conformity that the chief of one Japanese company actually issued the following order to his employees: "Have an opinion, and state it to your superiors."[9] Can't you just picture the response? "*Hai!* My opinion is that your opinion is an excellent opinion, sir!"

Yarikata, then, is hardly the stuff of a "superior people" in an age where everything from the mass audience to

mass production seems to be withering away. But if the
West has swallowed simplistic explanations of Japan's
success, the Japanese have clung to yet a simpler one:
their unique Japanese spirit, abstractly expressed as *wa*.
It would be hard to overstate the importance of *wa* in the
Japanese view of their own success. Countless books
have been published in Japan on the uniqueness of the
Japanese spirit; indeed, there is a entire genre called *nih-
on-jin ron*, or "theory of the Japanese people," a subject
we'll return to in the final chapter of this book.

It is not my aim to write a history of Japan, and if the
brief reprise of events that follows seems selective, let me
concede the point. I simply intend to show that *wa*,
though usually translated as "harmony" or "peace," has
always implied conformity and obedience. In this sense,
at least, the Japanese spirit may rightly be said to be ex-
piring.

Wa appears as the cardinal principle in Japan's first constitution, written by Prince Shotoku in A.D. 604 It was
less a constitution than a list, derived from Confucian
and Buddhist writings, of the duties owed by subjects
to their rulers. Chief among these was the preservation
of *wa*.

Unfortunately, *wa* proved hard to keep. The Japanese
are as conflict-prone as any other people. In propounding
the official myth of Japan as a peaceful agrarian country,
apologists stress how seldom the Japanese were involved
in foreign wars. They conveniently forget that from the
twelfth century on the Japanese hacked away at each
other in quite merciless civil wars, until a military
strongman named Hideyoshi united the country in 1590.
By then the Japanese spirit was distinctly martial. Hideyoshi's successors, members of the Tokugawa clan, took
the title *shogun*, or "military commander." The period
that followed is usually described as one of exceptional

peace and stability. This, however, depends on one's point of view.

To scuttle any threat to *wa*—and their own dynasty—the Tokugawas took an extraordinary step: They sealed the country. They expelled all Christian missionaries and all but a few of the Dutch traders who had been doing a roaring business out of the port of Nagasaki. Any Japanese who were outside the country at the time of the decree were forbidden to return.[10] The Tokugawa regime gently persuaded Christian converts to renounce their faith: It threw their children into volcanic pits, crucified their priests, and imprisoned the faithful without food. Before long, the 300,000-strong community of Christian Japanese had been virtually wiped out. To survive, the remnant had either to renounce their faith by grinding their feet on an image of Christ or to go into hiding in the remote mountains of Kyushu in southwestern Japan.

Of course, at about the same time, Catholics and Protestants in Europe were merrily roasting their own for heresies discovered or imagined. Then again, no sane person would ever claim that Europe has a peaceful history.

The Tokugawa treatment of foreigners was no softer. When a shipload of Portuguese merchants docked at Nagasaki in the mid-seventeenth century to request a reopening of trade, the shogun had all but a few beheaded. The survivors were sent back with a message for the outside world:

> You are witnesses that I caused even the clothes of those who were executed to be burned; let them [hearing this message] do the same to us if they find occasion to do so; we consent to it without demur. Let them think no more of us, just as if we were no longer in the world.[11]

These are not events the Japanese dwell on when they describe themselves as a peaceful, harmonious nation. Nor do they mention the subjugation of the Ainu people in the north, or of the Ryukyu kingdom in the south, though these events are scarcely more than a century old.

Of course, life was not uniformly grim in the feudal period: Edo, as Tokyo was then known, offered many delights, even to the common people. (We'll glimpse these in chapter 4.) Nevertheless, it must be acknowledged that peace for many came at a dreadful price.

And there was worse to come. In 1853 Congress sent Commodore Matthew Perry along with a quarter of the U.S. Navy to force Japan to trade with America. Japan's policy of isolation had lately been challenged by several nations, including Russia, and the United States didn't want to fall behind in the race for influence in the Pacific.

The ferocious Japanese spirit had dwindled considerably by the time Perry's fleet of Black Ships sailed into Tokyo Bay. The samurai were floundering in debt. With no wars to fight, the best of them cultivated learning, but many others wasted themselves in drinking, gambling, whoring, and fighting. (In this way, the samurai gave rise to both the bureaucrats and the *yakuza* gangsters, arguably the two most influential groups in postwar Japanese society.) After 250 years in power, the line of shoguns that began with the mighty Ieyasu had dwindled to a figurehead presiding over a tottering government.[12]

When Commodore Perry strutted ashore with the U.S. fleet at his back, the frail shogun Ieyoshi and his advisers meekly acknowledged the superior firepower of the United States. They requested time to deliberate how best to reply. A month later, Ieyoshi died.

The following year, when Commodore Perry returned for an answer, Ieyoshi's successor agreed to open trade with the West. However, it couldn't all be done at once, the shogun's advisers explained. For starters, they would open the port town of Shimoda, 150 miles south of Tokyo, and a little fishing port called Hakodate far to the north.[13] The rest would take a little time, they said. Some Americans are still waiting.

The arrival of Perry's Black Ships sparked a fierce blaze of nationalism among the samurai. Other Asian nations had already been colonized, but Japan regarded itself as different. In all its recorded history, it had never suffered an invasion. When Kublai Khan tried it in the thirteenth century, his armadas were swept away by freak storms, which came to be known as *kamikaze*, the "divine winds."

Revolution followed in Perry's wake. The shogun was overthrown and the Tokugawa clan, which had kept Japan isolated for more than two centuries, lost power, largely because it could no longer keep the door shut. As European and American diplomats poured into Japan, the cry in the mouth of every samurai was: "Expel the Barbarian, restore the Emperor!"

Emperor Mutsuhito, a bewildered sixteen-year-old who would come to be known as Meiji, was indeed "restored," but on the question of how to deal with the West, cleverer heads behind the throne prevailed. Rather than try to reseal the island nation, Meiji leaders set about trying to beat the West at its own game. In the late nineteenth century, this meant becoming a military, colonial, and industrial power. The hotheaded samurai were disarmed and disbanded. A mostly meritocratic school system took root and guided the finest male minds in the country into a burgeoning bureaucracy. The Meiji government launched a campaign to study and re-create Western products and practices, everything from top hats and tails to a modern military based, fatefully, on the German model.

At the same time, the *genrō*, or "elder statesmen," who ruled Japan from behind the facade of democracy, cultivated a highly nationalistic view of the world. The country's ambitions were captured in a slogan that every citizen could understand: *Fukoku, kyōhei*—"rich country, strong military." The citizen's role in this mission was defined with equal clarity in the Imperial Rescript on Education. By 1892 every schoolboy started the day by vowing to sacrifice his life gladly for the Emperor.[14]

Nationalism eventually became a cult, grounded in the native Shinto religion and embodied in the emperor as divine father of the Japanese family. The rapid conversion of a feudal nation into a modern industrial state during Emperor Meiji's forty-five-year reign was capped by an unexpected victory over the Russians in a territorial war that ended in 1905.

Japan experienced a brief flowering of democratic impulses between 1913 and 1932, a period that came to be known as the Taisho Democracy because it overlapped, roughly speaking, with the brief reign of Emperor Taisho. It was a period in which voting rights ballooned from 2 percent to 100 percent of the male population; a vigorous labor movement conducted strikes, rallies, and riots; and the intelligentsia toyed with radical ideas of socialism, feminism, and free love.

But with the onset of depression in the late twenties, Japan's shallow democracy was uprooted. A police state emerged. Feminists, socialists, and other "deviants" were jailed and their leaders hanged. As the world sank into the Great Depression of the 1930s, military-backed fascism prevailed in Japan. The "thought police" closed theaters, purged bookshelves, and marched nonconformists off to prison. All over Japan, the nail that stuck up got hammered down. This was *wa* at its worst.

THE FOUNTAIN OF WEALTH

Daylight in Tokyo revealed anachronisms: As I wandered through Ueno Park, I came across an ancient shrine fronted by weather-beaten stone lanterns and a robotic fortune-telling machine. In western Tokyo, I stumbled across a moss-covered farmhouse (in the city!) with chicken coops out back and a shiny Toyota coupe in front. At Nihon-bashi, I found that the site of the old stone-and-timber bridge so often seen in Japanese prints now had a superhighway passing over it.

Clearly the pace of change was something Tokyo could not keep up with. During that first visit to Japan, the enormity of its evolution was put into human scale for me by a Japanese business professor whom I'd met in the States. "Tom" Takahashi was a cheery, elfin man in his late fifties who taught at one of Japan's most prestigious private universities.

A convivial man who, like me, enjoyed nothing so much as a first-rate meal paid for by someone else, Professor Takahashi invited me to lunch with his publisher at an exceptionally fine Italian restaurant. After we had washed down lunch with several bottles of wine, the publisher obligingly paid and then wobbled off. Professor Takahashi and I went for a stroll. Leaving the restaurant, we paused to admire the entrance. I hadn't really noticed it going in, but the thing was done up like a miniature Italian piazza, complete with one of those marble fountains that is replenished by a rascally bronze cherub pissing from atop a pedestal.

*I smiled, but Professor Takahashi clutched my arm
with sudden emotion. I was alarmed to see tears welling
up in his eyes.*

*"I can't believe what we've done," he said proudly.
"When I was a boy after the war, we had nothing. Nothing. One bowl of rice a day! And sometimes we had to
share it. Now Italian restaurants!"*

OCCUPIED WITH REFORM

The U.S.-led Occupation at first tried to reshape Japan
into an American-style democracy. It broke up big business, promoted strong unions, and gave farmers land,
women rights, and tenants protection. Though in many
ways the Americans who conducted the occupation
were self-righteous, clumsy, willfully ignorant, and hypo-
critical, the result was nevertheless perhaps the most
mutually beneficial conquest in history. However, the
Occupation's ideals were corrupted within a year by the
onset of the cold war. From 1947 on, MacArthur's officers
cracked down on militant unions, then "de-purged" wartime leaders and allowed them back into positions of
power. Despite lofty claims about forever disbanding Japanese armed forces, the Occupation soon created the nub
of a new Japanese military. All this was done in the spirit
of anticommunism.

Once the Occupation had ended in 1952, little more
than an appliqué of Western institutions could be found
in Japan. Democracy remained, but politics collapsed
into single-party domination. Land reforms held, but
farmers were reorganized into a virtual arm of the government. An antimonopoly law stayed on the books,
but the old industrial groups soon reunited under the

wing of MITI, the Ministry of International Trade and Industry.

Everything was subordinated to the goal of rebuilding the nation. The national mantra was that Japan (bereft of its empire) was "a small island nation with no resources other than the industry of its people." Factory floors were bedecked with slogans urging workers on to victory over the competition—while the government ensured that no established Japanese company would face external competition or internal upheaval.

After the 1964 Olympics were staged in Tokyo, Japan began to reassert nationalist self-confidence. *Wa* was back. World War II was, in official terms, recast as a tragedy in which Japan was the prime victim. (America, it was said, had goaded Japan into bombing Pearl Harbor.) Some cabinet ministers continued to assert that Japan had been defending Asia from Western colonialism, though none of the countries that had been occupied by the Japanese agreed. But for the most part, Japan simply pulled a curtain down over the war.

As with everything Japanese, there was a cultural explanation for this: Buddhist-influenced societies, it was said, prefer to sweep away bad thoughts rather than confront the guilty past. I don't dispute this. However, it's one thing to ignore the past and quite another to suppress it.

Under the long rule of the Liberal Democrats, official regrets for atrocities committed during the war were merely diplomatic niceties. For more than forty years, Japan officially denied its role in the enslavement of thousands of young women from the countries it conquered to serve as sexual "comfort women" to its soldiers. At home, the Education Ministry sanitized textbooks of historians' distressing claims that Japan had invaded China during the thirties, while right-wing thugs enforced a

public taboo on criticism of Japan's wartime conduct. To
be sure, public school teachers, struggling against these
official and unofficial pressures, tried to teach the evils of
war to their students. Nevertheless, with entrance exams
focused mainly on the premodern past, the most important event in recent Japanese history remained largely
a haze in the minds of Japanese students.

Except for the atomic bombs. All Japanese children
learned the horror that Japan suffered at the hands of the
Americans. Every year, thousands were taken to Hiroshima on school trips to see for themselves the scarred
survivors, the outlines of victims seared into walls by the
A-bomb flash, and the shattered dome in the Peace Park.
This was fitting enough and undoubtedly helped promote
pacifism, but it also helped sustain the official myth of
Japan as the victim of the war.

Then, in 1988, Hitoshi Motoshima, the mayor of Nagasaki, the other "A-bomb city," said in public that he felt
Emperor Hirohito shared some blame for Japan's role in
World War II. Though millions of Japanese agreed, the
ruling party expelled him. Not long after, the leader of
one of Japan's many right-wing paramilitary groups shot
and nearly killed him outside City Hall (just as in 1930
their predecessors had shot a legal scholar who claimed
the same emperor should be bound by the constitution.)
Fortunately, Mayor Motoshima recovered and remains in
office, despite being excommunicated by the party elite.

This pattern of suppression hardly accords with Buddhist precepts. On the contrary, it reflects the altogether
worldly needs of the ruling elites to conceal how little
had changed in their ranks since the war's end. Indeed,
national guilt could hardly be admitted while many of
the guilty still ran the country.

It was not until 1993, forty-eight years after the end of
the war, that a Japanese prime minister admitted plainly

that Japan had been an aggressor in World War II. Even then, Prime Minister Morihiro Hosokawa, the upstart who led the coalition that ousted the Liberal Democrats, had to weather a storm of criticism for his frankness. Ironically, but perhaps fittingly, Hosokawa was the grandson of Prince Fumimaro Konoe, himself a prime minister and the man who announced Japan's wartime plan for a "co-prosperity sphere" in Asia.

Of course, the curtain Japan pulled over its past was never meant to be impermeable. The switch to industrialism brought with it many trappings of militarism: The Prussian school uniforms, the morning calisthenics at companies, the salutes thrown to corporate brass as they entered the building. And running through it all, like a current of electricity in the air, was a slogan that had come to embody the Japanese spirit since Commodore Perry's arrival: "Overtake the West."

Japan has done it. That is its biggest problem.

NOAH'S INVISIBLE HAND

I moved to Japan in 1987, just as the country was on the verge of achieving its century-old goal. It was an odd moment to arrive. I had come as a correspondent for a banking newspaper. This was a leap of faith, considering how ignorant I was of banking and things economic, but even to me it was clear that the Plaza Accord had failed. The 1985 Plaza Accord was the Reagan administration's plan to cut Japan's exporters down to size. The idea was to raise the value of the yen so high that many exports would become unprofitable while all imports would become attractive. To borrow America's favorite trade metaphor, the playing field would be tilted in our favor for a change, so that U.S. products would just roll into Japan, while the Japanese would have to push theirs uphill. But instead of buying U.S. products, Japan tended to buy the means of production. What's more, as I was to discover through my wife's experiences, some Japanese were quite willing to charge uphill even if it killed them.

As to my wife: Shortly before moving to Tokyo, I had married Rumiko Hirata.[15] She was a Japanese architect I had met five years earlier when she began her graduate studies in America. We moved into a three-room apartment in Fuyo, a "city" set in the western expanse of Tokyo. Though well within Tokyo's boundaries, it was an hour (and two train rides) from the financial district where I would work.

When I say our new apartment had three rooms, I mean one room, approximately eighteen feet by twenty-seven, divided into three by sliding paper doors. This was what Japanese realtors call a 2LDK, or two bedrooms plus living room, dining room, and kitchen. The boundaries of the L, the D, and the K were left to the imagination to draw within a nine- by fifteen-foot parquet-floored space. It offered few hints. There was no refrigerator, no stove, and no dishwasher, only a sink, a drain, and a few built-in shelves. The rest of the "mansion" (that's what they call such apartments) was split into two straw-matted bedrooms, each smaller than a typical American parking space. The apartment had its own bath, however: It was a kind of squared-off plastic barrel. Once inside, your chin could rest quite comfortably on your knees.

The rent was extraordinarily reasonable by Tokyo standards: about $700 a month. Downtown, a fully equipped Western-style apartment could cost $10,000 a month. Even in our neighborhood, $1,300-a-month rent was far from rare, so we felt lucky. True, no ray of sunshine ever found a direct path into that apartment. That *it backed onto a factory may also have contributed to its affordability. Forklifts roared to life outside our bedroom window every morning at seven.*

As for the stiff terms on which we rented—five months' deposit and "gift money"; no stove, refrigerator, heater, or cooler provided; all utilities, including water, at the expense of the tenant; all repairs, as I discovered when the water heater broke down, likewise at the tenant's expense—these were standard.

My first morning there, yearning for something familiar, I went into the Mr. Donut shop on the opposite corner and in halting Japanese ordered a couple of doughnuts and some milk. Giggles sprang up around me. I got the terrible feeling I'd said something awful. In fact, it was only the presence of a foreigner that amused the salesgirls.

I soon found that our subdivision of Fuyo was really a village, one of the thousands that have congealed to form the Japanese capital. I seemed to be its only foreign resident. Like all villages, this one was wary of strangers, especially strangers from abroad.

When I ventured into the shōtengai, the long, narrow shopping arcade that led to the train station, I felt all eyes were upon me. Soon, though, shopkeepers up and down the length of the arcade got word that I could speak some Japanese and became eager to chat. After a few words of awkward conversation on my part, they would praise my skill lavishly—and, I had no doubt, laugh themselves to tears once I was gone.

While Rumiko was busy setting up an architectural practice with some former classmates, I spent a lot of time hanging around the shōtengai, trying to get a fix on how things worked. It seemed to me that if I were going to report on the headwaters of the economy, I had better understand how it flowed in the delta. Besides, it was

*cheaper than riding the trains into the financial district
every day.*

*The arcade appeared to have been designed by a Japa-
nese Noah. There were two of every kind of shop. Two
shoe stores. Two women's boutiques. Two drug stores.
Two vegetable stands. Even two supermarkets. And yet
far from slugging it out with each other, all the competitors seemed quite friendly. They had chipped in to fes-
toon the arcade with plastic flowers and apparently
shared the cost of the tinkly Japanese music that filled
the street.*

A peaceful sense of wa *prevailed. No price wars broke
out. A single tomato cost as much as a dollar; a head of
lettuce might be triple that, depending on the season.
Milk topped $6 a gallon, and bread was as much as 20
cents a slice. (At those prices, you could buy unbeliev-
ably small quantities: hence, the four-slice loaf of
bread.) Many stores took the same day off, so they would
not steal each other's customers.*

Still, it was a charming place, that shōtengai, *full of
the spirit of older times in spite of the Mr. Donut shop
at one end and a McDonald's at the other. Just next to
the doughnut parlor was a little wooden stall where a
man with a traditional rolled-up headband sold pickled
vegetables. He seemed to be a holdover from the medi-
eval Edo era. A dour fellow who looked as though he
lived exclusively on his own wares, the shopkeeper held
to many of the rituals of his forebears. Every morning,
he brought out a watering can and sprinkled the area in
front of his shop. This was undoubtedly a public service
when the roads were dirt, but the advent of paving
seemed to make it unnecessary. However, he was not a
solitary anachronism. Even those up-to-the-minute employees at Mos Burger—home of the famous "rice-
burger"—started their day by sprinkling the walkway.*

Mrs. Sato, who ran an old-fashioned mom-and-pop liquor store near our home, was most friendly. She peppered me with questions whenever I went in to buy beer or sake in her cramped little shop. As months passed, she began to give me little freebies with my purchases: hand towels, ceramic cake plates decorated with cartoon cats, and the like. These seemed more in the way of friendly overtures than sales incentives. Of course, since the price of beer was fixed throughout Japan by the four major domestic breweries, she would not dream of offering me a discount. The giveaways, supplied by the brewers, helped her form a personal bond that would keep me coming back.

The other liquor shop (two of everything!) was closer to our apartment, but the Mrs. there was distinctly cold, while her ancient mother, who sometimes filled in, made things so warm I fled in terror. The moment I said anything as simple as "Konnichi wa" ("Hello"), the mother would smile her toothless smile and begin exclaiming "Ah, jyōzu desu ne!" ("Oh, you're so skillful!"). If I came within range, she would stroke my hand while she repeated the phrase over and over. She made me feel like an idiot child who had just blurted out the Pythagorean theorem.

So I continued to give Mrs. Sato my custom. After a while, Mrs. Sato's daughter, Keiko, began working in the shop. Keiko was a garrulous young woman fond of wearing Guess jeans, perhaps just a half-size too small. Her earrings jangled merrily as she went about her work. One evening when I stopped in to buy a bottle of beer on the way home from work, she floored me by saying, in perfect English, "Have you ever been to Hawaii? I'm dying to get back there."

"Hawaii?" I mumbled.

Yes, Hawaii. She had gone to the University of

Hawaii. I was stunned. Mrs. Sato seemed like the sort of person who had never been more than a day's journey from home. That her daughter would go to college overseas was mind-boggling.

"But you should be doing something better with your life than working in a liquor store," I told her. (If that seems an insensitive comment, I can only plead that I was truly discombobulated by her revelation.)

"Yeah, but for now it's only right that I help out my parents with their store," she said with a sigh. "Pretty soon, though, I'm getting out of here."

Over the years I was in Japan, whenever I saw Keiko in the store she invariably told me that she couldn't wait to get back to Hawaii. I came to think of her as being like George Bailey, the Jimmy Stewart character in It's a Wonderful Life—*always packing, never leaving. But my last week there, she proudly announced that she had landed a job with an international airline. She could hardly wait to get to Waikiki.*

The shōtengai *left me very confused. Everyone seemed to be trampling on the fundamental laws of economic self-interest. But Keiko came to embody a clear lesson for me. The young Japanese were vastly different from their parents, and, though patient with the demands of the system, they were ultimately self-seekers.*

SO LONG, PEBBLE BEACH

The late eighties were a disheartening time to be an American in Japan. Although conflicts with the West threatened to erupt into trade war, Japan's companies continued to expand overseas.

As cash-rich Japanese corporations and speculators

began to make what they called "trophy purchases" of American skyscrapers and golf courses, Americans debated whether or not "the Japanese" were buying up America. Some insisted that they were; others retorted that Japanese investors should be as welcome as any others. Few paused to note that the vast majority of Japanese owned not a particle of American soil. The point missed in the West was that many ordinary Japanese were as disgusted as anyone by these displays of ostentation and power. They began to worry that their country had overshot its goal and was rolling on aimlessly. The *Yomiuri Shimbun*, the nation's largest daily newspaper, echoed this in a 1989 editorial:

> If Japan continues on its present course, Western companies will be defeated and the lifestyle and culture they worked so hard to establish will be destroyed. Can Japan be allowed to destroy Western cultures?[16]

I brooded on that question at length. Deep down, I felt sure the answer was no. I just couldn't figure how, short of war, Japan was to be restrained. Disheartened though I was on New Year's Eve, 1990, exactly five years after my night on a mountain in Kyoto, I had a small revelation—call it a *satori*, if you will. It led to this book.

THE PIED PIPER OF DISNEY

On New Year's Eve, 1990, I was sitting in the snug living room of my Japanese in-laws' house, trying to balance a laptop computer on my knees as I perched on a tiny chair. By now I was a correspondent for United Press

International. Having drawn holiday duty, my task was to capture the flavor of Japan's most important holiday in a few hundred words that I would soon deliver over our wires to newspaper readers around the world. I had done my on-the-street reporting earlier and was now watching NHK, the national broadcasting service, for its annual midnight roundup of temple visits in hopes of wrapping up the story and getting on with celebrating the New Year myself.

As I looked on, it wasn't the Buddhist temples that caught my attention; it was that shrine to American fantasia, Tokyo Disneyland. More than 50,000 Japanese in their teens and twenties had shouldered into Disneyland that night, NHK reported, and thousands more waited in a three-mile-long traffic jam outside the gates. They had passed up the traditional temple visits to go there for a midnight parade featuring Mickey Mouse.

At that moment the flash of insight struck: Compared with the Enchanted Kingdom, young people find the temples and shrines of Japan as dead as the pyramids of Egypt.[17] All great countries draw strength from their national myths, none more so than Japan. But here was spectacular evidence that Mickey, Minnie, and Goofy had supplanted the native gods in the pantheon of Japanese youth.

They were not exactly rebels, those young people: All the popular magazines had assured them Disneyland was the place to be that night. And many would no doubt accompany their families to a shrine or temple the next day. Still, in the eight years since it opened, Disneyland had become the single most popular attraction in Japan. Not long after that New Year's Eve, visitors to Tokyo Disneyland passed the 100 million mark—equivalent to four-fifths of Japan's population.

The Way of the Warrior had dwindled into the Pursuit of the Cute.

ICON OR MERE CON?

Of course, this revelation hadn't come without foreboding. Living in a Japanese community, surrounded by Japanese family and friends, it had long before dawned on me that Japan the juggernaut was not troubling to foreigners alone. Many Japanese were, quite naturally, proud of their country's breathtaking accomplishments. But many others began to feel doubts, even pain and anger, at the turns Japan was taking. Old couples—shopkeepers and urban farmers—were run off their land by gangsters in the pay of speculators. So widespread was the practice that the "land shark," as this type of gangster was known, became a stock figure in movies and television shows.

Throughout society, a yawning gap opened up between the haves and the have-nots, the landholders and the landless. Japanese who had been raised to despise personal wealth and think only of the nation's well-being were shocked to see the ostentation of the newly rich, or *narikin*, as they called them.

Polls showed that young Japanese were the unhappiest people in the industrialized world. At a time when the *narikin* were drinking their sake flecked with gold, less than half the country's homes were hooked up to sewers. Everyone had a job, but few could afford to buy a house. Japan was, in the words of one Japanese critic, a "paradise of idiots."[18]

But in the end the Japanese were not idiots. For a time they may have been dazzled by the prospect of being number one, but the achievement made them realize how skewed their society was—how much of the nation's resources were directed toward beating the West and how few toward improving the lives of ordinary citizens. Newspapers and television talk shows began to register a drumbeat of dissatisfaction.

"Our society is rife with unfairness," seventy-eight-year-old Jiro Taguchi wrote in a blistering letter to the *Asahi* newspaper in 1990.

That same year, a remarkable survey found that although Japanese continued to identify strongly with their nationality, they expressed far less patriotism than Americans—or for that matter, Mexicans, Nigerians, Poles, and others.[19] Those who declared pride in their country amounted to just 62 percent, compared with more than 80 percent of respondents in the United States, Spain, South Korea, Canada, Mexico, Chile, Poland, Czechoslovakia, and Nigeria. Thanks, perhaps, to the efforts of teachers, only 10 percent of Japanese said they would be willing to sacrifice their lives for their country. Less than a third said they were proud of the nation's companies. Clearly, half a century after Pearl Harbor, the Japanese were a changed people.

Within the family, traditions were crumbling: Fathers had lost their authority and become absentee breadwinners; many grandparents were left behind in villages as young people flocked to the cities; children gave up the pastimes of childhood for the all-consuming competition to get into a "good" university. And finally mothers, pushed by the need to pay for their children's tutors and cram schools, and pulled by Japan's ever-growing need for labor, left home for the workplace.

In conversations with Japanese, I began to hear the same theme over and over: "We Japanese have ruined our nation." My friend Katsuo, a father of two young children who works for a large electronics company, told me late one night over beer, "We have lost our culture and we have destroyed our environment, all for GNP. What will happen to my kids? My daughter has rashes all over her body." He blamed them on chemicals in the food chain.

I encountered other Japanese who, in their own ways, were pushing against the grain. At a "Save the Rain Forest" rock concert, I met an employee of one of Japan's giant, timber-hungry trading houses. A few years earlier it would have been unthinkable for a Japanese employee to join in an event protesting the activities of his own company. (Maybe he was there to spy, but I doubt it. What could he report: "We observed people dancing, having a good time, and badmouthing us for cutting down the world's forests"?)

I met Japanese husbands who yearned to be nurturing fathers and Japanese wives who insisted on putting their careers first. I watched teenagers with rainbow-colored hair waxed stiffly above their heads or greased into pompadours gulp down amphetamines, break dance, duck into "love hotels" for midnight trysts, and block traffic at two in the morning while they cut figure-eights on a motorcycle. Wa-hoo!

Within the workplace, too, life was rapidly changing. What had seemed a glorious national mission—to hoist Japan up from the ashes of war and place it among the world's leading nations—now seemed a pitiless status game. There were still plenty of dedicated company men. Indeed, thousands worked themselves to death in the eighties. But among the young a poisonous cynicism set in, and with it a self-centeredness previously unknown in Japan.

Politics, never highly regarded, became even more widely scorned following a series of bribery scandals that were unprecedented even in this scandal-ridden nation.

The turning point came in 1993. Shin Kanemaru, a back-room political hack who could have given correspondence lessons to Boss Tweed, walked away with only a $2,000 fine from his conviction for accepting millions in bribes from a mob-related company. He disdained even to show up in court. The public howled. Protesters marched on the prosecutors' offices. The investigation was reopened, and, lo and behold, prosecutors found that Kanemaru had amassed a $50 million fortune from the largesse of Japanese companies. Kanemaru was rearrested.

Big business, the icon of postwar Japanese success, was tarnished by revelations of its involvement in this and numerous other schemes involving politicians and gangsters. The public had already come to feel abused, first by the bursting of their so-called bubble economy, then by revelations that big companies had been secretly reimbursed for their losses in the great Tokyo stock crash of 1990, in which many ordinary citizens had seen a big chunk of their savings go up the flue. As we'll see in chapter 3, whatever moral virtue business had been thought to possess shriveled.

What has any of this to do with real change? Some commentators say Japan is incapable of change. In a sense, they are right. Since reform would mean upsetting the balance of power and privilege among elite institutions, when confronted with demands for change Japan typically makes elaborate efforts to give the appearance of change while preserving the system's balance. A change of government doesn't necessarily mean a change of practice. But we should not assume that just because the Japanese have sacrificed in the past for the common good, they will continue to do so. In the past, Japan has always given the Japanese a reason to sacrifice. First it was Commodore Perry, the living embodiment of Western imperialism, then it was a fight for Japanese hegemony in Asia, and for the last half-century, it was the struggle to rebuild Japan and catch up with the West. Those justifications have expired. A 1993 government survey of 10,000 Japanese found that their top priorities for the future are personal happiness and leisure.[20] The Japanese people simply do not want to sacrifice anymore.

The opening of Tokyo Disneyland in 1983 appeared to be one of those demonstrations that Japan had arrived. But I came to see Mickey Mouse as a kind of Trojan horse. By showing the Japanese people that there was a good life to be lived out there, Mickey as much as anything else changed Japanese thinking.

"The young people today are getting the wrong information from the U.S.A.," sixty-three-year-old Sosuke Kato complained to the *Washington Post*. "Being lazy, having fun, enjoying life—that these are good things and that to sweat and work are not trendy."

Life in Japan was never supposed to be fun. There isn't even a precise equivalent for the English word *fun* in Japanese. But linguistic barriers can't hold back the changes sweeping Japan. The youngsters I saw clambering off Space Mountain at Tokyo Disneyland whooped *"Saikō!"* ("Tops!") and *"Suge!"* ("Wonderful!"). These do just as well.

Of course, learning to have fun was just the beginning. In the somber nineties, the Japanese have begun to concern themselves with weightier matters. Identity in Japan has always belonged to the group. For the group's sake, "face" has always been a thing to be saved. Now, however, one by one the Japanese are laying claim to their individual faces. And in doing so, they are re-creating their society from the bottom up.

2
ANYBODY HOME?

The first family I met in Japan was the one I married into. This was not a wild impulse; actually, nothing could have been more gingerly done. International marriage, I had heard, was no easy thing, particularly when it involved cultures as different as those of America and Japan. I knew of American men who in earlier days had married Japanese women only to find that the in-laws moved in with the bride, and I had heard of others who in more recent times had been chased off by outraged Japanese parents. And judging from Rumiko's determination to keep our relationship a secret, I had no doubt her family would be a terror.

So on arriving in Japan that Christmas Eve of 1985, I was defiantly set against marrying Rumiko. But locked away in the glove compartment of my mind, I suppose, the possibility must have been glowing. After all, I had passed up Christmas at home and endured a thirteen-hour flight at least partly to meet Rumiko's family. And, of course, to see Rumiko after four painful months apart.

We had met several years earlier in Philadelphia,

where she was a graduate student in architecture at the University of Pennsylvania. Our relationship was never supposed to happen and, once it did, was never supposed to last. She was then on leave from an architectural firm in Tokyo and was due back at her job in a matter of months. She had come on a Japanese fellowship that expressly required her to state she was not planning to marry an American man. (The question of male applicants marrying American women never came up, of course.)

My position was no stronger. I was struggling with the end of a marriage made too early and the start of a journalism career seemingly begun too late. Unable as yet to make a living off my scribbling, I had taken a job as a foreign student adviser in the university's international programs office while I pursued an abortive master's degree in communications. Although I was not officially Rumiko's adviser—we met over dinner in the university's dining hall—a love match between us was not likely to be smiled upon by the university administration. Not in the era of sexual harassment suits.

Then again, for a long time our conduct could have passed muster in a Disney film. It helped, perhaps, that we had almost nothing in common. I knew little about Japan, and even less about architecture. She seemed interested in precious little other than architecture. Indeed, we could barely communicate at first, since her English was still shaky and my Japanese was nil. But we did share a liking for classical music and autumnal strolls in the woods.

After several tramps through the falling leaves and up the stairs to the $2 seats at the Academy of Music, she gave me a box of Japanese tea. I gave her a Navajo vase. We were exquisitely chaste.

One winter evening, things changed. She came to my

apartment, distraught. The moment I opened the door I could see she was on the verge of tears. It was extraordinary to find her that way, since normally in public she wore the stern expression of a bill collector with bunions. (In Japan, she later told me, people who want to be taken seriously must look serious.)

Rumiko sat down on my rickety green sofa and unfolded her sorrows between sips of green tea. She was upset because it was the birthday of the man she used to love, the man whose intentions she had failed to discern before leaving Japan. Sympathetic, but with competitive instincts fully aroused, I sidled down the sofa and took her in my arms. The result was astonishing.

I don't know what she expected, but I can never forget the look of terror in her eyes as she reared back from me. Suddenly she was like a horse shying away from a torch. The legs on the old sofa gave way, and I slid painfully to the floor on my knees. I huddled there, stunned, wondering what I had done wrong. To me, a hug was no more than an everyday gesture. True, it was meant to lead to something more, but I had barely gotten out of the gate, so to speak. After a few minutes of silent contemplation, we began to talk. And then, just as suddenly, we didn't need to talk anymore. The problem had quickly become clear: Rumiko, like so many other Japanese, hadn't been hugged since she was a child.

WHAT'S LOVE GOT TO DO WITH IT?

To the Western observer, the Japanese family has always been somewhat different. Japan has no tradition of romantic love like that of the West. Not within marriage, anyway. You only have to see a kabuki play to realize this:

The weary samurai, returning home after years in the
battlefield, flings himself down on the stoop and bawls
to his wife: "Tea!"

Traditionally, children learned that they owed their
parents not love but an infinite debt of obligation that
outweighed any other attachments they might form. Author Michael Shapiro recounts an illuminating exchange
between Lafcadio Hearn, the writer who in the nineteenth century became one of Japan's first modern immigrants, and some of his students.

> "Teacher," he was asked, "I have been told that if
> a European and his father and his wife were all to
> fall into the sea together, and that he only could
> swim, he would try to save his wife first. Would he
> really?"
>
> "Probably," Hearn replied. . . .
>
> "And does a European love his wife more than his
> father and mother?"
>
> "Not always—but generally, perhaps he does."
>
> "Why, Teacher, according to our ideas that is
> very immoral."[1]

Of course, passionate love is a universal human emotion, but in Japan its place has generally been outside the
home. Within the family, duty outranks love; reserve is
valued far above expression. Until recently, marriages
were most often arranged by parents with the aid of go-
betweens. They sought practical matches rather than
affairs of the heart. The *o-miai*, or formal introduction,
normally permitted only a brief acquaintance before marriage. Often there was no meeting of the couple at all.
Love was beside the point. One woman, interviewed in
the 1960s for an academic study on Japanese marriages,
said:

My opinion was disregarded. I was at the mercy of other people. When I got engaged, I felt little affection. In fact, I rather disliked him, but I thought I could manage to get along once we got married.[2]

Her plight was typical of women under feudalism, not only in Japan but all over the world. That the comment was recorded in the 1960s simply testifies to how long the feudal customs of Japan have endured, despite the speedy modernization of the country over the last century.

Whatever its inequities, however, feudalism did not erode the family. Quite the contrary: It gave rise to the view that "the purpose of life was to maintain the family's status and to enhance its reputation," as the great Japanese sociologist Tadashi Fukutake writes.[3] This, however, was a received notion from Chinese Confucianism and could be said equally of, say, Arab culture, or indeed of many others.[4]

The distinctive point about social history in Japan is the way the state, reacting to the challenge presented by Commodore Perry and the rest of the outside world, took over the family for its own purposes.[5] This intervention began in earnest with the Meiji Restoration of 1868 and continues up to the present. It played a vital role in Japan's rapid economic development and ultimately accounts for many of the difficulties that lie in Japan's future. The sins of the state against the family are heavy. To put the case baldly, in the late nineteenth century it snatched daughters out of the home to work in factories; in the first half of this century, it snatched sons to fight in expansionist wars, and in the latter half it stole fathers to work in expansionist companies. It furthermore robbed children of their childhood by creating an education system so rigid and bottlenecked that

millions had to compete for a comparatively few places in
top universities or face a life of mediocrity.

At last, however, the authority of the system is tottering.

HORROR FLICKS

*Shortly after the couch tipped, Rumiko and I set up
household together in a Philadelphia version of the
brownstone apartment building. We shared an efficiency that combined cutlery and chopsticks, bags of
Doritos and sacks of rice, my slobbery and her style, all
with surprising harmony. I began to study Japanese.
Meanwhile, Rumiko's English got so good she was soon
creaming me in Saturday-night games of Scrabble.*

*Rumiko never said a word about our living arrange-
ments to her parents. I was under strict instructions
from her never to answer the phone, in case they were
calling.*

*It took two years, but in the fall of 1985 her parents
finally did call—to say that it was about time she came
home. Rumiko, tired, I suspect, of waiting for me to
raise the subject of marriage, returned to Tokyo, leaving
her doctoral studies and our relationship in limbo.*

*Rumiko had made it perfectly clear she would not be-
come an American. And I was not about to become a
Japanese. Besides, my career was finally moving. I had
landed a regular job as a reporter of sorts in the university's news bureau. Meantime, I'd had a column published in* Newsweek. *A play I'd written—a sort of comic
tribute to my grandparents' struggle to cope after one of
them went senile and the other frail—was in the running for a playwriting prize. (It eventually lost.) How
could I think of emigrating at a time like that? I made
a $40 phone call to Tokyo to say that I would not be*

pressured into marriage. But even as we bickered, I could not face the notion of ending our relationship. The best thing, we agreed, was for me to visit Tokyo; if all went well, she would return with me to continue her studies for another year. After that, the future could take care of itself.

My journey, then, was the culmination of four months of anxious planning on both sides of the Pacific. For my part, I carefully charted foreign exchange rates in search of the best moment to swap my pitiful bankroll for yen. When I wasn't playing at international finance, I agonized over presents for her family. In my anxiety, I crassly settled on a variety of winter wear imprinted with the University of Pennsylvania logo—a broad hint that I had an education. In one of her letters, Rumiko suggested I get some hand cream for her father; I got him a jar that would have seen Napoleon's army through the Russian winter.

Rumiko, meanwhile, was faltering in her effort to pre- pare the family for the arrival of her "friend from America." The Japanese, as I said, shy away from direct communication, even at home, and she was having a hard time conveying exactly who I was. The language didn't help. With six weeks to go, I learned to my horror that Rumiko had not even told them her friend was a man. (It's not really necessary to say "he" or "she" in Japanese.)

Imagining what would happen if I turned up and found a frilly nightgown laid out on the guest bed, I pan- icked. In feeble Japanese I began a letter of confession to her parents. I said we had met and fallen in love. Fortu- nately, I had to switch to English before I got to the steamier details concerning our living arrangements. Rumiko gave her parents a heavily edited summary of the letter. The invitation stood.

Now, as I boarded a Northwest flight at JFK Airport in the frozen tundra of Queens, came the ugly questions. The Japanese were notorious for their distrust of foreigners. Would her family allow her to return to the States with me? Would they want to interrogate me first? Or would they contract out the job? The Japanese, I knew, often investigated the backgrounds of potential suitors, even hiring private detectives to check their pedigrees. At a glance, my family looked respectable, but seen in a certain light, wouldn't they appear . . . eccentric? We were a bewildering mix of ethnicities: Arab-American on my father's side, Anglo-American on my mother's, with dashes of French-Canadian, German, Welsh, and Irish thrown in for seasoning. Completing the circle, more or less, one of my great-aunts had married into a Jewish family. Like many ethnic families, we were prone to loud arguments and frequent laughter.

Then there was me: a divorced, underemployed journalist! Rumiko had somehow accepted all this, but it seemed unlikely that her parents would. But why worry about it? I asked myself. I had no intention of marrying her anyway.

I declined the flight attendant's offer of headphones; I was too engrossed by the horror film in my head. Reel Two: What if her father wasn't even interested in my family? What if he accused me outright of defiling his daughter? Seen from a certain point of view, the facts were on his side. What was I supposed to do then, go down on one knee (or was it two in Japan?) and ask for her hand in marriage? Rumiko had told me, shortly after we became lovers, that without her virginity there was no hope of marrying a Japanese man. Was there such a thing as a shotgun marriage in Japan? Or did they do it at sword-point? I wondered.

For thirteen hours my mind and stomach churned in

dreadful unison. In all that time, I never once imagined the actual horror that awaited me: a slavering hound from hell in the shape of the family dog.

At last, as the sun eased into the Sea of Japan, the 747 circled for a landing and I saw the perfect cone of Mount Fuji, symbol of an unchanging Japan, silhouetted against the incarnadine sky. Excitement and wonder banished my fears.

THE FAMILY TOOLS

Under the reign of the Tokugawas, running from the seventeenth to the nineteenth centuries, class mattered more than family. The shoguns were obsessed with keeping everyone in his place. They codified the feudal system, creating four social classes. Samurai warriors were at the top, followed by farmers, artisans, and, at the bottom of the heap, merchants.

Razan Hayashi (1583–1657), a neo-Confucian philosopher who served as adviser to the first three shoguns, recorded their views on the importance of class distinctions:

> . . . [W]e cannot allow disorder between the ruler and the subject, and between those who are above and those who are below. The separation into four classes of samurai, farmers, artisans, and merchants . . . is part of the principles of heaven and is the Way which was taught by the Sage.[6]

Tokugawa family policy mainly affected the *daimyō*. To keep these great provincial warlords from rebelling, the Tokugawa shoguns perfected a system of hostage taking. Each *daimyō* was required to put up his family in

the capital as hostages whenever he returned to his es-
tates. This neatly foreshadowed the day when the shoguns of business would require salarymen to leave their
families and go off on long-term assignment to some
godforsaken corner of the country, or indeed of the globe.

While the Tokugawas made darn sure everyone stayed
in their place and paid their taxes, they generally allowed
ordinary families to manage their own affairs. These consisted mainly of struggling to survive. Although the spectacular two-sworded warrior stands as the symbol of
feudal Japan, only 6 percent of the Japanese were samurai.[7] The vast majority of Japanese, more than 90 percent,
were villagers engaged in farming or trade.[8] The typical
Japanese family at the time lived in an *ie*, or household,
which was part of a *mura*, or village, made up of inter-
twined *ie*.

Such people learned to submerge their egos, even their
lightest desires, to serve their *ie*. "Absolute obedience
served to preserve the harmony of the family, of which
the household was the kingpin," writes sociologist Fukutake.[9] Family members worked together and cooperated
with their neighbors in a common enterprise. The family
may or may not have been happy, but it was unquestionably close-knit.[10]

When samurai upstarts finally put an end to the Tokugawa regime in 1868 and made the emperor the nominal
ruler of the country, they changed its dominant metaphor. Japan was a single family, they declared, and the
emperor, descended in an unbroken line from the goddess
Amaterasu, was its father. But the Meiji government's
plan to galvanize the economy and strengthen the army
went far beyond metaphor. It abolished the samurai warriors and created a modern military. It refashioned the
social order into something resembling Britain's: an aris-

tocracy, a fledgling middle class, and a broad working class. Under color of tradition, it gave its "state as family" policy the force of law by writing the *ie* into the constitution. In so doing, the Meiji leaders began a process that would substitute martial values for domestic loyalties and, in the twentieth century, hollow out the emotional core of the Japanese family. Historian Janet Hunter writes:

> For the cardinal virtues and family structure, the Meiji "tradition" drew on the ethos of the warrior class. . . . The persistent dominance of military society in Japan was crucial to this change. In Japan the supreme virtues were loyalty to one's ruler . . . and filial piety. . . . [W]here the two virtues conflicted, loyalty tended to take precedence over filial piety.[11]

The results were soon apparent. Family life had been regulated by families within villages; now control would flow directly from the state. "This change alone," writes Fukutake, "transforming what had been a self-governing unit into a segment of a larger administrative village, represented a very great change indeed."[12]

Wherever possible, tradition was put to new uses. The *ie*, for example, held one key advantage for a country bent on rapid industrial and territorial expansion. By making the eldest son sole inheritor, it assured that a steady supply of impoverished daughters and younger sons would be available for the factories and the military. "This *ie* system had a good deal to do with the industrialization of Japan after the Meiji period," Fukutake observes.[13] Even after the Pacific war, when the *ie* was abolished and democracy set in place, the lesson was not lost. Japan continued to shape its families into cold tools of economic growth.

DOGGIE DEAREST

*As to the dog: The trouble began with my gray, pin-
striped suit. This was actually the first suit I'd ever
owned. I dislike formality and, when asked to dress up,
I had always managed to get by with a blazer and
slacks, whatever the occasion. But I'd gone to a lot of
trouble and expense in picking out this suit, because I
thought it would appeal to conservative-minded Japanese parents such as those I had expected to encounter.
I never dreamed it would appeal to the dog.*

*Rumiko met me at my hole-in-the-wall hotel and we
boarded a commuter express train for her family home
in the western arm of the city. Incredibly, an hour later
we were still within the vast sprawl of Tokyo. We got off
at a station overlooking what appeared to be a doll-
house village. I'd never seen anything like it before. Gaz-
ing around from the platform, I could see dozens of tiny
houses with blue-tiled roofs jumbled together at crazy
angles. Here and there irregular patches of green showed
through. They were, I later learned, tiny farms—left-
overs perhaps from the Occupation's redistribution of
land.*

*We waded through a shopping plaza in front of the
station, bumping elbows with busy housewives at every
turn, crossed a four-lane thoroughfare, and then suddenly we were enveloped in the silence of an empty sub-
urban road barely wide enough for two compact cars to
pass. We walked in the street—there was no sidewalk—
and the echo of our heels played back to us off the
cinder-block walls on either side. I peered over one. A
cat could not have squeezed through the dark, mossy
space between the wall and the house it contained. Ner-
vously, I rehearsed my greetings in Japanese.*

My misgivings were misplaced. As we approached a

tiny two-story house wedged in between several larger ones, Rumiko's whole family spilled out to greet me— everyone but her father, who was still at work. At the gate was her mother, Tatsuko, a small, energetic woman of feline elegance and a disarming smile. On the stairs behind her posed sister Megumi, tall (among Japanese), slim, and relentlessly sexy in her hip-hugging jeans and sunset eyeshade. In the doorway, her grandmother, known as Obaa-chan ("Darling Granny"), frail but the picture of dignity in a chiaroscuro kimono of black and green. Bounding among them was the dog, a scruffy little white Maltese who yapped ferociously at me.

I don't remember whether I uttered my introduction correctly, but I'm sure that with all the yapping it was never heard. I was swept into the house in a flurry of bowing and greeting. We regrouped just inside the door in the genkan, the entrance hall that symbolically divides the inner world from the outer. The family was already on the wooden floor, which counts as inside, while I remained on the stone part, which belongs to the outside. I was about to become the first foreigner ever to cross the threshold. There was an expectant silence. I handed over the bouquet of flowers I'd brought along as insurance in case I got tongue-tied and, with all eyes upon me, I struggled out of my shoes—big, black lace-up things that no sensible Japanese would ever wear. Then, in stockinged feet, I stepped up onto the wooden floor. A sigh of relief filled the narrow hall, followed by the urgent sniffing of the dog.

Feeling a bit more confident, I accepted Mrs. Hirata's invitation to step into the yōma, the Western-style sitting room found in many Japanese homes. It was small, no more than four paces across, but before I made it to the sofa, I was tackled from behind. I stumbled and managed to land on the sofa. Looking down in horror, I saw what everyone else politely declined to see: the dog was furiously humping my leg.

I shook him off. He came right back for more. Tea and cakes were placed before me. Smiling tautly, I punted the dog halfway across the room. No use. Half his teeth were gone and he was stiff with arthritis, but in me—or rather in the irresistible wool of my suit— the cur had discovered his second youth. He cartwheeled to a stop on the shag rug, bounded onto the sofa, and went to work on my arm. It was a hideously embarrassing situation. His bright red erection seemed impossible to overlook, but the party went on as if nothing were amiss.

I felt myself to be in something of a dilemma. My new pinstriped suit was in danger of getting some hard-to-remove stains if I could not persuade the nice little doggie—whose stylishly Western name, by the way, was Jon—to back off. And yet, in my experience, thrashing the family dog as soon as you walk in the door does not generally leave a good impression on a girlfriend's parents.

Mrs. Hirata had gotten out an old album and was showing me sepia-toned pictures of Rumiko as a child. My head swam. I tried flashing urgent messages with my eyes to Rumiko, seated across from me. She smiled back demurely. It was at this point that I learned something interesting about Rumiko, and about Japanese culture at large. Whenever we were in her family's house, she was part of their team, not mine. Inside and outside, I thought sadly, the only principles from which the Japanese never stray.

Finally some merciful soul—I think it was Rumiko's little sister—pried loose the canine Casanova and locked him up somewhere.

Years later, Jon died, probably of terminal lust. I can rise above petty grudges as well as the next man, and

*did not refuse to attend his funeral. It involved a full
Buddhist ceremony with a monk chanting over his cremated bones using gongs and candles and incense. Very
solemn and mournful it was, but I'm ashamed to say
that even at that moment I could not in my heart forgive
him. If I shed any tears, they were for the grieving family.*

WE ARE STILL MARRIED[14]

As in every other society, women have always been the
linchpin of Japanese families. Yet, in Japan, as in all too
many societies, they have been valued as little more than
chattel. A proverb describing children went: "One to sell,
one to take over, one to stand by."[15] The one to take over
was the eldest son, and the one to stand by was his
younger brother. The one to sell was, of course, the
daughter. Once she came of age, you would get a price for
her in marriage (or in prostitution) and be done with her.
If you had more daughters than you could manage, you
would "thin out" the family by *mabiki*, that is, infanticide.[16]

The Meiji reforms, though they opened some educational doors for women, served mostly to cement these
inequities. Industrialization opened up the new alternative of leasing the family daughter to a factory owner for
years of hard labor before marrying her off. Marriage continued to mean that the groom's household acquired a
servant. "Before the war marriage was usually for the
sake of the *ie* and the woman became more a daughter-
in-law of the *ie* than the wife of her husband," Fukutake writes.[17] The bride answered primarily to her
mother-in-law. Indeed, *yome*, the word prewar Japanese used for wife, also carried the meaning of daughter-
in-law.[18] In Western cultures, the bullying mother-in-law

has long been the butt of husbands' jokes. In Japan she
was a terror to the wife. "Even after marriage," says one
commentator, "a girl was often little more than an ap-
prentice for sometimes as much as twenty years, until
her mother-in-law died."[19] As matriarch of the household, the mother-in-law held the awful power to expel
the wife at whim. This privilege, it seems, was often
invoked: The divorce rate in the Meiji era was triple
the postwar rate.[20] Although the mother-in-law could
give the order, traditional divorce was a male prero-
gative: All the husband had to do was hand his wife
a brief notice, called the *mikudarihan* ("three-and-a-
half lines"), and throw the "baggage" out.[21] Even though
Meiji rulers made mutual consent a requirement, the
wife's views were generally ignored.[22] If the unfortunate woman's family would not take her back, she often had to choose between prostitution and starvation.

The Meiji government, reviving Confucian notions of
family, decreed the ideal role of a woman to be *ryōsai
kenbo*, or "good wife, wise mother." And woe betide the
woman who failed to live up to that ideal. "The lot of a
childless wife in Japan is a sad one," wrote Alice Bacon,
author of the first book on Japanese women by a Westerner, in 1891. "She is an object of pity to her friends, and
well does she know that Confucius has laid down the law
that a man is justified in divorcing a childless wife."[23]

Even if she had children, the nineteenth-century Japanese wife gained little more by it than mere acceptance.
Bacon observed the woman "has so few on whom to lavish her affection, so little to live for besides her children,
and no hopes in the future except through them, that it
is no wonder that she devotes her life to their care and
service."[24] Only when her first son married would she
gain a measure of power, and then it would be mainly to

inflict on her daughter-in-law the same treatment she had received at the hands of *her* mother-in-law.

As Japan veered toward twentieth-century militarism, the state, having wrapped itself in the metaphor of the family, claimed absolute authority over the real thing. Sons were taken in growing numbers to serve in the military. The 1925 Peace Preservation Law created a thought-control system of appalling efficiency.[25] While the infamous thought police scoured the country to break up meetings, burn books, and interrogate citizens, families were kept in line by *chōkai* (neighborhood governing associations).[26]

After Japan's defeat in World War II, General Mac-Arthur's occupation forces wrote the *ie* out of the nation's new constitution. In principle, women gained equal rights, and primogeniture was abolished so that all children could inherit. The unabashedly Western idea was to place the dignity of the individual above the authority of the family. Instead, whatever sanctity the family may once have held was trampled in Japan's rush to rebuild.

Husbands and wives who once worked side by side in the fields or shops found that in the postwar industrial landscape they had become strangers. The Meiji ideal of *ryōsai kenbo* was tailored to the new economic reality. In the early 1960s, Ezra Vogel, a renowned Harvard Japanologist, noted the results in his milestone book, *Japan's New Middle Class*:

> The housewife generally knows little and cares less about her husband's daily activities at the office. She has virtually no opportunity to go out with her husband to meet other men in the company and their wives. . . . Because she is so completely sepa-

rated from the husband's daily world and he knows so little about her community activities, the area of their mutual interest tends to be the children and the relatives."[27]

As Japan's economy boomed, things got worse. Lacking time and common understanding, couples communicated less and less.[28] Even in the most intimate sphere of marriage, a terrible malaise drifted between many husbands and wives.

Traditionally, the Japanese, lacking the puritanical norms of Christianity, are said to have been quite uninhibited about sex. Young people often lived together in trial marriages. Mixed bathing in public bathhouses was commonplace. Even religious rituals sometimes involved explicitly sexual images.

However, as the bawdy Edo period gave way to the anxious modern era, the Japanese somehow became quite inhibited about sex. Even in marriage, researchers found that men and women lacked the ability to discuss and, in many cases, to enjoy sex together. "There are a number of signs that a larger proportion of Japanese women reject sexuality or derive less pleasure from it than do women in the West," notes researcher Samuel Coleman. "Surveys conducted in Japan in the early 1950s . . . found that it took longer for Japanese women to experience orgasm in marriage than in the United States, and that the percentage of women who had not experienced orgasm after fifteen years of marriage was twice the United States figure."[29]

Men, in their own way, were equally cold. For all too many, marital intercourse quickly became a mere obligation (called *giri man*). All too many sought gratification with prostitutes or mistresses.[30] Infidelity occurs everywhere, of course, but few cultures denigrate marital love to such an extent as Japan's. This, too, grew out of military values. "In the army and navy, until the end of the war, love was thought 'effeminate' and 'unmanly,'" according to one Japanese writer.[31] To describe the dearth of marital affection, Japanese sex specialists coined a unique term meaning "sex without a heart."[32]

It is often said that Christian missionaries were responsible for introducing sexual shame to Japan. No doubt this is true to a degree, but it is worth noting that Japan never became a puritanical nation. It has a huge sex industry, ranging from pornography to sex clubs of every variety. And, as noted, men, especially wealthy and powerful men, feel no restraint about infidelity.

What's more, if missionaries could persuade only one in a hundred Japanese to adopt the Christian faith, how can we suppose that they succeeded in changing the view of the entire society about sex? A more plausible explanation lies in the authoritarian roots of the Meiji government. Authoritarian regimes typically impose sexually repressive mores on the populace, especially on women, while reserving sexual freedom to themselves.

Sexual mores in Japan over the last century comported more with authoritarian views than some Christian notion of propriety. In prewar rural Japan, an unmarried woman who became pregnant was often expected to kill herself for the sake of the *ie*. In the cities, the police kept boys and girls from mingling in the cinemas.[33] Sexual repression, in short, has been part and parcel of the general repression of the Japanese people under the rubric of public order.

Taken together, the Meiji-invented "tradition" of placing loyalty to authorities above duty to family, the absence of marital romance, and the repression of sexuality go a long way toward explaining the mutual disdain of husbands and wives that is so common in Japan today.

However, the alienation became complete only when the postwar economic system came into force. Just how much that system relies on the distortion of the family will become clear further on.

If marital alienation were the only problem besetting Japanese families, it could be easily dismissed. After all, marriage hasn't been perfected in any society and rarely assures unalloyed happiness in life. As it happens, the Japanese family faces many other difficulties. But before moving on to them, I want to shed a bit more light on marital discord in Japan. I do this not to rub dirt in anyone's face but because here we encounter another facet of Japanese life that is often presented as a picture of harmony.

Japanese wives have long tolerated, and even facilitated, their husbands' peccadilloes. I knew of a truck driver in Japan whose wife gave him a monthly allowance specifically for entertaining his girlfriend. At higher reaches of society, male infidelity was practically institutionalized, as Vogel found:

> If a man carries on an affair with a girl in the office, it need not disrupt his relationship with his wife. . . . Some wives even say their husbands are milder and easier to deal with if they have a sexual outlet outside the home.[34]

To many, this state of affairs appeared to be a stable cultural phenomenon. It wasn't. Men's brazen infidelity to their wives resulted from an almost total disparity in power. The Japanese man, it was said, had three mothers: the one who gave birth to him, the one who took care of his house and children, and the one outside the home who gave him comfort and solace from the harsh world.[35] It may have been paradise for men, but "[t]he maternal trinity gave wives the worst deal of all," remarks female historian Etsuko Yamashita.[36] Women tolerated bad marriages because the alternative was intolerable. Even in postwar Japan, divorce left women virtually unprotected and cast a lifelong stigma on the children, cutting them off from a good job or marriage.

Those who see harmony and happiness in Japan's comparatively low divorce rate should note this: A 1993 poll of Japanese found that less than half of those interviewed said they would marry the same person if given the chance to do it over again.[37] A full 36 percent said they definitely would not marry the same person, and more than 40 percent of the middle-aged respondents said they had actually considered getting a divorce. The most commonly cited benefit of marriage was not love or companionship but acceptance in public as full-fledged members of society.

And those who believe that women rule the roost should talk to Yukiko Tsunoda, an attorney who handles cases of battered wives. In a survey she conducted, Tsunoda turned up hundreds of battered women, many of them the wives of respected managers. Despite beatings with baseball bats and golf clubs, scaldings with hot tea, and other atrocities, 53 percent of the battered women remained with their abusive partners.[38]

Of course, there are numerous happy marriages in Japan. But what holds many other Japanese couples together is not domestic bliss but the punitive effect of divorce: loss of social status and, on the woman's side, economic security; on the man's, the household services of a wife. In many homes, then, there is a *katei-nai rikon*—"divorce within the household."[39] Husband and wife simply glide past one another, interacting only when necessity dictates.

The fundamental cause of such alienation, I have suggested, is the intervention of the authorities—government and employer—in the family. The responsibility for change, however, lies with the people themselves. The Japanese are gradually realizing this. There is a broad perception in Japan that all the well-defined family relationships of the *ie* have gone askew. In a letter to the *Yomiuri Shimbun*, Japan's largest daily newspaper, a middle-aged Tokyo housewife named Motoko Ogura pinpointed the problem:

> It may sound good to regard Japanese men as "worker bees," but the results of ignoring families clearly appear [in the rising divorce rate] . . . . When I traveled to Italy, I heard Italian husbands say to their wives every morning: "You look really pretty this morning. I love you." Most Japanese wives hardly ever hear those words. They devote their days to raising children. It is almost like they are single mothers, as they do not get any help from their husbands. . . . [U]nless men gain awareness of family issues, wives will continue to want their husbands not to be home.[40]

Mrs. Ogura's notion of the chivalry of Italian husbands may be exaggerated, but her perception of the state of marital relations in Japan is not.

In the seventies, the Japanese started fretting about their *chichi naki shakai*, the "fatherless society" brought about by the company demand for total devotion to work.

In the eighties, they began worrying about children who were becoming sociopathic bullies under the pressure of their round-the-clock quest for admission to high-status schools.

Now, the establishment is in a sweat about women. As hard as it has tried to keep them in check, they are stepping out of their roles. On the cusp of the nineties, 50 percent of women surveyed by the government disputed the notion that men should be breadwinners and women housekeepers.[41] The proportion among working women was naturally much higher. Back in 1972, tradition had been disputed by only 10 percent of male and female respondents alike.

It's not mere opinion that has changed: As late as 1985, only one of every five Japanese women with preschool children held a job. Now more than one out of three return to work as soon as they can arrange day care. By the time children enter school, two out of three of their mothers are back at work outside the home.[42]

The social framework has hardly adapted to these changes at all. Day care remains scarce and its hours short. Counseling is primitive. In place of solutions, nostalgia abounds. Many older women pine for the old *ie*, where at least everyone's roles and duties were clearly defined.

A perennially popular cartoon show captures this nostalgia, much as the old "Father Knows Best" TV program did for Americans. The "Sazae-san" show portrays a family in which everyone from Grandpa to Baby Sis sticks to role, and all conflicts are resolved in the mildest of ways. Not much happens on the show. The Sazae family sits around in traditional cotton robes eating traditional Japanese meals (no Big Macs for them!) and soaking in hot baths. The humor is quaint, the pace is slow: The satisfaction arises mainly from seeing all family members present and interactive.

Even before the big domestic upheavals of the eighties had begun in earnest, Keiko Higuchi, a sociologist and critic who writes on social concerns for the *Asahi Shimbun* newspaper, noted: "Perhaps the major problem is that we still pursue the old image of home life, without realizing that times have changed. Do we not build a homelike facade for the family to conceal a hollow interior?"[43]

FATHER KNOWS BEST

Mr. Hirata, the one I really dreaded meeting, proved to be all gruff and no bite. After tea and cakes, we rode the train back into central Tokyo, to the neon-lit canyons of Shinjuku. There we met Mr. Hirata on a crowded street corner. He was thin and wiry, with a craggy face and a shock of thick white hair. He walked with a pronounced limp and wore a brown beret. To my fevered imagination the combination appeared, well, soldierly.

In truth, as I was to learn, he was a gentle, thoughtful, and indulgent man who had managed to sit out the war in an agricultural college until they were handing out bamboo stakes for a last, desperate defense. Yet in some ways he was the epitome of his generation of men: born a country boy, grown an urban businessman. He wore well-cut suits but retained the tough hands of a farmer. If he came across a potato bug while tending his potted chrysanthemums, he would crush it between his forefinger and thumb and flick it aside. You didn't have to be strong to do that, but you certainly couldn't be squeamish.

Mr. Hirata, like all the men of his generation, had been honed to discipline in a military-style school where he had to march about in uniform and venerate the emperor's picture every morning—that is, he would venerate the locked cabinet that held the picture. Until Japan lost the war and the emperor his divinity, Hirohito's face was too sacred for mere schoolboys to gaze upon.

After the war, he became a high school teacher, mar-

ried a fellow teacher from Tokyo, and returned to his hometown in the region called Fukui, on the Sea of Japan. It was there, in the Snow Country made famous by Yasunari Kawabata's novel of that name, that Rumiko was born.

And Rumiko might well have lived out her life there, except that one of Mr. Hirata's old students called one day from Tokyo to say that he was starting a construction company and needed an older, respectable man to serve as a director.

It was a good move. The company prospered in a small way and the family benefited from being in the nation's capital. Mrs. Hirata was able to land a job with an education magazine, a move that would eventually lead her to become a publisher herself. Rumiko was able to enter the first of a chain of prestigious public schools that would bring her the greatest educational prize the country has to offer: admission to the University of Tokyo. Megumi was able to grow up with all the stylishness and frivolity that Tokyo has to offer young people: She was totally free of the small-town quaintness that stuck to her country cousin Sawako like a Quaker bonnet.

Moreover, the new career suited Mr. Hirata well. He was full of those virtues that led to the Japanese economic miracle: loyalty to his company, a relentless drive to do things right, and a bottomless capacity for suffering and self-sacrifice. How much he embodied these qualities was to become clear when he died in harness, three years past the date he was supposed to retire. But before that awful time, I would learn of many other, more individual qualities he possessed—his sense of humor, his stubborn idealism, and his broad-minded tolerance, none of which I had expected in a Japanese father.

But all of this lay shrouded in the future. As we stood

on the street corner, buffeted by the crowds and chilled
by the winter winds, I whipped out a business card and
attempted to introduce myself—a ritual that requires a
lot of bowing and mumbling and sucking of teeth.

"This is not the time!" Mr. Hirata snapped. I was hor-
rified. He turned to lead us into the restaurant where we
were to have dinner.

"What did I do?" I asked Rumiko hoarsely.

"It's okay," she reassured me. "Just wait for him to
do it."

To my further embarrassment, I discovered that he
had reserved a private room for us in a renowned beef
house. Renting a private room in a restaurant is not all
that rare in Japan, though I didn't know it then. What I
knew beyond all doubt was that the expense would be
unspeakable. All the more so in a restaurant that
served beef.

Beef! Not any tough, stringy, imported beef, but finely
marbled Kobe beef, more precious than pearls. Beef from
cows that lead the lives of idle noblemen, passing the
time with daily massages, buckets of beer, and, for all I
know, indulging nightly poker games before they get it
in the neck.

Beef like that could not just be cut into slabs and
tossed on the grill. The restaurant sliced it into paper-
thin sheets for use in shabu shabu, a kind of stew made
at the table.

We were led into our room by four or five kimono-clad
women and seated on embroidered silk cushions on the
straw tatami mats. As we settled in, Mr. Hirata finally
presented me with his card, which showed him to be a
managing director of the Ichimaru Construction Company. I offered my card with a meek "hajimemashite"
(the Japanese equivalent of "nice to meet you"), and followed up with my present—a ski cap emblazoned with

the words UNIVERSITY OF PENNSYLVANIA. *It suddenly seemed completely the wrong gift for a Japanese businessman with a limp, but he accepted it with grace.*

It soon became clear that whether or not I was enjoying myself, the whole family was enjoying watching me. If there's one thing that really stands out among the things I've never mastered, it's how to sit cross-legged on the floor. Within minutes I felt as if I were resting on a bed of sea urchins. Mr. Hirata's eyes crinkled in mirth as I squirmed from haunch to haunch. Finally he burst out in a high-pitched laugh that was startling in a man with such a gravelly voice and told Rumiko to let me know it was okay just to put my legs out straight under the table. After I had settled in, the beer was poured and Mr. Hirata raised his glass to offer me "kanpai," the Japanese equivalent of "cheers." Downing the beer, I felt a warm sensation of relief coursing through my veins.

STRANGER IN OUR MIDST

Without question, the most dramatic shift in the Japanese family has been the emasculation of fatherhood. Traditionally, the father was sovereign of the household; according to an old saw, the four scariest things in life were fire, earthquakes, thunder, and Father. This was not for lack of familiarity. In what used to be mainly a land of farmers and merchants, Father was rarely far from home. By contrast, the modern-day salaryman (as the white-collar worker is known) is rarely home and scarcely welcome when he is.

"Oversized trash" has become a common expression for husbands among Japanese wives. Fully 83 percent of the housewives surveyed in May 1991 by Japan's largest newspaper said men are useless around the house. (The occasion for the poll was Father's Day.) Even after death, husbands aren't getting the respect they used to: A growing number of women are resorting to *shigo rikon*—"divorce after death."[44] Wives refuse to have their remains interred with their husband's in the family grave.

The open contempt of many women for their husbands astonished me. I had subscribed to the stereotype of the passive, deferential Japanese wife, even though I knew from the start that Rumiko in no way fit it. One day I ran into the wife of a salaryman friend. I asked how he was.

"Oh, that crybaby! He kept me up all night with his complaining," she replied. Startled, I asked why. Her husband, it turned out, had torn a muscle in his back playing golf while she was taking care of the kids. Reason enough, I would have thought, for a little moaning and groaning. Of course, in a country where a few generations ago men of honor were frequently expected to slit their bellies without complaint, stoicism remains a virtue. What really startled me was the woman's undisguised scorn for her husband. Her response did not seem to be the kind of ritual humility that Japanese often employ when talking about their families or companies. Hers was a put-down *con brio*.

Japanese fathers fare no better in their children's regard. Here is the Japanese version of *Home Alone*, in the words of critic Keiko Higuchi: "A child feels that nobody is at home when the father happens to be home early but the mother and everyone else are out."[45]

This is not merely some elitist critic's view. I knew a Japanese man whose kids bawled in fear and clung to their mother on those rare occasions when he happened to return before they were asleep. He was a sober, soft-spoken man of gentle habits, but a stranger in his own home.

Popular culture has pegged the typical father as little more than a lout. While I was living in Japan, the makers of a videocamera capitalized on this view to promote a new use for their product. Their TV ad shows a father bursting in through the front door late at night, tie askew and hair matted, roaring like a gored bull. As his young son and daughter cower in the folds of their mother's nightgown, she videotapes the scene so she can show him his disgraceful behavior in the morning. In America, this would be the solemn stuff of a public service spot against child abuse or alcoholism. In Japan, it merely provoked roars of laughter.

Fathers are also figures of ridicule on many television shows. I was shocked when I tuned in to a popular cartoon show one evening and saw a kid's-eye view of Father: Two children are watching their father sleep on a Sunday morning. As they look on, he wakes, scratches his belly, sneezes, and breaks wind.

"Wherever Dad is, he cuts huge farts," says one little kid to the other.

"Yeah, he's so gross!" says the other.

Dad slurps some tea. Then he pads off to the toilet. After he finishes, the kids look at each other and exclaim, "Wow, it really stinks!"

The father stumbles back to his futon and falls asleep again. End of scene. Set alongside such caricatures, Homer Simpson would be a safe bet for Father of the Year.

Men have worked hard to earn the contempt of their families. Putting company business above all else, many do not bother to be around for the birth of their children, and leave the subsequent upbringing entirely to their wives. Two Japanese men of my acquaintance were away on business for six months when their first children were born. Even those who are nearby frequently miss the birth of their children. Of 210 husbands in one study, only a fourth were present for the great event. The rest, with few exceptions, were all at work or at home.[46] Our neighbor Mr. Inahoso was one of Japan's half-million *tan-shin funin*, men who are dispatched by their companies to live far from their families for years at a stretch. He saw his teenage daughter just a few times a year. I met dozens of men who could not recall the ages of their children. Some have trouble coming up with their names.

Unsurprisingly, Japanese men have come to feel that home is not a safe place to express their feelings. In some cases, the distress becomes acute. Japanese psychologists have recognized this with a term that means "phobia of going home." Still, there are fathers in Japan who share in family life and many more who yearn to. Articles such as one titled "Most Young Fathers Like Parenting, Survey Finds" attest to the change.[47] A journalist whom I'll call Daisuke Matsunaga went through the transition before my eyes.

Matsunaga had gone to college in Florida and returned with a serious case of good humor. He frequently peppered himself with it, always joking about how henpecked he was and how miserable his home life was. Through his jokes, however, I could see the shadows of a pathetic situation. Money was the focus of his complaints. In order to buy a tiny house in Tokyo's outrageously inflated market, he had taken out a mortgage that claimed nearly half his monthly check and virtually all of his semiannual bonuses. And still, he had been forced to borrow half the down payment from his in-laws, which he would pay back God only knew how, hitched as he was to a lifetime job that offered steady but unspectacular annual raises. But his troubles weren't entirely about money. His daughter, who was seven or eight at the time (he didn't seem quite sure which), virtually ignored him when he was home. If she had anything to say to him, she relayed it through her mother.

Yet, cowed though he was by this daunting domestic scene, Matsunaga clung to his macho prerogatives as husband. One evening, when some news story was keeping me longer than I had planned, I phoned Rumiko to let her know I'd be late.

Matsunaga, who happened to be nearby, overheard. As soon as I put the receiver down, he laughed jeeringly.

"You call your wife to tell her when you'll be home? Hah! I'd never do that," he crowed. Our relations cooled for a while.

But a couple of years later, I ran into Matsunaga again. A big change had come over him. Intimations of mortality, or perhaps just irrelevance, had taken hold of him. He was now forty and his daughter had just turned tcn.

"I'm quitting," he announced.

"You're what?" I said, thinking of his mortgage and the hardship that any Japanese forty-year-old would have in finding a new job. "What are you going to do?"

"I'm going to spend a couple of months just being with my family," he said proudly.

"That's great!" I said. "You can do things with your daughter for a change."

His face clouded over and his voice sank. "I don't know my daughter very well. Frankly she doesn't seem to like me."

I couldn't think of anything to say. Suddenly I was angry with him—no, for him, for all the Japanese men I knew who were blindly throwing their lives away in service to the company. They did it, I knew, because they felt they had no choice. They had been raised to regard working for a company as the prime duty of their lives; any streak of independence had been ground out of them, first by the school system and later by the grueling indoctrination that new employees undergo. And even those who shook off the blinders and looked around saw nowhere to turn. For decades, the curse of the lifetime employment system was that the only direction you could move was down. Companies that hired midcareer people were inevitably the weaker, second-tier suppliers. In rare cases, blue-chip companies would hire a specialist in midcareer, but that person would be frozen in place with no chance of climbing the management ladder, let alone joining in the mainstream social life of the company. But now cracks were appearing in that system, and Matsunaga, who remembered the openness of America so well, evidently thought he could squeeze through one.

After a long pause, I came up with a platitude: "Well, buck up," I told him. "It's never too late to start over."

TO THE EDGE OF DOOM[48]

In the warmth of that first meeting with the Hirata family, my doubts about marrying Rumiko began to melt away. After the Hiratas took me on the trip to Kyoto— during which I accompanied my friend the English teacher on our New Year's visit to the temple—I felt absolute certainty. What a fool I'd been to think that Japan would stand in the way of our getting married! With sudden clarity I realized that for a journalist this was the place to be—the techno-frontier, to be sure, but also the locus of an ancient civilization that ten centuries earlier had produced the world's first novel. Japan, moreover, was rising like Godzilla out of the Pacific as America's most fearsome competitor, a fact that was bound to keep it in the news for the foreseeable future.

More important than all this, of course, was the realization that I genuinely liked Rumiko's family and felt

*I could, well, live with them. And at the heart of it all
was the secure knowledge that I really, truly, deeply
loved Rumiko and trusted that we could manage our
lives together even if that required shifting halfway
across the globe from time to time.*

*All these ideas coalesced as we flew back to Philadel-
phia together. I didn't speak my mind right away but
mulled my thoughts like warm winter ale. Rumiko's parents had seen us off at the airport—no mean feat of gen-
erosity, considering that Narita is a three-hour drive
from their patch of Tokyo. Walking down the ramp to
Customs, I looked back to say good-bye one more time.
Mrs. Hirata, I observed, had tears in her eyes. She said
something to me. My Japanese was still very weak and
it wasn't until we were out of sight that I worked it out.
I may, of course, have been wrong, but it seemed to me
that she had said, "Please come live in Japan."*

*A few days after our return to Philadelphia, I took Rum-
iko out to a dim little piano bar. There was a hard freeze
outside. The wind had numbed my lips and fingers. Perhaps fear, too, made it difficult to speak. At any rate, I
couldn't seem to find anything to say. We just sat, listening to the soothing vagaries of New Age piano music.
An aperitif of brandy, however, thawed me nicely. I began by telling Rumiko how much I had enjoyed meeting
her family—leaving out my impressions of the dog, of
course—and how surprised I'd been to find Tokyo so fascinating.*

*"I told you Philadelphia wasn't a real city," she said
mischievously. This was a running gag with us, but for
the first time I had to concede my end of it. Finally, I
got to the heart of the matter: I told her I had a new
vision of our relationship. I thought we could get married and go live in Tokyo. Not forever, perhaps, and not*

right away. Landing a journalistic assignment there would take some time. But I was certain now that this was the path I wanted to follow, in step with her.

She listened thoughtfully, so much so I began to worry that I might have waited too long. But as it happened, Rumiko too had been rethinking our relationship. She agreed that getting married would be the right thing, despite all the difficulties of an international marriage. There was only one snag: While I had been deciding that I wanted to move to Tokyo, Rumiko had decided that she wanted to settle in America after all. A few months back in Tokyo had convinced her that life there would stunt her career and cramp her newfound joie de vivre.

I stared at her in open-mouthed astonishment. Then we both began to laugh. Out on the frosty street again, I began to sing, "I say to-may-to, you say to-mah-to . . . ," which, as it happens, was true. Just the same, we didn't call the whole thing off.

Rumiko and I were married a year and a half later, in a five-minute ceremony conducted by a federal judge on his lunch hour. We very nearly didn't get married at all on account of the shortage of available magistrates. It was only by appealing to the federal judiciary that we were spared the embarrassment of having to postpone the ceremony till after the reception party. There was never any question of a church wedding. Rumiko was nominally a Buddhist, while I, though nominally raised a Christian, was not attached to any church.

District Court Judge James McGirr Kelly, a kindly man who took his duties so seriously that he wrote an original and profound address for the occasion, married us in his antechamber on June 19, 1987. Passing through the courthouse on the way to his chambers, we attracted a good deal of attention. Prisoners in shackles, hardened men who had probably seen and done a good *deal of the outrageous in their time, stopped in their tracks to stare. Rumiko was swathed in a gorgeous white kimono embroidered with a pattern of cherry blossoms and verdant leaves. Her parents and sister, who had flown over for the wedding, were dressed in Western clothes. However, they insisted that Rumiko should wear her kimono, even though she had already bought a wedding dress. I was modestly attired in a cream-colored summer suit, but my brother Derek, a born showman, had turned up in a brilliant white set of top hat and tails. Hand him a whip and he'd have been a perfect Barnum & Bailey ringmaster. Up and down the halls he smilingly acknowledged congratulations as the lucky groom, while I wandered on in happy anonymity.*

Even the judge very nearly married off the wrong man. However, once we had straightened out our respective roles, we soon got down to business. All went smoothly until the judge's interrogatory to the bride. You know, the one that goes something like: "Do you, X, take this man to be your lawfully wedded husband, etc., etc.?" A long silence followed. The judge looked up. I looked up. The judge raised his eyebrows encouragingly. Finally, out of the side of her mouth, Rumiko whispered to me, "What am I supposed to say?" This was the first, and perhaps the least profound, of many communication problems in our marriage. But, like the others, I'm pleased to say it was eventually resolved.

Our marriage hasn't been perfect, and it certainly hasn't been easy, but if we have come this far it is largely because we tried to take to heart a piece of advice the judge laid down in his address to us:

> *As time passes, romance will diminish. The physical attraction you have for each other will lessen. There may be financial problems. The ex-*

pected promotions may not come about. There may be illness. We are all faced with the vagaries of life. Each of you must commit yourself to ardently and earnestly build a friendship with each other. If this marriage is to last, you must become best friends.

IN MY BEGINNING IS MY END

The traditional Japanese wedding, conducted by a Shinto priest, is a gorgeous and solemn affair. However, it need not be elaborate. Until recently, some Japanese chose simply to hold an austere but dignified wedding at the home of the groom. From the Meiji era on, the only requirement was that the couple register their marriage at the local government office. The only religious elements would be the honoring of the home's Buddhist altar and the Shinto custom of bride and groom sharing cups of sake. There were etiquette guidelines, of course, and the Meiji government went so far as to legally define formal wear for men, but a good deal of discretion remained with the families.[49]

Rumiko had told me of one such wedding she recalled from her childhood. It took place in the Hiratas' home in the village where she grew up. All the paper doors were taken down to open up the house into one big space. As the guests knelt on the *tatami* mat floors, the bride and groom took their vows unattended by any priest in front of the family altar. Then they drank sake in the ritual fashion and shyly bowed to the witnesses. That done, food and drink were brought in and a feast was held on the spot. Rumiko's grandfather sang.

The contemporary Japanese wedding is often a pastiche of Japanese tradition, Western sacrament, and epic ostentation. Commercialism, though hardly unique to Japan, has made an especially virulent intrusion into family rituals there. Ever anxious about social status, many Japanese place themselves entirely in the hands of wedding arrangers. These professionals display all the demure taste of the late Liberace—with none of his originality. The cost, even by Japan's pricey standards, is appalling: On average, weddings run to 8 million yen—more than $75,000.[50] In recent years weddings have been known literally to bankrupt families.

Since at least four out of five weddings now represent a *ren'ai* ("love match") rather than an arranged marriage, the hotels pander shamelessly to youthful conceits. And since the unmarried are thought to be childish, those conceits are very youthful indeed. You cannot ride a train in Tokyo without seeing ads for "the Tom and Jerry Wedding," or, perhaps to soothe the man who feels threatened by the newly independent woman, the "Young Love" wedding featuring a bride who appears to be not a day over twelve.

As in America, the pattern is set not by tradition but by celebrities. It has become *de rigueur* for a successful Japanese actress to turn her wedding into a three-hour television event, complete with Jell-O-ey songs quivering with sentiment, heavenly clouds of dry-ice fog, and at the right moment, a tight close-up of a single pearly tear carving a gully through the pancake makeup on the bride's right cheek.

The biggest choice most couples must make is whether to have a traditional Shinto ceremony or a mock Christian service. About a third of Japanese couples opt for the latter, though fewer than one in a hundred Japanese is Christian.[51] The attraction is purely atmospheric; brides, a Japanese informant told me, find Christian weddings "irresistibly romantic." The hotel supplies an imitation chapel and priest to perform the wedding sacrament, replete with genuflections, mumbled Latin, and organ music.

The first Japanese wedding I attended did not involve quite that much fakery, but it was a depressing experience all the same. Chieko, whom I had met in the States while she was studying there, was marrying a banker. She herself had gone to work for the bank in its head office, but her tasks had little to do with banking. They consisted mainly of serving tea and answering the telephone in a breathless falsetto.

To my surprise, Chieko did not object. She had intended to launch a career, but on learning how much time the bank demanded of its "lifers"—7:30 A.M. until nine, ten, or even eleven at night—she saw it would be impossible to launch both a career and a family, and opted for the latter. That meant going off the career track to the "Office Lady" siding. There, her actual role was to serve as wedding bait for bachelor bankers, a role in which she soon succeeded.

The day of her wedding began with a genuine Shinto ceremony. Normally, this is attended only by family members, but knowing of my interest, Chieko invited me. As I slipped into the back of the hall in the posh Tokyo hotel, I had a shock. Chieko the bride was unrecognizable. She looked more like a bird of paradise than a human being. Her moon-shaped face, emerging from the collar of a spectacular kimono, was painted a deathly white and her lips cherry-red. (This ghostly appearance, I was told, symbolizes her death in her family and rebirth in her husband's.) Chieko's dark hair, augmented by a wig, was piled and skewered on her head. Atop it lay a huge white headdress. This, I later learned, was the *tsunokakushi*, intended to shield the groom from the bride's "horns," a symbol of feminine wickedness.

The groom sat bareheaded (no horns on him), in a long-tailed morning coat and striped pants. Together, they waited quietly before a portable Shinto shrine about the size and shape of a street vendor's cart. Apples, strawberries, sake, seaweed, a melon, a pile of salt, and a pile of rice were placed neatly on the shelves of the shrine. This may sound like a buffet wagon, but it was a beautiful and inspiring sight. Shinto, an animist religion, honors natural things and seeks to offer the young couple all the symbols of plenitude.

The Shinto priest, a small, spare man in wizardly robes and a peaked cap, shuffled about in huge black clogs. He said a few quiet words to the immediate family and then "purified" the couple and all the witnesses by shaking a wand hung with thick white paper strands. Setting this down, he chanted a prayer to invoke blessings on the couple.

The bride and groom then performed the key ritual of drinking sake together from three bowls. Now thoroughly fortified, the groom stepped up to the altar and read a formal marriage vow, to which the bride quietly assented. Then everyone rushed off for the formal photograph, while the priest refilled the sake bottles for the next couple waiting patiently in the lobby.

I hesitated. The ceremony, though impersonal and, to the politically correct, swinishly sexist, had an undeniable cultural integrity. I didn't sense any of the joy or excitement of a Western wedding, yet I felt moved.

It was the rest of the wedding that left me cold. The *hirōen*, or announcement feast, proceeded along a rutted and ruinously expensive path. In every country and cul-

ture, a wedding feast gives the hosts a chance to demonstrate their standing in the community. But in Japan, it
often raises ostentation to a kind of performance art.

Guests were seated at two long tables, one for the
groom's associates, friends, and relatives (in that order),
and another for the bride's. They were bridged at the top
by a short table for the newlyweds and their chaperons. I
was placed fairly far down the bride's table. On my right
was a young woman with a girlish manner and extrava-
gantly long hair with bangs that curled stiffly above her
forehead. She responded to my greeting with a panicky
giggle. I took it she was single. To my left began a string
of Chieko's relatives who, contrary to Western practice,
took the humblest spots near the exits. It didn't take me
long to figure out how I rated. I was the buffer between
the VIPs and the relatives. But where was Chieko? I wondered. Then the lights went out.

The couple entered the darkened wedding hall in flush
Las Vegas style, with clouds of dry-ice vapor swirling at
their feet and spotlights playing about their heads.
Chieko had changed from her kimono into a sparkling-
white wedding gown. Her husband, Tetsuya, had traded
in the striped pants and swallow tails for a mere tuxedo.
They glided along to the lilt of Mendelssohn's wedding
march, performed by a small but competent orchestra.

After taking their places, Chieko and Tetsuya were introduced by a frosty old gent with snowy eyebrows who
was apparently some business colleague of Chieko's father. He and his wife, who sat next to Chieko, were the
nakōdo, the official go-betweens for this marriage.

Even though, as I said, most Japanese marriage partners are self-selected these days, few couples get married
without a nakōdo. Appearing to have wed on their own
judgment would be unseemly, I suppose.[52]

The introduction was a very dry and humorless proceeding, and I was getting hungry. Delicious fragrances wafted into the hall, but I seemed to be the only one who noticed. Everyone else sat stiffly, faces blank of all expression. At last the old gent sat down, and I heard the soft tread of servers approaching.

But I was disappointed. They came only to fill our sake cups for a toast. A professional emcee, an employee of the hotel, gave the mike to a prosperous-looking, middle-aged man who turned out to be the groom's boss. He gave the next of what seemed like an endless series of dry, humorless speeches, alleviated only by the sake. A professor spoke. A politician spoke. Everyone but the local undertaker spoke, excepting that all the women remained silent.

My empty stomach burned and my head swam. Just when I though I might have to slip away to the McDonald's down the street, there was a sudden slumping of shoulders, as if a platoon had just got the "at ease" order. Waiters burst in with wine, pâté de fois gras, consommé, fish in sauce a Frenchman would kill for, sorbet, medallions of buttery beef, and shoots of tender asparagus, altogether the very picture book of French cuisine. I was delighted, and, evidently, so too was Chieko. I looked up and caught her smiling for the first time that day.

With the speeches over, the couple retreated to make another of what would eventually be three or four costume changes. I lost count. Once again, the lights dimmed, and they reappeared to perform the candlelighting ceremony, a bit of romantic Western schmaltz. A Disney tune—I think it was "When You Wish Upon a Star"—filled the room. With only the butane flame of a wand and the glitter of a mirrored ball to guide them, the happy couple flitted around the guest tables, lighting the

centerpiece candles. Other smatterings of Western custom, such as the cutting of a lofty wedding cake, followed. The band played on.

As I ate, I thought over what I had heard in the speech
by Tetsuya's boss and wondered what Chieko had to be
happy about—or Tetsuya, for that matter.

The boss had addressed part of his speech to her,
along these lines: "Please accept that your husband will
have to work very hard. He will often come home late
and leave early. Please do everything you can to see
that he can rest at ease in his home and come to
work refreshed."

So there it was: The wedding marked the end, not the
beginning, of their full relationship. From here on, it was
to be mechanical, not personal. If they were lucky, Tetsuya would come home to sleep. Many young bankers
were expected to spend years running small-town
branches while their families remained in Tokyo. But
even if he managed to stay at headquarters, his weekends
were to be the bank's property, not theirs. If I knew bankers, Tetsuya would probably sleep Saturday afternoons
and go golfing with his boss on Sundays. Very sad.

Interestingly, though, by the early nineties, young Japanese were reconsidering the marriage ceremony, just as
they were reconsidering marriage itself. A small but significant number of couples began to turn their backs on
the grandiose, hotel-run wedding and opt for a private exchange of vows before an assembly of relatives and
friends. It was to be followed by a comparatively simple
celebration at a restaurant.[53] No priest, no go-betweens,
no well-paid consultants. This new trend, called the
"witnessed wedding" is obviously a throwback to the
kind of wedding Rumiko saw when she was a child, but
it also marks a hope-laden step toward the autonomy of
the married couple.

US AND WE

Following our move to Japan, it gradually became apparent to me that the Hirata family was somewhat unusual. Tatsuko Hirata, Rumiko's mother, was a remarkable woman, a living paradox. Exquisitely mannered, she somehow managed to seem perfectly natural with a foreigner like me. A postwar pioneer in women's rights, she was largely deferential to her husband. A leading advocate of educational and parental reform, she left the upbringing of Rumiko mostly to her mother-in-law. And though she worked tirelessly to shape Japan's future, she was in many ways a creature of the gracious past.

Her speech was studded with all the pearly courtesies that Japanese has to offer. In a cultivated hand, she wrote letters almost daily and kept a diary without fail. She never arrived anywhere without a gift, and never returned without omiyage (souvenirs) for friends and family. On the few occasions when she would take time from her writing, lecturing, and campaigning to see a movie, tears would spring to her eyes during the sentimental parts.

I liked her from the instant she took out the photo album on my first visit to show me Rumiko as a child. It was a gesture that relieved me from the stress of making conversation in Japanese and, at the same time, signaled her acknowledgment of my feelings for Rumiko.

Soon after we had moved to Japan, Mrs. Hirata commissioned me to write a series of articles for We, the magazine she published for educators. Her offer was a flattering overestimate of my ability to write in Japanese, let alone my analytic powers in a country where just figuring out how to enter a room taxed

*my mind. (The shoes/slippers/bare feet rules baffled
me.) Mrs. Hirata sensibly labeled the series "Mysterious
Japan."*

*The commission gave me an opportunity to see, close
up, what We magazine embodied. It was, above all, the
product of Mrs. Hirata's determination to bring fresh
thinking to an education system framed by bone-hard
ideology. On the one side was the ultranationalist, ultra-
conservative Education Ministry. On the other was the
largely leftist national teachers' union. Wedged between
them was this small, cheaply printed monthly journal.
Ostensibly concerned with modern home economics, it
dared to venture diverse opinions on how to raise boys
and girls, combat prejudice in society, protect wetlands,
and involve fathers in the lives of their children and
homes. And, of course, for a year it contained my sublit-
erate ravings on such topics as the inhumanity of putting young department store employees into bizarre
uniforms and making them stand all day in an elevator
so that customers won't have to bother pushing the
buttons.*

*Tatsuko had been steered into home economics at an
early age because that was considered the appropriate
slot for a bright young woman harboring ambitions to
teach. When the family moved to Tokyo, she took a job
with an established education magazine but left as soon
as she was able to start her own. That she was able, it
should be noted, was due in no small measure to Mr.
Hirata's support and tolerance.*

*I say tolerance because We was produced entirely out
of two spare rooms in the tiny Hirata home. An editorial
staff of three was crammed into one room, while equipment and supplies filled the other. The Hirata living
room served for interviews and business meetings. We*

had a circulation of only about 3,000, but its impact seemed to be all out of proportion to its size.

A We support group had formed, composed mainly of teachers and college students, and met several times a year for field trips or meetings on issues that concerned them.

Mrs. Hirata was frequently invited to speak at conferences around the country, and was appointed a part-time faculty member at the Japan Women's University, a position that consumed her Saturdays.

She obliged nearly all requests, even though toward the end of the eighties she was afflicted with arthritis that made it painful for her to write or even to climb a flight of stairs. Besides the official invitations, she accepted numerous appeals from women who called her in distress of one sort or another. Once when we were visiting, she got a call from a troubled woman. Although we had been about to leave, she spent three-quarters of an hour making soothing remarks over the phone to her.

Later, I suggested getting an answering machine so she could screen her calls. She turned the suggestion around and invested in both an answering machine and a fax machine to serve as a hot line for anyone who wanted to sound off to her, in speech or in writing. Predictably, the result was more, not less, work for her.

All the same, at the time I got to know the Hiratas, it seemed to me they were conducting a fairly normal Japanese family life. Tatsuko laid aside her work at five or six most evenings to make dinner. Typically, she and Megumi would eat first. Since the house had no dining room, they sat at a table that occupied most of the kitchen. Mr. Hirata usually came home by about 8:30 and would eat alone while Mrs. Hirata and Megumi watched TV in the living room. Ichio was a finicky eater (astonishingly for a Japanese, he disliked fish), and when

*something on the table didn't agree with his tastes, he
would throw it out with no apparent regard for his wife's
feelings. Like many Japanese husbands, Ichio was apt to
coarsely demand this or that from his wife.*

"Oi!" he would call when he wanted her attention.

*Tatsuko would unprotestingly oblige. In the way of
many Japanese wives, she used polite, though not the
politest, forms of speech in addressing him.*

*After dinner, he would decide the order of bathing.
This matters, because in a Japanese bath everyone soaks
in the same hot water over the course of an evening. The
soaping and scrubbing and rinsing take place before-
hand on the tiled floor area outside the tub, where a tap
and drain hole are provided. As father, he was entitled
to go first, but he sometimes passed up the privilege if
he wanted to linger over coffee or watch TV.*

*A perfectly normal Japanese household. And yet I
gradually realized that these formal habits of speech
and precedence masked a quite different reality. To a
degree rare even in America, there was an underlying
equality of burden in the relationship of Ichio and Tatsuko Hirata. They treated the household as a shared responsibility. If she cooked, he washed up. If he did the
laundry, she hung it out to dry. They shopped together
on weekends. True, he sometimes demanded tea, but at
other times he made coffee, grinding the beans in an old,
hand-cranked grinder. Often on a Sunday evening, he
made dinner and proved a fair hand at it, too. His best
dish was sukiyaki, a kind of sweet beef stew made in a
deep skillet at the table. When he was making this, a
look of fierce concentration would pinch his snowy features. Soon his daughters would tease him about putting
in too much sugar or setting the fire too high, and then
he would burst into that absurdly high-pitched giggle of
his and start telling some story about how, to keep his*

belly full during the war, he had filched sweet potatoes from a farmer's field. On such occasions, Tatsuko would sit back and quietly sip a glass of wine. Afterward, they would relax on the living room couch, he puffing away on a Seven Stars cigarette, she nibbling at a sweet rice cake, while they watched NHK's weekly historical drama on television.

It would be many years before I learned the origins of their unusually equal relationship. And by then it would be clear that they had simply been ahead of their time.

DIVIDE AND CONQUER

In the postwar era, Japanese family policy seemed to be concerned with balancing traditional family values with modern concepts. In truth the policymakers never took their eyes off Japan's economic goals: If tradition served those aims, they exploited it; if tradition obstructed those aims, they found a way to vitiate it. In the 1950s, with a population boom under way, the government reversed a prewar ban on birth control and actually subsidized contraceptives to prevent overpopulation.[54] In the sixties, when the economy boomed, it tried to boost the birthrate by restricting abortion. But abortion was profitable, and the powerful doctors' lobby succeeded in getting around the restrictions.

However, the cornerstone of postwar family policy lay not in birth control but in division of labor. Men became *kaisha ningen*, or "company men." To quote a semiofficial publication: "It has long been considered a virtue of Japanese company employees that they completely neglect outside interests and their families as they devote themselves entirely to their own advancement at work

and the development of their company."[55] Women were
stuck with the old "good wife, wise mother" formula.
This policy was doomed by its own success. As Japan
grew rich and its economy shifted from heavy industry to
services, women saw greater possibilities for themselves,
and inevitably grew disenchanted with their role.

It was easy to see why. Though the Occupation had
written guarantees of gender equality into Japan's constitution, those rights proved hollow. Women remained sub-
servient in everything, except, arguably, the home. There,
they had responsibility for everything, including the
household budget and savings.

Even the Japanese language divided the sexes: Outside
of formal occasions, men spoke in clipped, guttural
tones, while women maintained a sing-songy rhythm,
accented by soft, feminine notes. Where men might emphasize a statement by ending with *"yo!"* women would
close with a gentle *"wa."*

To be sure, the spread of laborsaving devices such as
washing machines gave housewives more leisure time.
But this did not necessarily equate with more freedom.
The Occupation had abolished the local governing bodies
called *chōkai*, but in their place sprang voluntary
housewives' associations, called *fujinkai*, along with supposed consumer groups, parent-teacher associations, and
a variety of other local organizations. Such activities typically demanded team effort, consensus, and conformity,
and thus exercised a restraining influence on members.

Serious activism of any sort aroused general suspicion.
Researcher Anne Imamura reports, ". . . [W]omen who
attempt to bring about local improvements risk being labeled 'pink' (having communist leanings) and suffering
isolation."[56] She recounts how, after a little boy was hit by
a car in front of a company housing complex, one mother
started a drive to have a fence put up to protect the chil-

dren. "Neighbors accused her of being pink, and she never made friends within the housing project."

As we'll see in chapter 6, some housewives, rightly or wrongly, took brave stands on real issues, such as pacifism and opposition to nuclear power. But most housewives' groups were noncontroversial to the point of seeming mindless. In a wicked satire titled "Perfectly Lovely Ladies," novelist Yasutaka Tsutsui depicts a group of bored and acquisitive housewives who take up robbery as a pastime. The group invades the home of a cultured woman on the pretext of being from the PTA, strangles the maid, and then cheerfully butchers the mistress of the house as they help themselves to underwear, asparagus, and other trifles.

"She was a true lady, wasn't she?" one of them sighs as they stare at the bloodless corpse admiringly.[57]

I spent an afternoon watching a *fujinkai* group who were almost as fierce, if not quite as deadly. They had formed a volleyball team, and I watched them in practice. Their leader was a squat little dumpling of a woman in her early fifties. She drilled them like a marine sergeant, hurling balls at the floor for them to dive after. Fun did not seem to be the order of the day. Between every drill, she led them in a cheer, which at first I could not understand. After a while, though, it clicked. *"Fighto!"* she was yelling. "Fight on! Give your all! Struggle to the end!" Whew . . .

However, by far the most debilitating aspect of being a housewife was having to become a *kyōiku mama*, or "education mother," so as to steer one's son through the vast competition that every year produces a few lucky winners who gain admission to prestigous colleges—and millions of despairing losers. Under the banner of educational egalitarianism, the government policy made a woman's status depend entirely on her success in guiding her children through the fires of what came to be called "entrance exam hell."

"The cultural ideology makes the mother solely and totally responsible for the well-being of children," writes Mariko Fujita in a study aptly titled "It's All Mother's Fault."[58] It's been that way since the Meiji era, Fujita says, but there is evidence that prewar fathers, being better educated than their wives, took at least an occasional hand in their children's education. For example, the following caption appears in a book of photographs published in 1933 by the *Asahi Shimbun*, one of Japan's leading national dailies: "Father takes pleasure in helping his children with their home lessons, and sometimes is prone to overdo it."[59] The photo above it does not seem to justify quite so florid a statement, but it is significant all the same. It shows Father at the kitchen table, cigarette in one hand, newspaper in the other, supervising his son and daughter as they study their Japanese reading and writing.

The withdrawal of Father from this scene has created a painful dilemma for many working women. Not even a full-time job excuses the mother from absolute responsibility for the progress of her children through Japan's educational maze.

No sensible person would quibble with the notion that parents should be chiefly responsible for the education of their children. But the Japanese system gives the mother so little control over the outcome, and measures success so narrowly, that the chances of a gratifying outcome are slim.

Manipulation is the only tool the *kyōiku mama* possesses. She is expected to make her child feel highly dependent and then use her love as a motivational lash, tirelessly driving the youngster through the countless hours of mind-numbing study required for entry to a desirable kindergarten, primary school, junior high, high school, and, ultimately, university.

Once a boy—it is chiefly boys who are the focus of this effort—begins school, the *kyōiku mama* encourages him to abandon all other responsibilities or pursuits. His life becomes her preoccupation. She cooks his meals, washes his clothes, cleans his room, helps him with his homework, and drills him on material for his exams. As he reaches puberty, she struggles to discourage him from all outside interests, including dating, until he has won acceptance to college. Of course, not all mothers or children adhere to this pattern, but it is common enough to stand as representative.

All this may seem admirable. Certainly the keen educational competition in Japan is an attractive contrast— from afar—to the slouching apathy of American education. But it is not a healthy existence for mother or child. Aside from distorting their relationship (even in the context of Japanese culture, it is widely recognized that this is a distortion), it places enormous stress on them.

In the eighties, this stress worsened as the competition intensified. The struggle to beat out millions of other youngsters for a seat in one of the top universities now started before kindergarten. Health officials, alarmed by a rise in stress-related disorders in Japanese children, such as ulcers in boys as young as three, issued dire warnings.[60] The Education Ministry itself recognized the ill effects on children: In 1991 a panel advised the education minister to "restore the humanity of children by correcting the distortions in the current education system and by lessening their mental stress, rather than determining what education should be in accordance with . . . plans and objectives as an industrial nation."[61]

Incidentally, there is strong evidence that the competition was rigged in favor of the privileged. Many private

elite universities maintain their own network of affiliated private schools, running all the way down to kindergarten, whose graduates are virtually guaranteed admission. Scandals involving bribed admissions officials have
proliferated. One academic study of Japan's universities
concludes: "Access to higher education has become more
dependent on social background in Japan, despite the
expansion of the higher education sector. . . . [It is] no
more open than in the U.S. and Britain."[62]

Nevertheless, keeping up with the Tanakas has become a kind of mania. When the Education Ministry
finally put an end to Saturday classes in public schools,
many parents filled the void with additional cram-
school sessions.

As the competition heated up, researchers found signs
of maternal strain, too. Kyoko Kubota, a sociologist at
the Tokyo Metropolitan University, noted that alcoholism among women, once rare, was on the rise. "There is
a noticeable tendency for women to be solitary, late-night
drinkers, who use alcohol to escape an unhappy situation," Kubota wrote in the mid-1980s.[63]

Popular culture echoed the discontent: By the mid-
1980s, researchers found a sharp increase in the portrayal
of unhappy wives on television. More important, women
in television dramas stopped being silent sufferers and
began to take destiny in their own hands. "Women are
apparently less willing to submit to male domination,
and their refusal to make sacrifices is having a very disruptive effect," wrote television researcher Yasuko Muramatsu.[64]

But in reality the change was less a disruption than
a natural outcome of events the government had set in
motion. The *kyōiku mama*, though rooted in Confucian
tradition, was the education bureaucrats' invention. The
idea was to maximize competition and discipline, so as

to produce an obedient and highly skilled workforce. However, from the individual mother's point of view, anything that would increase her child's chance of success in the competition was good. In the early eighties, cram schools opened to drill students in English, the *kyōiku mama*'s weakest subject. The diligent mother had no choice but to enroll her child. She then naturally took a job to finance the cram-school tuition. As these costs escalated—on average, cram-school costs tripled in the eighties—women began to work more and more, transforming their role from moms who worked to working moms.[65] This coincided with a labor shortage that opened many doors for women in the working world. By the end of the decade, the percentage of Japanese and American mothers of school-age children who worked outside the home was at 67 percent, virtually identical.[66]

As their foothold in the working world grew more secure, women began to assert themselves as never before. Their bottled-up resentments against their husbands gushed forth. In 1992 Japan saw a record-high 180,000 divorces—up more than 10,000 from the year before, and more than four times the number seen in the fifties, according to the Ministry of Health and Welfare. Before long, it was estimated, one in four marriages in Japan would dissolve.[67] Reversing the old pattern, women now initiated 60 percent of divorce suits. What's more, divorce among older couples quadrupled, not because men wanted younger partners—they were free to philander anyway—but because women could not stand the thought of having their husbands on their hands after retirement. One such woman caustically remarked: "It is much easier to be lonely alone than to be lonely together."[68]

The only ones casting off the yoke in greater numbers were the young. Indeed, some young women became so restless that on returning from a less-than-thrilling honeymoon on the sands of Waikiki or some other foreign shore, they sought divorce the moment they passed through Customs at Tokyo's Narita Airport. This happened often enough to become known as the "Narita divorce."

"The decision maker is the bride," Tsuneaki Iki, executive vice president of the Japan National Tourist Organization, told me.[69] For many young women, untrammeled by the conventional male fear of vacations, the honeymoon represents their second or third trip abroad, he explained, while their workaday husbands have never been out of Japan. "The bride knows more about travel outside. She knows all the requirements, all the habits of travel in other countries, and that causes a situation where the bride is disappointed by the unfamiliarity of the husband."

And those were the ones who had deigned to marry in the first place. Until recently, all Japanese women were expected to be married by the age of twenty-five. According to a popular saying among men, women were like Christmas cakes: only good until the twenty-fifth. The point of getting married was to have a child, and the point of having a child was to become whole. Indeed, to be childless was to be a child in Japan. Only after giving birth was a woman said to be *ichi nin mae*, "fully a person."

Nevertheless, by the early nineties, the average bride was over twenty-six, and more than 40 percent of Japanese women were still unmarried by the age of twenty-nine.[70] In Tokyo, the nation's trendsetter, fully half of young women remain unmarried by their thirtieth birthday.[71] Indeed, Japan had more single women under the age of thirty than any other nation but Sweden.[72]

It certainly wasn't that Japanese women had suddenly

become unattractive. On the contrary, men began complaining to the Japanese press that they were finding it difficult to get married because women were so reluctant to give up their freedom. "There is less social pressure for women to marry, and women feel they do not have to compromise on their spouses," the Asahi News Service reported in 1991. "Women are becoming more demanding in what they look for in husbands."[73] A school for bridegrooms opened up, teaching men for the first time how to become "a good catch."

Single young women, living at home but earning a good wage, became the powerhouse consumers of the country. Unburdened by mortgages, rent, or education bills, they had more disposable income than any other group. A typical young Japanese woman in a clerical job put more than $1,000 a month—about 80 percent of her income—into dancing, dining, and buying clothes, the *Economist* magazine calculated.[74] One scholar marveled: "Women and teens in Japan are champion shoppers, and their search for novelty is matched by their search for quality. . . . Parisian shopkeepers, for example, know Japanese women are in town when all the Yves St. Laurent scarves and Louis Vuitton bags have been sold."[75]

Women not only staked a claim to careers and conspicuous consumption, they entered the world of politics. In 1989, when Prime Minister Sousuke Uno was exposed as a tightwad philanderer by his former mistresses, women hounded him out of office. Socialist leader Takako Doi, a fiery feminist who became the first woman to head a Japanese political party, rallied women to the polls to vote out the ruling party from one house of Parliament in elections that summer. The issue that stung them into action was the Liberal Democrats' broken pledge not to impose a national sales tax. When the Liberal Democrats regained their balance in the next election, the women's political fury was thought to be spent. Actually, the revolution was just beginning. The cynical notion that women would be interested only in domestic issues and would follow their husbands' lead on international questions died a painful death in the Persian Gulf crisis. In the months that led up to Operation Desert Storm, Japan's government was frantic to make at least a showing of participation with its allies. Prime Minister Toshiki Kaifu had promised "sweat," along with checks. Foreign Ministry bureaucrats prepared a bill that would have worked around the constitution to allow Japanese troops to be dispatched to the Gulf as noncombatant support.

Women, however, had another idea. Reminding everyone of the suffering of World War II, they insisted Japan adhere to its constitutional pacifism. That stand was personified by the Socialist leader, Takako Doi. Reacting to none-too-subtle hints from the U.S. administration that Japan's presence at the liberation of Kuwait was awaited, she exploded. "This time," Doi thundered, "no means no!"[76]

However, Doi's Socialists lacked the power to block the government on their own. It was the Buddhist Komei party, in which women are a majority, that dashed the government's hopes. The Komei party's leader had been promised heaven and earth by the Liberal Democrats if he would go along with their plan. By all reports, he was prepared to cooperate. But, as the war against Iraq drew near, he called the defense secretary of the ruling Liberal Democrats and said, "Sorry. The women won't stand for it."[77]

America's view of Japan as a strategic ally nosedived. I did not agree with the pacifist reaction to Iraq's invasion of Kuwait—certainly, oil-dependent Japan had a huge stake in the outcome—but I admired the guts of the women who took a stand on what they felt was a sacred principle. For better or worse, women had for the first time altered the course of Japanese history.

Bear in mind that all this happened before a proper revolution in consciousness had even gotten off the ground. For the most part, Japanese women have yet to make the connection between male society's treatment of them as childlike sex objects and the discimination they suffer in jobs, the media, and politics. Indeed, many young women don't object to being regarded as sex objects. Quite the opposite: They revel in being labeled "bodi-con girls" (short for "body-conscious"). It's not rare for a group of young women to leave the office, change into skimpy clothes, and, just for fun, mount the platform of one of Tokyo's special discos, where men pay to watch them disrobe as they dance.

Young women have made Japan the world's largest cosmetic surgery market. Undergoing what the Japanese call "Cinderella surgery," they have their eyes rounded and their noses pared in hopes of looking less "Japanese" and thereby more employable and marriageable.[78]

In short, ideological feminism so far appeals to only a tiny, faction-riven elite.[79] So far, the mainstream Japanese woman couldn't care less about ideology. So far, she has been interested mainly in self-fulfillment. But after being pushed so far by callous husbands, exploitive employers, and indifferent bureaucrats, she is beginning to catch on. When her rage ignites into conscious reaction, watch out.

THE CAT'S MEOW

The youngest child in a family is often the one most reluctant to leave childhood behind. I was reminded of that as I watched Rumiko's little sister play with her cat, Niao. Megumi cradled her cat like a baby, rubbed her nose against his, then marched him around on his hind legs. Niao, a big orange lump of fur with the figure and temperament of Garfield the cartoon cat, yowled pitifully, but Megumi would not relent.

There was nothing particularly odd about her behavior; lots of people like to engage their pets in a kind of child's play. But it revealed a lightheartedness in Megumi that Rumiko simply lacked.

For Megumi childhood had been good. Her older sister, Rumiko, had been born in the mid-1950s, when Japan, still recovering from war, ranked with Brazil, India, and the rest of the developing world. But Megumi had been born in 1964, the auspicious year Tokyo hosted the Olympics and Japan vaulted into the league of advanced industrial nations.

Rumiko had spent her early years in a village surrounded on one side by rice paddies and on the other by craggy bluffs leading down to the sea. In winter, the incessant snows piled up far above her head. She had to gather wood to heat water in the big iron bathtub and cook meals while her parents worked. During the growing season, she sometimes helped her grandmother in the rice paddies and vegetable patches that surrounded their home.

Megumi had grown up in Tokyo, where hot water ran from the taps and where, except for a jolt or two during the oil shocks, year after year the neon lights got brighter and the music got louder.

In America, when we spoke of the generation gap in the sixties, we meant the gap between parents and children. But here were two sisters, separated by nine years but divided by an enormous chasm of change.

Rumiko belonged to the driven generation, the one

that by sheer effort and skill carried Japan on its shoulders over the shoals of development and into the promised land of economic supremacy. Japanese youth born in the chaotic aftermath of the war had thrown a radical fit during the sixties, but by and large Rumiko's generation took hardship for granted and duty for its watchword.

Yet as much as Rumiko may have been a part of her generation, as a woman she stood out against it. Against huge odds, she got a berth in the University of Tokyo, the pinnacle of Japan's hierarchical education system. Rejecting the usual women's majors of education, literature, or home economics, Rumiko went into physics. Later she switched to architecture, becoming one of just five women to go into the field there that year. At the induction ceremony for the new class, the chairman of architecture declared that the admission of so many women would ruin his department.

Many of Rumiko's male classmates told her that no one would marry her if she persisted, but Rumiko remained undaunted. She was determined to have a career of her own, rather than live through a husband.

Megumi came of age in the eighties, in the midst of Japan's own Lost Generation, the one older Japanese call shinjinrui, "a new species." The label is not meant as a compliment.

Like many of her well-nourished generation, Megumi was tall and slim and sexy, given to wearing her hair long and her skirts short. For her, going to college was more or less a normal expectation. (The percentage of Japanese women in higher education now exceeds that of men: 36.8 percent to 35.8 percent as of 1989—though, to be sure, women are clustered in the junior colleges and less prestigious universities.[80] When Rumiko entered university, women trailed men in higher education by more than 10 percentage points.)

Megumi shared much of her mother's social conscience. She spoke out fiercely about discrimination against Koreans in Japan, whom many have compared to blacks in America. So it was not entirely surprising that she set her ambition on becoming a social worker. The trouble was, she didn't have the same drive and discipline that carried Rumiko over the hurdles. As in America, life in Japan now offered too many distractions for a young person who was not entirely single-minded about what she was doing.

She failed the entrance exams to college. This is by no means rare, and reflects nothing on her intelligence. To pass the exams requires an almost inconceivable amount of memorization. The student must have a command of such arcana as the succession of thirteenth-century Chinese kings and the chief industrial products of Pennsylvania. (If the latter seems easy, see if you can recall any product of Kumamoto province. Hint: It's in southwestern Japan and is home to a former prime minister. Time's up. The answers are oranges and Morihiro Hosokawa.)

Eventually, on a retry, Megumi passed and entered a junior college. But along the way, she got fed up with studying and living at home. She suddenly took off, rented an efficiency, and landed a job as a waitress. Megumi was starting on what would prove to be a highly independent path.

THE FADING FAMILY

Educated young Japanese women reject the notion "that women's fulfillment is to be found only in the self-sacrifice and hard work of motherhood," sociologist

Brenda Bankhart found in a 1989 study of university women.[81]

For some educated young couples, the American yuppie concept of the "DINK" lifestyle (double income, no kids) became an ideal. It has spread like a brushfire. By 1990, one in seven Japanese couples under the age of thirty-five was childless. By the end of the century, the Ministry of Health and Welfare predicts, the figure will be one in four. My favorite Japanese DINKs were Mayumi Okada and Teruo Maruyama. I liked them because they chose to be DINKs for principle rather than to free up their cash flow for imported wines and caviar. Mayumi was the one I really knew: She was an accountant who had helped me on a story involving corporate spending in Japan. Her husband was a writer, of the serious variety. He had published a book of poetry and was working on another. As a rule, poetry does not sell much better in Japan than it does in America. I knew they were dependent on Mayumi's salary, and I confess to having been intensely curious about this unusual arrangement, partly because I too had been dependent on my first wife's salary early in my career. But I was American. In Japan, I thought, a man simply does not stay at home while his wife goes to work.

Some months after we worked together, I ran into Mayumi at the Foreign Correspondents' Club and we had coffee together. After chatting about my newborn daughter, I steered the conversation to her plans: What would she do when the time came to have kids? Would she keep her job? She reddened and said (with what Victorian novelists would call considerable asperity) that they did not intend to have any children. Trying to make a joke of it, I blundered ahead. Why not? I asked. Didn't all Japanese couples aim to have two kids, preferably a girl first, then a boy?

Mayumi stared angrily at me. Only an American would persist in these rude questions, her expression seemed to say. After a long pause, she blurted out: "Because they would be illegitimate, that's why!"

I was stunned.

"Sorry, I thought you were married," I mumbled.

"We are."

"I don't get it."

Mayumi's jaw was clenched in fury, but I began to sense that I was no longer the object of her anger.

"We were married in a private ceremony, but the government won't accept the registration of our marriage, so we are not legally married," she said.

"They won't recognize a civil ceremony?" I asked.

"No, that's not it. They won't let me keep my name. The government insists that I have to take my husband's family name when we register, and I refuse to do that. So they refuse to register us."

I don't recall how I responded to that. I only remember being filled with awe at the courage of this tiny woman in defying the government and social norms. For in Japan, as the saying goes, the nail that sticks up gets hammered down. In Mayumi's case, the nail penetrated to the core of her identity.

As the decade wound down, other women like Mayumi emerged, and their cause—essentially, the right to individuality—began to get play in the press. The government made some show of reconsidering its position, but insisted that the difficulty of tracking children would be too great without unitary family lines. And it pointed out that its policy was not sexist, because it allowed men to take on their wives' names if they chose to do so, which happens occasionally for business purposes. (Some names are valuable to inherit.) But in 1993 a Tokyo district court judge ruled that Reiko Sekiguchi, a professor of sociology, had no right to use her family name at work, as she had been doing throughout her academic career. Sekiguchi had sued her university, which was insisting that she use her husband's last name. Siding with the university, Judge Atsushi Fukui ruled that making couples use the same family name "fosters a sense of oneness."[82]

When Rumiko and I went to register ourselves, we found that foreigners were not permitted to register as the head of household. Legally, I had to be incorporated into the Hirata family register, with Rumiko as head of our household. Xenophobia took precedence over sexism. Additionally, as a foreigner, I had to be fingerprinted. The official who attended to us seemed quite worried that I would take offense at this double whammy to my dignity, but I just laughed it off. What did I care how the Japanese government recorded my identity? I was American. I could be whoever I wanted to be.

But for Japanese women like Mayumi, identity represents an enormous struggle. In America, identity is a blend of personality and role, but we tend to honor the person more than the role. We expect our president, for example, to have "character," and when we are displeased with his character, we largely withhold our respect in spite of his position. In Japan, by contrast, a person is not expected to reveal his character to the public. The personality of most Japanese prime ministers has been a complete mystery to the public. Indeed, the exposure of Prime Minister Uno, the tightwad philanderer, underscored the dangers of letting one's character show. Except in the most intimate situations, the Japanese traditionally consider identity and role to be the same. Kurt Vonnegut's phrase "You are what you pretend to be" is far more suited to Japan than America.

If men's personalities have had limited room for expression, women's have been bound tight as a kimono. Not even their voices are their own. A young woman is expected to chirp in a falsetto pitched at least a third above normal. Once she becomes a mother, though, the voice drops. Older women sometimes affect a bearish growl.

Few Japanese women are like Mayumi, consciously rejecting motherhood in their struggle for identity. But Japanese women have clearly begun to reject the idea that their identity is entirely dependent on marriage and motherhood. A government poll of single women found that their main reasons for remaining unmarried were a reluctance to trade their freedom for housekeeping and child rearing, and an unwillingness to adapt to the ways of a husband.[83] The upshot is that, although many polls show Japanese women want to have at least three children, most are starting later and limiting themselves to smaller families.[84] Other women, like Mayumi, are forgoing motherhood altogether.[85]

As a result, the traditional family no longer makes up a majority of Japanese households. In 1991 households with children under age eighteen fell to just 38.3 percent of the total, down dramatically from just a few years before.[86] The number of single-member households climbed to 21 percent. By any measure, then, the traditional Japanese family is rapidly sinking into myth.

In its place, however, a new, more balanced, and more egalitarian notion of family is rising. Many obstacles stand in the way of a couple who want to have dual careers and to share the burdens and joys of child rearing. Companies still expect men to give their all; nurseries and schools still demand that mothers accommodate them in countless petty and time-consuming ways. But faced with the prospect of a population dwindling to the vanishing point, institutional Japan is gradually, grudgingly giving way.

3

OF HUMAN CAPITALISM AND ITS CORPSES

I went to work for the Japanese, or more particularly for the Japan Times, filled with an unnameable dread. I had been warned. Well before moving to Tokyo, I had been warned.

"Don't take a job with a Japanese company. They will kill you with work," Noboru, my language partner, had said. Noboru was well qualified to speak on the subject: A bright young salaryman in the ranks of one of Japan's giant trading companies, he had been sent to the States to get an M.B.A. at the Wharton School and had reacted like a man unchained from a dungeon. He cruised downtown Philadelphia in an old Chevy Impala (Japanese often seem to buy American cars when in America), exploring restaurants, bars, and dives that I, a fifteen-year resident, had no idea existed. I liked him because, unlike many dour, serious-minded men of business, Noboru was unshakably cheerful. Many of his countrymen sent by their employers settled into little Japanese ghettos in the suburbs and rarely deviated from the straight line between school and home. Not so Noboru. Tall,

handsome, self-possessed, but supremely naive, he wandered blithely through nooks of the city that I wouldn't
have entered without a police escort.

Noboru and I had teamed up to exchange language
skills but wound up spending more time playing tennis
than correcting each other's grammar. Still, I learned a
lot from Noboru. Over a beer after one of our tennis
games, he laid it out for me in a splendid mixture of
Japanese and English: "Za Japanezu lifestyle is too tsurai
(hard) to you," he said. Using pretzel nuggets and gold-
fish crackers, he made a crude map of Tokyo on the bar.
"Zis is Yamanote Line of train," he said, pointing to a
ring of pretzel nuggets that encircled his model of Tokyo.
"Usual person cannot live inside zis line."

Noboru went on to describe his former life of rising at
5:30 in the morning to catch a train for an hour-and-a-
half commute to his company, where, by an unstated
code, he was expected to be at his desk an hour and a
half before the official starting time. All he had to do in
those early hours was read the morning newspaper and
drink coffee, but to be seen doing so was important.
Come evening, if there was no pressing work at hand,
he was obliged to go out drinking with his boss in the
company of people important to their firm. They were
not necessarily clients, he said, but just kankeisha (connected people). He would get home between eleven and
midnight, giving him just enough time for five hours'
sleep before it started all over again.

His warning came swooping back to perch, vul-
turelike, on my shoulder as I rode the second of three
trains that would deliver me to the Japan Times. (Noboru had been quite right: No way could I live within
the boundary of the Yamanote Line.) Of course, the Japan Times was not exactly one of the nation's corporate
behemoths, and anyway, it wasn't like I was signing up

to be a salaryman for life. I was an American, damn it. I could walk away anytime I chose.

This was a comforting lie. Five months after landing in Japan, I was earning 25 percent less than when I started, thanks to the shift in exchange rates, and Rumiko had not yet started working. A welter of unexpected costs, such as the $400 charge for a phone line, had drained our savings. I still had the honor of being the American Banker's accredited correspondent in Tokyo, but prestige would not pay the bills. With the dollar sinking under my feet, I just had to have yen.

So, on a bright January morning I stepped off the Yamanote Line, shouldered through a numberless throng of blue-suited salarymen, and made my way to the drab three-story concrete-and-steel building that was home to Japan's oldest English-language newspaper. Once I got past the doorkeeper, Shimamura-san, a senior editor, rose from his cluttered desk to greet me with all the beaming charm of a tubby Fred Astaire. He had hired me with astonishing alacrity a week earlier on the strength of my résumé, a few clippings, and a brief conversation in Japanese. (I had improved a bit since my doughnut days.) Now he whirled me around the smoky, cluttered newsroom like a new son-in-law, introducing me with lavish praise to a bewildering variety of Japanese and gaijin (that is, foreign) editors and writers. One of them, a hatchet-faced Japanese with a permanent frown, said sternly, "I understand you are an expert in finance. I will call on you for help."

My guts trembled. Is that what they thought they had hired? An expert? I had only a few months of work for the American Banker under my belt. I hadn't even gotten straight all the names of the Japanese banks yet, let alone the securities companies. Come to that, what exactly was a security, anyway?

Fortunately, Shimamura-san spun me away from the business features desk and deposited me at a terminal on the domestic news desk, where I was to edit copy all day. To sit down to this work was a great relief: Copy-editing was something familiar and welcome.

I had only to master the computer system and I felt sure I would soon be a highly productive employee. Unfortunately, the system appeared to have been manufactured in Bulgaria in the early 1950s, though I couldn't be sure. The nameplate was obscured by a coat of cigarette ash that had gelled into tar. How to operate the damn thing was even more obscure. It certainly wasn't a Sony.

Eventually, after typing in codes that resembled ancient cuneiform, I succeeded in conjuring up a story to edit. After a good quarter-hour or so spent cleaning it up, I zapped the story into oblivion with one false stroke.

On reflection, it seemed to me that an intuitive comprehension of this swamp-life technology was a bit much to demand of me. I peered around helplessly and saw that I was being watched by one of the Japanese editors. He had the same young-old look I had noticed in some of the others. His skin was sallow and soft, as if he hadn't been out in the sun for years. But he had not gone to fat in the way of so many Americans (this writer included), and his youthful aspect was accented by a Beatles haircut. It was as though he had walked into the Japan Times *twenty years earlier and never found his way out the door. (Which, in a sense, proved to be true.) But what struck me most at the moment was that the older part of him—his tired face—looked kindly.*

Perhaps, I thought, he will come to my aid. He did not appear to be particularly busy at that moment. Some sort of functionary, I concluded—possibly even a member of the famous mado-giwa zoku *(the "win-dowside tribe"), those middle-aged Japanese company men who find themselves out of the running for executive positions and are consigned to a spot by the window with nothing to do. Still, he ought to know how to run the computer system. I smiled and bowed simperingly. He did the same, in a more dignified way, and carried on watching me. I began to feel like a rare finch in the presence of a dedicated member of the Audubon So-ciety.*

Just as I was despairing, a tinny American voice rose behind me. "So you're the new guy," it said. I turned and, through a haze of cigarette smoke, discerned the thin, bored, and vaguely hostile features of a young man, apparently just out of college and clearly on his way to something far more important. He looked me over in a brief, dismissive way and allowed that his name was Alan.

Alan aside, I was the only native English speaker on the domestic desk that morning. Feeling somewhat bewildered, I hunkered down to edit copy. My confidence soon crumbled. Some of the wire stories were already in English, of a sort, but many others had been translated at the desk into an almost indescribably barbarous form of the tongue. Japanese grammar, though fairly consistent, is completely alien to English speakers, while English grammar is utterly bizarre to Japanese. In a fast-paced news operation, the result was frequently a horrible mishmash.

But it wasn't only the computer system or the fractured English that troubled me. Japanese news has tons of precision but often lacks an ounce of analysis.

One of the first stories I got opened like this: "The Education Ministry released a report Monday showing the data of 695,000 students in kindergarten, primary,

*junior high, and senior high school who experienced
health checkups between April and June last year."*
  *Having told the reader almost nothing in the lead, the
story then plunged into the nitty-gritty:*

> *Ninth-grade boys averaged 155 centimeters in
> height. Ninth-grade boys averaged 58.2 kilograms in
> weight. Their chest measurements were 0.1 to 0.3
> centimeters larger than those recorded in the pre-
> ceding year. Ninth-grade girls averaged . . .*

You get the idea.
  *I felt sure that tailors across the nation would find
this information valuable, but I had qualms about foist-
ing it on the general public. Wading through the bog of
statistics, I created the following lead: "The physiques
of Japanese children, once thought to have peaked, are
still improving, the Education Ministry reported Monday." Eventually, I sent a completely rewritten story to
typesetting and waited. No one objected.*
  *Emboldened, I plowed into the next story. I would
soon regret my brashness. What (if anything) it was
about, I cannot recall, except that it concerned matters
nautical. I do, however, clearly remember that it began
with the phrase "In 1874 . . ." and took at least ten para-
graphs to wend its way to the present. News, as Turner
Catledge, the former* New York Times *managing editor,
once said, is supposed to tell you something today that
you didn't know yesterday.[1] And it's supposed to tell you
right away. Taking a deep breath, I set to work on the
story with an editorial jackhammer. It took what
seemed like hours, but at last I got the gist of the news
into the lead and relegated the historical background to
the end, where it could be safely cut away by the page
editor if the story ran too long (which seemed a safe bet).*

But no sooner had I sent the story up to typesetting than its author came charging in, blazing with fury and trailing the offending manuscript behind him. He was a small, proud man with a remarkable fluency in English, which he now demonstrated to good effect. Slapping the manuscript down on my desk like a twenty-eight-count indictment, he tore into me for ruining his story.

"You are here to correct the English, if you are even capable of that," he sneered. "You are not here to pass judgment. And besides, you put an aircraft carrier in my story." (It was true. To this day I have no idea how an aircraft carrier drifted into his story. I suppose I must have misinterpreted something.)

"It's too stupid for words!" he railed. "An utter disgrace! Anyone who knows anything about Japan knows that we do not have aircraft carriers. They are considered weapons of aggression." He went on to recite all of the transgressions he had suffered at the hands of stupid copy editors and lay them at my feet.

Meanwhile, to my acute embarrassment, a small crowd of curious onlookers gathered. "Wa!" I thought. "Harmony! You're disrupting the wa!" When he at last paused, I apologized for the aircraft carrier and asserted, as mildly as I could, that editing meant something more than correcting spelling, but that in the spirit of compromise I would withdraw my aircraft carrier forthwith. To my infinite relief, he accepted.

Returning to the desk, I found the in-basket towering over me. Suddenly, Alan announced to no one in particular that he was going to lunch. I was alone in a paper jungle. Panic flowed like a dark river within me. Deadline was four o'clock. How could anyone even think of lunch with so much work to be done in little more than three hours? I hacked my way furiously through tangled grammar and knotted narratives. My eyes watered

and my lungs ached from the pall of cigarette smoke.
Pythons slithered around in my stomach.

Then a rescue party came striding through the vines.
Sophie and Carl, the afternoon shift, logged into the system and calmly hewed a path through the story pile.
Carl, tanned, balding, and cool, was so relaxed he put
his feet up on the desk as he edited. I half expected to see
him do it with his eyes shut. Sophie, meanwhile, chuted
stories to typesetting without ever breaking her steady
patter. She would sling barbs, jokes, commentary, even
weather bulletins at anyone in her range, which was at
least fifty feet.

At about three, proof sheets started coming down
from the print shop, and just as I feared, they contained
masses of white space, whole continents of unexplored
territory between stories. People began to shout across
the room about line corrections. Alan, my erstwhile
trainer, had returned from lunch and was roaring about
some piece he didn't think was fit for toilet paper. The
desk editor was roaring back in that it was too late to
kill it. Everyone but Sophie and Carl seemed in a panic
now. And no one was more panicky than I. I was stuck
trying to make sense of a particularly gruesome piece of
copy about how farmers in some backward part of the
country were using a government grant to try to cure
stomach cancer with tea leaves. If they had provided a
sample, I'd have been tempted to try it: My stomach was
killing me. Teeth clenched, I soldiered on, trying not to
consider the consequences of being late. Who takes time
more seriously than the Japanese? I had been on deadline before, but never quite like this.

And then, suddenly it was over, and everyone was
smiling, putting their feet up on the tables between the
empty paper cups and bags of shrimp-flavored puffed

rice. My story was still in a shambles before me. I had failed.

The editor who had been watching me all day, the one with the Beatles haircut, put a hand on my shoulder. I felt my brief career at the Japan Times drawing to an end.

"Naff-san," he said, "don't worry about it. They can use it in second edition. And Naff-san . . ."

"Yes?" I looked up at his kindly, drooping face. It struck me that he was addressing me with respect. San is an honorific title, like "Mr." or "Ms." A superior need not use it in addressing his employee.

"You don't have to work through lunch," he continued. "There is always time to get something to eat. The paper will go out."

I was stunned. For even as he said these comforting words, it dawned on me that this was Kuroishi-san, the deputy managing editor. The only coherent thought I could form was: So much for killing you with work. I was to learn, however, that as a foreigner in a small and humane company, I had it easy. I was also to learn, in a lesson that struck much too close to home, that for those who labor by Japanese rules, work can indeed prove a fatal pursuit.

ALL IN THE FAMILY

The family metaphor did not die in World War II. The state, having exhausted its claims after its military adventurism, passed it on to the company. Ever since, Japanese executives have tirelessly repeated that their companies are actually "families" of employees. They have succeeded in passing this message along through the Western media. For example, in a front-page *Washington Post* story about the 1992 employee induction ceremony at NEC, Japan's giant electronics company, personncl manager Makoto Maruyama tells us: "In America you have a marriage ceremony, don't you? This is a similar thing. These new entrants have become members of the NEC family now."[2]

For all the talk of "family," though, the typical Japanese worker has never really merged his identity into the company the way his ancestors fused theirs in the *ie*. As far back as 1968, a study comparing attitudes toward employers in the United States and Japan showed only 9 percent of Japanese respondents regarded the company as "the central concern in my life and of greater importance than my personal life."[3] A nearly identical percentage took completely the opposite view; the company was "strictly a place to work and entirely separate from my personal life." The majority quite sensibly placed company and personal life on an equal footing.

Nevertheless, the constant repetition of the family metaphor has led many otherwise perceptive Americans to latch onto a Disneyland image of work life in Japan. Take Alan Blinder, for instance. He's a bright guy: A Princeton economist and a Federal Reserve Board member, he's even spent time in Japan. And yet, in the pages of *Business Week* he can write such blather as this:

> To a degree that Americans would find astonishing, large Japanese companies are run for the benefit of their employees rather than their stockholders. . . . It is in managing people, I believe, that America can learn the most from Japan.[4]

Pray that he's wrong. For, while it's true that Japanese stockholders have no rights, such remarks grossly distort the truth about workers. If women had a heavy burden at home, men were no less exploited at work. As we'll see in the pages that follow, in the postwar decades the Japanese worked themselves to exhaustion and beyond, making Japan one of the richest countries in the world. In return, they received an income with only 69 percent of the purchasing power of their American counterparts and job guarantees that, when the crunch came, proved worthless for some.[5]

A growing number of disillusioned Japanese are recognizing that the company claim to being a family is a sham. Tear away the facade, they say, and what you find is a feudal system.[6] And they are right. The same martial values that reshaped the family have been imposed on men in the workplace. The martial emblems are everywhere: in the uniforms, the salutes at the entrance, the ranks of the hierarchy, and the fight-to-the-death mentality, which, I'm sorry to say, is all too literal.

Thus, whatever private feelings of independence the worker may harbor, his life, for all practical purposes, belongs to the company. Soldiers may grumble, but they may not disobey.

Between the sixties, when most American executives dismissed Japan as a laughable producer of cheap toys and gadgets, and the late seventies, when the country became a formidable competitor, Japanese working hours, as recorded by the Ministry of Labor, eased by about 14 percent. Even so, they remained well above the Western norm. Average annual work hours (the standard measurement in Japan) fell from 2,426 (a workweek of about forty-nine hours) in 1960 to 2,077 hours (roughly forty-two hours a week) in 1975.[7] Sounds right, doesn't it? As a nation grows richer, you expect leisure time to expand.

But heading into the eighties, as Japan swelled into an economic behemoth, a strange thing happened: Vacation time withered and working hours crept up again. By 1988 the annual workload had risen by a week earlier to 2,120 hours (about forty-three hours a week).[8] In other words, even as Japan's wealth indicators hit new heights, its workers were putting in the equivalent of five more workweeks a year on the job than Americans, who were already working much harder than Europeans.

Even so, the official numbers pale before reality. To anyone who has observed work habits in Japan, the claim that the average Japanese works just forty-three hours a week strains belief. Not even the trend toward the five-day workweek (down from six) necessarily means shorter working hours. Unrecorded overtime is a widespread if not universal phenomenon in Japan.

The salaryman, who may nominally work a forty-hour week, is expected to put in enormous unpaid overtime. It may not be productive time (it may only mean reading the newspaper), but as long as one is there, all must be there. In 1988, when banks announced they would start giving employees Saturdays off, I called an acquaintance who was a rising young manager at the Mitsubishi Bank. "What are you going to do with that free time?" I asked him. He laughed and said, "Well, we're all happy to have Saturdays off, but I don't think we'll work any less. We'll just have to stay even later on weeknights." This was a man who was already routinely working from eight in the morning until nine or ten at night.

Of course, managers everywhere have to be prepared to sacrifice personal time for their careers. But during the boom years of the late eighties, things only got worse farther down the line in Japan. Large manufacturers pressured assembly workers to put in huge amounts of overtime. Businesses, many desperately short of labor, routinely falsified the worksheets they handed in to the

Labor Ministry, as an investigation of banks by the Tokyo metropolitan government showed.[9]

Union-backed researchers calculated that the time the average Japanese worker spent on his job was nearer to 60 hours a week.[10] And for some, the hours were much longer.

Even part-timers could find themselves working to the limit of human endurance. In the course of doing a story on working hours, I interviewed a former employee of a small manufacturing plant. He was a lean, raw-boned man in his early thirties. He climbed mountains as a hobby and looked capable of doing a good day's work. Although he was a part-timer, when the parent company sent down a rush order for parts, he was compelled to work nearly 100 hours a week. (That's the equivalent of working a double shift for six straight days.) Naturally, this could not be reported to the authorities, as it would require the payment of overtime wages, so he was also required to sign papers saying he had worked no more than forty-eight hours in any given week. Trained to obedience, he complied.

All this hard work naturally took a toll. Japan's Institute of Public Health found that 40 percent of the 24,000 workers it surveyed felt "a continual sense of fatigue."[11] It is probably no coincidence, then, that more than 40 percent of the 500 subjects in a study conducted by the Fukoku Life Insurance Company reported they feared dying from the strain of their jobs.[12]

But a raft of statistics cannot convey the reality of Japanese work life half so vividly as a letter to a newspaper from an ordinary housewife:

My husband is a thirty-eight-year-old clerk who has been working at a major bank for fifteen years.

He works an average of fourteen hours a day, spends
more than three hours commuting to and from the
bank, and puts in over 100 hours of overtime every
month. He sleeps only a few hours a night and is
suffering from a chronic lack of sleep. He is always
tired. . . . Although he gets both Saturday and Sunday off, he spends both days sleeping like an infant.
What kind of life is this? What does he work for?[13]

She goes on to say that when their daughter was ill,
her husband took the morning off to accompany her to
the hospital, only to be scolded by his superior at the
bank for wasting time on "such a trivial matter."

The Japanese miracle is, above all else, that so many
Japanese have worked so hard for so long.

FOREIGN STOOGES

*It took me awhile to comprehend the lessons of that first
day at the* Japan Times. *There might not be a policy of
apartheid, as some had bitterly put it, but foreigners like
me were in a distinctly different class from the Japanese
sei-sha-in, the lifetime employees. We worked by different rules. Curiously, though, to a large extent the difference was expressed through indulgence to foreigners.
We were not expected to work beyond the terms of our
contract. No unpaid overtime was demanded of us; indeed, on those occasions when we did work beyond the
call of duty, Kuroishi-san and the other supervisors
would see to it that, in addition to overtime, we got extra pay. On a slow news night, some of us would be
allowed to go home early, though all the Japanese staff
stayed on to the bitter end.*
We were indulged in other ways as well: our slovenly

dress habits, our constant and sometimes uproarious banter, and even, in the case of certain hostiles like Alan, our shocking rudeness. At first, I was amazed at what we got away with. Gradually, I began to feel that there was something condescending in the way the Japanese treated us. We were not consulted in any decisions except those where our supposed expertise came to bear: headlines, grammar, that sort of thing. I concluded that the Japanese felt it would have been more trouble than it was worth to attempt to discipline us. After all, it takes a lifetime of effort to produce a Japanese worker. The process begins on the first day of school, and often includes a full year of company training provided to new recruits. There was no point in trying to remake transient foreigners in their image. As the Japanese are fond of pointing out to foreigners who try too hard to fit in, you cannot learn to be Japanese.

The fascinating thing was that, like schoolchildren who are tracked into "behavioral remediation classes," we lived down to their expectations. A rowdy insolence became the group ethic for all gaijin *editors. This was not without benefit. The companionship was great. Handed a piece of "Japlish"-sodden copy, the cynical, nicotine-stained editor came alive. Suddenly, an arc light snapped on in his mind and he heard an offstage announcer intone, "Live, from Tokyo, it's 'Saturday Night'!" While his fingers did the editing, he loosed a stream of biting satire. A favorite theme was matching Japanese politicians with look-alike comedians: Sousuke Uno and Milton Berle. Shintaro Abe and Shemp. This process led, inevitably, to reenactments of Three Stooges routines. To the utter bewilderment of the Japanese editors, the* gaijin *would suddenly start poking, slapping, whooping, grabbing a shirtfront, and cocking a fist while growling, "Why, I oughtta . . ."*

Banter inhabits all newsrooms and is rarely suitable for church teas, but the tension between the gaijin and the Japanese lent a peculiar intensity to the newsroom at the Japan Times. *It could not have been pleasant for the deskmen to hear their translations ridiculed with hoots, guffaws, and vile obscenities. Nor was it pleasant to deal with gaijin whose commitment to the paper fell somewhat short of wholehearted. Alan, who soon departed to pursue something more worthy of a Harvard man, took a parting shot at the paper. His last headline, over a story about a conference sponsored by the* JT, *read:* EGGHEADS MEET IN OSAKA. *Somehow it snuck into the paper, to the amusement, no doubt, of our 60,000 readers.*

This juvenile prank scarred relations between the news desk and the copy desk for quite some time. However, it also set in motion events that would bring dramatic changes in the way we worked together.

Still, Kuroishi-san seemed to take a personal interest in my progress. One night, after we had put the second edition to bed and were relaxing before the third-edition rush began, he came over to the domestic desk. Most of the staff had gone out to grab some dinner from a nearby curry shop, so we were alone, except for Sophie, who was off in a corner playing a computer game that she had installed on the system. I had stayed behind to dine on a box of Oreo cookies while I tried, once again, to master the Computer from the Black Lagoon.

Kuroishi-san put a hand on my shoulder. Startled, I looked up into his tired eyes.

"Naff-san, you are not working too hard, I hope?" He gave a nervous little laugh that indicated I was not to take offense at this question. When I am nervous, I talk too much. By now I was aware Kuroishi-san, far from being a slacker, routinely worked double shifts and

more, seeing the paper through from its early story con-
ference at 10 A.M. until its last edition at something after
1 A.M.

Thinking I must be slacking, I launched into a long
recital of how my day began with a noon interview for
American Banker *and would not finish until after mid-*
night.

"But that's okay," I concluded fatuously, "I like to
work hard. It keeps my blood moving."

Kuroishi-san was all sympathy. He warned me not
to push myself too far. And then he said something
curious.

"We should find a way to blend your efforts, so you
can work more efficiently. Maybe you can work for us
full-time and report part-time for the American Banker.*"*

I didn't know what to say. As an accredited foreign
correspondent with a genuine trench coat hanging in my
closet, I remained a bit wary about throwing in my lot
with the Japan Times. *It was one thing to work there*
part-time; it would be quite another to make it my pri-
mary affiliation. The JT was widely mocked among the
barflies at the Foreign Correspondents' Club, where
I was still a neophyte member. Though everyone read
it, and not a few cribbed stories from its pages, they
sneeringly called it a tool of Japan's Foreign Ministry.
The paper, as old-timers well knew, had been taken over
by the government during the war and turned into a
propaganda tool. To my astonishment, I learned that
some of the foreigners and dual citizens pressed into
service at that time were still working there. Among
them, Sophie told me, was the ex-husband of Tokyo
Rose.

However, by the time I'd worked there for half a year,
I knew the Japan Times *was as independent as any other*
Japanese newspaper—which is to say that it was not ad-

versarial toward the Establishment, but neither was it a stooge. When it came to the news, I never saw a paper with a more democratic, not to say anarchic, system of deciding what went into its pages. Aside from the brief news conferences, the desk editors had enormous discretion about what to run in the paper. They also had an amazing span of individual fixations, ranging from archaeology to the glandular progress of the nation's youth. Such stuff did not set any Foreign Ministry hot line to ringing.

And neither, so far as I know, did any of the more controversial reports the paper carried on Japan's discrimination against Korean residents, or the government's revision of history textbooks to mask the atrocities of the Imperial Army during World War II. Eventually, I would be able to discern how the government shaped news in Japan, but even then I was certain that the JT was no more in thrall to it than any other Japanese news outlet.

I managed to hold both jobs for about six months, until Bill Zimmerman, the American Banker editor who had hired me, left and was replaced by a man whose interests apparently did not extend as far as Japan. After a string of my stories ended up on American Banker's spike, I reconsidered Kuroishi-san's offer of a full-time job involving both reporting and editing. Actually, it would be more than a full-time job, because I had to edit five shifts a week and report in the time that I used to devote to American Banker.

I didn't mind. I was used to the routine and had come to like the copy desk immensely. My only hesitation was whether the Japan Times would be respectable in the eyes of the mainstream American press, whose ranks I eventually hoped to rejoin. But Sophie, that font of all *news, assured me that others had gone on to glory in the American media after working there. So I resigned my post, retired my foreign press card, and settled in to work full-time at the* Japan Times.

After a brief period of squeaky-clean earnestness, I fell in with the class clowns. Sophie, the brash, voluble, chain-smoking Canadian was our ringleader. She also happened to be a terrific editor and the only one who fully understood the computer system. Best of all, she knew where all the bodies were buried within the organization: who was feuding with whom, which deskman was likely to be kicked upstairs, and most important, what management was thinking of doing with us.

Sophie was half Japanese, but she was hardly shy or deferential. She swooped in on her Japanese bosses, giving them a hug or a punch in the arm, depending on how the mood took her, tousling their hair, bumming their cigarettes, and generally allowing herself other such breathtaking liberties. She nicknamed them mercilessly—poor Nakamura-san became "the Nakster." Sophie was heart-stoppingly bold. Whenever the paper's owner visited, even he, an auto-parts magnate of no small dignity, got the treatment from her, in an ever-so-slightly restrained way.

In short, she treated everyone like a family member. This caused the Japanese visible discomfort. Theirs is a land where touching is reviled; where one normally addresses a boss by his title rather than his name (from shachō-san, "honorable company president," on down), and where extraneous chat at work is a venal sin. Only Sophie had the natural charm, the lack of guile, and the sheer brass to get away with taking to heart the family metaphor.

SWORD IN HAND

Of course, the family myth is only one of many confusions in the West about the nature of work in Japan. Ever since Japan reappeared on the world stage as host of the 1964 Tokyo Olympics, Americans have been searching for the "secret" of its economic miracle. The hunt turned a bit frantic in recent decades, as American industries found themselves outhustled and then outmuscled by the Japanese on the field of commerce. All sorts of nonsense was proposed, while the one obvious and well-supported explanation was ignored.

So desperate did the search for an explanation grow that Miyamoto Musashi became a best-selling author. His *Book of Five Rings* went through at least a dozen printings in the seventies and eighties and was a Book of the Month Club selection. The paperback edition's cover claimed it was "Japan's answer to the Harvard M.B.A.!" and carried a quote from *Time*: "On Wall Street, when Musashi talks, people listen."

But Musashi did not exactly bring tidings of the latest stratagems in the Mitsubishi boardroom. He was a seventeenth-century samurai who had been obsessed with *kendō*, the Way of the Sword. He liked killing, and he wasn't scrupulous about it. Part of his reputation was made by leaping out of some bushes to ambush a boy, not yet in his teens, who had challenged him to a duel. A sort of martial Machiavelli, this Musashi wrote down a good deal of advice on how to cut people to bits before they did the same to you.

Picture an American semiconductor manufacturer poring over this passage:

The best use of the [short] companion sword is in a confined space, or when you are engaged closely with an opponent. The long sword can be used effectively in all [other] situations.[14]

Would this really prove valuable in his next round of negotiations with NEC? Could he even get both swords past Customs?

Despite being armed with such potent Oriental wisdom, America's business leaders went on losing the battle with their Japanese opponents. In truth, the whole search for a mystical explanation of Japan's industrial success was bunk. But at least it had the virtue of being so preposterous as to be easily debunked.

Not so the cultural argument. An entire school of thought, heavily promoted by Japan itself, claimed that the postwar Japanese economic system was a vital expression of Japanese culture.[15] In trade negotiations, Japanese officials dragged things that seemed entirely remote from what we would call culture under that umbrella to shelter them from the fury of American competitors. Japanese bureaucrats, for example, argued long and strenuously that Japan's closed bidding system for public works contracts, and the price-fixing cartels that accompanied it, were a cultural phenomenon. Then, in 1993, prosecutors began to follow up leads found in the files of the fallen LDP kingpin Shin Kanemaru. They arrested a string of provincial governors and mayors, along with construction executives and even a former cabinet minister, on charges of massive bribery in return for contracts. As the arrests rolled on, people began to wonder aloud if any politician or executive would be spared. The system, it seemed, was more criminal than cultural.

Still, culture plays its role in Japan's work life. The Confucian emphasis on rote learning and obedience has some obvious advantages, especially in training for industrial jobs. Japanese companies have made use of the

yarikata—"way of doing"—tradition to ensure that each
employee does each task in the same way. Friendships
often take the form of *kōhai* and *sempai*, "junior" and
"senior." Hierarchy is embodied in the very language: A
pair of Japanese can hardly exchange a word without ex-
pressing their relationship in some detail. The powerful
sense of *uchi*, "inside," undoubtedly hardens company
solidarity. The cultural precept of *wa*, or harmony,
though it cannot extinguish conflict, helps prevent it
from openly combusting.

One other "cultural" explanation of Japanese work
habits must be considered: nationalism. Japanese who set
out to explain their country to foreigners often cast nationalism in extraordinary terms. In the late 1960s,
Ichiro Kawasaki, a former Japanese diplomat, wrote:
"The individual Japanese identifies himself more intensely with the nation than does the Westerner, who
seems more capable of cosmopolitan nonchalance toward
national issues."[16] Granting for argument's sake this de-
batable proposition, does that make nationalism a cultural feature, bred into the bones of Japanese workers?
Hardly.

Just over a century ago, European observers regarded
ordinary Japanese as surprisingly apathetic about the fate
of their country. A German visitor in 1876 recorded in
his diary that "people in general have seemed to me extraordinarily indifferent, quite unconcerned about politics and such matters," and, on the occasion of the
emperor's birthday in 1880, "It distresses me to see how
little interest the populace take in their ruler. Only when
the police insist on it are houses decorated with flags."[17]

That phrase, "only when the police insist on it," suggests the true source of Japanese nationalism. It was
whipped up by Japan's rulers to engage the common
people in the rapid industrialization and overseas expan-

sion of the country. Despite the injection of nationalism, however, from 1905 on riots by working-class Japanese became commonplace. Many of these disturbances took place in Tokyo's Hibiya Park, just a stone's throw (and many stones were thrown) from the Imperial Palace. By 1920, 10,000 workers turned out at Ueno Park in Tokyo to observe May Day.[18] Unionists employed as violent a rhetoric as any rabble-rouser in the West. "In order to live we must attack capitalism at its roots; we must entirely destroy the existing social order," thundered a speaker at a union rally in 1921.[19]

For its part, the state reacted to the rise of organized labor with the infamous Public Order Police Law, giving police broad powers to suppress unions and strikes. When the military ruled, in the thirties and forties, it found it necessary to crush the existing unions and create special units to control workers. Japanese historian Kazuo Okochi describes the phony union set up by the secret police:

> Sanpo [Patriotic Industrial Association] units were organized in every workshop by the military clique, right-wing bureaucrats, and great war industrialists, with the collaboration of right-wing labor leaders, using coercive methods on the lines of the Nazi Labor Front. There was no pretense of voluntary action. The object of the organization was to compel the workers to submit unconditionally to forced labor, overwork, and low wages in wartime.[20]

Could all this have been necessary if the harmonious, familylike Japanese company had flowered out of the soil of Japanese culture? Or could it be that "culture," like "family," was just a little too neat an explanation for Japan's success? Koji Taira, a Japanese-born economist, scorns our romantic ideas about management in Japan:

It is widely assumed among Western scholars that "employer paternalism" fully explains the fundamentals of the Japanese industrial relations system. . . .
. . . [T]his phenomenon, popularly attributed to unchanging Japanese traditions, was in fact a new institutional invention in response to the labor market conditions which prevailed during the first cycle of Japan's industrialization.[21]

In other words, the truly distinctive features of the postwar Japanese management system—lifetime employment, seniority-based wages, and company-based unions—were a reaction to the chaos in prewar Japanese industry.[22]

BORN AGAIN

For my part, I tried to thaw relations with the frostiest of Japanese deskmen. Following the "egghead" incident, their attitudes toward us ranged from open contempt to polite wariness. Still, I eventually found it possible to strike up conversations with the friendlier of them. One day we carried a story on Greenpeace activists roaring about in rubber dinghies to try to prevent Japanese trawlers from catching minke whales. Under the International Whaling Convention, Japan was allowed to catch some 300 of these whales a year for "research." (There were no white-coated scientists lurking around the chunks of whale meat I saw in supermarkets.) Greenpeace opposed even this limited catch and, while I didn't harbor any strong feelings on the subject, my sympathies were generally with them. Curious, I asked Nakamura-san, the cherubic and mild desk manager,

*how he felt about Greenpeace. To my astonishment, he
exploded in anger.*

*"They are so arrogant!" he shouted. "Whale meat is a
traditional food for Japanese. We don't tell you Westerners not to eat beef, do we? Cows are sacred in India,
aren't they? But you don't think about that. Even though
you might be ruining the rangeland by raising cattle."*

*I was surprised and actually a little pleased to
find that he held such strong, considered opinions.
Nakamura-san's view jibed with the official line, but his
argument was intellectually stimulating. If the whales
could be saved by giving up hamburgers, would Americans be willing to make the sacrifice? I doubted it. Of
course, it was disturbing to find that Nakamura-san per-
ceived a continuity between the Greenpeace activists in
their rubber dinghies and the foreign copy editors who
ate Big Macs in his newsroom. But his outburst was for-
givable. After all, he was under a lot of pressure.*

*The Japan Times faced more competition than virtu-
ally any American newspaper. It was up against three
other daily English-language newspapers, published by
the three national giants of Japanese journalism: the Yomiuri, the Asahi, and the Mainichi. With vernacular cir-
culations running into the millions, they could afford to
run their English dailies at a loss. Only the Japan Times
would suffer if it went into the red. So while we transients were lightheartedly making a living, the Japanese
staffers were, in principle, fighting for their livelihoods.
They put in long hours, certainly longer than most of the
foreigners. Nevertheless, we occasionally had to roust
an editor out of a deep slumber to put the final edition
to bed.*

*Considering the Japanese penchant for order, the
physical surroundings were rather sloppy. Battleship-
gray steel desks were piled high with back issues, faxes,*

reports, press releases, and oddly enough, toilet paper.
(This, I learned, served in place of tissues, which were
more costly.) In the crannies between the piles were
half-drunk cups of coffee, tin ashtrays with mountains
of butts in them, empty beer cans (from the night shift),
as well as pizza crusts, dried strands of Japanese noodles,
and other debris of meals past.

Still, work at the JT could get intense. The method of
setting type was still fairly primitive. It involved crowds
of pressmen wielding razor-sharp XActo knives. As we
editors ordered last-minute changes and corrections, the
pressmen would slash at the pasteup sheets, replacing
single lines and even single words. It was here that
the culture conflict became most acute. As a rule, the
pressmen spoke little English and regarded copy editors
who did not speak their tongue with scalding contempt.
My halting, fractured Japanese seemed to qualify me as
an amiable half wit in their midst. In the mad, multilin-
gual scramble to get the paper into the presses, errors
occasionally remained or were compounded.

To my undying shame, I contributed a whopper to the
most important story I would ever handle at the Japan
Times. It was the morning Emperor Hirohito died. This
was an event we had been preparing for around the
clock for nearly four months. The emperor had fallen ill
in mid-September and we were now in the depths of
winter. Although it was taboo to say so, we all knew
he had intestinal cancer. Indeed, the Japan Times had
been printing, with somewhat questionable taste, daily
charts of his rectal hemorrhages. We had dummied obits
and miles of features ready to go. On at least two occasions when the end seemed near, I had spent all night
and all day at the paper, standing by. Finally, on the
morning of January 7, 1989, I rose early, flipped on the
television, and saw that regular programming had been

bumped from the air. Instantly, I knew what had happened. Hailing a cab, I raced to the JT. Sophie was the only other gaijin on hand.

The publisher called with orders to get out a one-page extra in an hour. For some reason, the deskman in charge decided to throw out most of our prepared text and write nearly an entire newspaper page from scratch. Fortunately, there was a large photo on it. Sophie and I split up the text and combed through it. As we worked, a crowd formed around us. To say the least, I felt under pressure. And of course, the eyes do tend to see what they want to see. Still, there is no excuse for what I did: In a line meant to refer to the former Son of Heaven's last birthday, I let it go into print reading "on the occasion of the emperor's eighty-seventh birth."

In spite of that error, which for all I knew might have been seen as blasphemous, no one berated me. I apologized profusely, but Kuroishi-san just smiled and said, "Don't worry. We'll fix it in first edition."

Compared with life at some companies, the Japan Times was a paradise. But, like all Adam's children, we were in for a fall. It was Sophie, naturally, who first got wind of management plans for a big change in the way we worked.

Dismayed by the "egghead" incident, Kuroishi-san and the managers above him had decided that we needed a full-time overseer. On a trip to China, the publisher had located just the man for the job. He was an American newspaperman who had fled the horrors of the East Coast for the mysteries of the East.

Thus forewarned, we kept a sharp eye out for him. When a tall, austere white man in tooled banker's shoes and a suit fit for a funeral strode into the newsroom, we knew we were in for it. He disappeared into the publisher's office. "They're issuing him the official whip and

chair," Carl growled. However, the stranger soon reemerged empty-handed, and Kuroishi-san brought him
over to introduce us. Sweat glistened on the newcomer's
bald scalp, and a nervous smile twitched across his lips.
He shook my hand with the earnestness of a man in
need of allies.

And so it was that I met Philip, one of the most brilliant and quixotic men I have ever known. He lived a
solitary, monkish life, without benefit of television, telephone, or even a refrigerator. A teetotaling vegetarian,
his one passion, apart from editing, appeared to be
books, and he remembered everything he read, down to
the original meanings of obscure ideograms used in Buddhist rites. In keeping with the management's desire, he
attempted to play the martinet, and indeed he quickly
imposed order on what had been a chaotic system. But
in the end there was too much humanity and humor in
him for the role of chief ogre. The banter quickly resumed, and he soon became a prominent voice in the
chorus.

The management strategy was obviously to make one
gaijin responsible for the conduct of all the others, and
thereby to isolate the problem. Philip, responding in
good bureaucratic fashion, concluded that he needed to
spread some of the responsibility around. Accordingly,
Sophie and I were elevated to night slot editors. This
meant we were charged with reviewing copy that others
had already edited to see that it conformed to style requirements, did not conflict with other stories already
slated, and, above all, made sense. Caught between the
wash of statistics and weird grammar churned out by
the deskmen and Philip's mountain of style rules, I
sometimes wished he'd picked someone else for the job.

Philip raised standards, all right, but his approach to
editing tended to be prim. One one occasion, he bawled

me out for a headline that ran 2 DEAD, 3 MISSING IN BOATING ACCIDENT. Using figures marred the page, he insisted. Better to spell everything out. Enraged, I responded by gathering copies of leading papers from around the world from the Foreign Correspondents' Club to show him that numerals appeared in headlines everywhere. He remained serenely indifferent.

However much I may have resented his stylistic straitjacket, I had to admit that Philip had made a significant accomplishment, one the management had never anticipated: By force of personality, he had brought the gaijin *editors much deeper into the workings of the paper. To be sure, things had been tending in that direction. Before my arrival, I had been told, the foreigners used to be segregated on a floor of their own. By the time Philip left, the* gaijin *not only shared offices with the Japanese but had a voice in the daily story conferences and even some committees. Relations had undergone a change that fell just short of revolutionary. Oh, there was an actual revolution brewing in the newsroom, but to everyone's surprise, it would erupt on the Japanese side.*

PRESS, PRESS, PULL

Could it possibly be that militarism had merely delayed the flowing of a natural proclivity for harmonious labor relations in Japan? To reject such a notion, you have only to reflect on how different Japan's postwar labor history might have been had MacArthur's social engineers been allowed to fulfill their intentions. When the Occupation briefly took the lid off the Japanese labor movement, unionism flourished. Membership shot up more than tenfold in a year, from 380,000 in 1945 to 5 million in

1946.[23] Workers at enterprises ranging from mines to newspapers spontaneously seized control.[24] Overnight, they turned the *Yomiuri Hochi* newspaper into first a liberal and then a left-leaning daily.[25] But once having confused democracy with communism, the union movement was doomed. General MacArthur, Supreme Commander of the Allied Powers, or SCAP, as he was known, reversed course. Things came to a head on February 1, 1947, when communist-led unions called for a general strike to demand a tripling of wages and the resignation of the conservative prime minister, Shigeru Yoshida. Nearly 2 million people were prepared to join. They weren't necessarily communists; indeed, they joked that their unions were like cranes: red-crested with snowy-white bodies. Nevertheless, they were determined to win "economic democracy," and might have done so had the strike come off. "[T]he Japanese government—unpopular and, having been disarmed by SCAP, still very weak in terms of police power—could not have withstood on its own a general strike of anywhere near the magnitude of the one being planned for February 1," a labor historian has written.[26]

But it was not to be. MacArthur cracked down. The strike was canceled, and the movement faltered. This was undoubtedly fortunate for the nation. The Soviets were eager to exploit any chance for revolution in Japan. But whether the Japanese would have been worse off with a strong, communist-dominated system of unions is irrelevant. The point is that there was a power struggle, not a cultural evolution, and because of U.S. intervention, labor lost.

Once the Occupation ended, Japanese managers still had to work hard to tame their workers. They feared a communist uprising, yet knew that brute repression had led the nation into disaster. Faced with this dilemma, Japan's leaders now conceived perhaps the most effective tool of social control ever devised: the Japanese-Style Management System, an almost perfect array of carrots and sticks. What American visitors so often mistook for egalitarianism in postwar Japanese companies was in fact hierarchy honed to a fine point. As a Japanese-American scholar put it, "Vertical alliance with a superior, necessary for one's status and elevation, may involve virtual slavery."[27]

Before this system could be put into operation, however, management had to win back "the right to manage." It was a bloody effort. Executives and unionists alike were murdered in shocking fashion. But with the conservative Liberal Democrats in power and with secret support from the United States, business leaders succeeded in breaking any real opposition in the ranks of labor.[28] Ichiyo Muto, a longtime Japanese labor activist, observes:

> The conventional mainstream thinking is that the Japanese are collaborative by culture. That is not true. . . . In the early postwar years the Japanese workers' movement actually paralyzed management. . . . It took 25 years or so for Japanese business to win a real, total victory. The device to get back the "right to manage" was basically the creation of a "company world" with the workers as its citizens or [rather] slaves.[29]

With the formation of the "company world," union membership as a proportion of the workforce dwindled to about half its peak. More important, the unions were tamed and caged. Trapped within the embrace of each company, the individual unions became at best mediators between management and workers, rather than representatives of labor. Before long, typical strikes took place on lunch hours, or at most over a day or two.[30] In 1988 Japan lost 163 work days to strikes, compared with 4,364 days lost in the United States.[31] It became difficult to draw a line between union and management. When Tokyo's Metropolitan Labor Standards Bureau found that bank employees were regularly performing unpaid overtime and were exceeding the legal thirty-six-hour-a-week overtime limit, unions representing each bank's workers joined management in denying the practices existed.[32]

The new Japanese management system had taken shape. Without question, it brought many improvements to the lives of employees. For those working in the top third of Japanese companies, there was the promise of lifetime security and steadily increasing pay, as well as an astonishing array of benefits. (Smaller companies, being at the mercy of large ones, could not offer such guarantees.) Without question, their workers were motivated to work hard by the admirable desire to rebuild the nation and see it take its place among the world's elite. And no doubt workers had more say about the running of the company than in the past. Managers solicited opinions from all employees on how to improve productivity and quality. But in return they required a commitment of unquestioning loyalty. Within the velvet glove remained an iron fist.

There are many answers to the riddle of Japanese success. Most lie outside the scope of this book. But nearly everyone agrees that a diligent workforce has been one of Japan's greatest assets. Therefore, we must revisit the question: Why do the Japanese work so hard? How can they pass up their vacations? Why don't they take sick days when they are sick, or strike for easier working conditions? The quick and dirty answer has been to label the

Japanese "economic animals." It's a horrible slur. Japanese workers are made to sound like sheep tended by wise shepherds. I'd much rather be called lazy: That at least is a time-honored trait of humanity.

In truth, Japanese companies devised many new ways of ensuring that their workers would cooperate. In 1972 the writer Satoshi Kamata went to work in a Toyota assembly plant on a six-month contract. He soon discovered that the pay system was designed to make each worker liable for the group's monthly wages.

> Should someone in the team make a mistake, the [team's] wage would decrease correspondingly. Tied to the conveyor belts, everyone works desperately, hoping that he is not a burden to the others. This is the "relationship of a community bound together by a common fate."[33]

Among their punitive powers, companies could transfer troublemakers to distant posts at will. When a few working couples challenged such transfers as a violation of their right to live together, they found the bureaucracy and courts basically unsympathetic. Or the company could simply consign a malcontent to the *madogiwa-zoku*, the "window-watching tribe." Like a naughty schoolchild being forced to sit in the corner, the disloyal worker suffers humiliation and isolation.[34]

So the messy but truthful answer to the Japanese puzzle lies partly in a tangle of cultural traits and personal motivation. Aside from plausible cultural traits such as devotion to the group, experience tells me that the very things that push Americans to work—to earn money, to support our families, to fulfill our ambitions, and so forth—press the Japanese to work. But in addition to push, there is in Japan an awful lot of pull.

Here, then, is the answer to our mystery: At root, what drives the Japanese to excesses of work is the *excessive* power of the authorities standing over them.

LOVE'S LABOR'S LOST

The Japan Times, *although not particularly authoritarian, consciously tried to be a traditional Japanese company. It made a clear distinction between the "lifetime" employees and the contract-based help. It had a company union. Big decisions were subject to ringi, the passing around of a proposal to all permanent employees for them to approve by affixing their personal seals.*

Hardly anybody took their full allotment of personal vacation. In lieu of this, the Japan Times, *along with all the other national newspapers, observed seven or eight "newspaper holidays" a year, most of which fell on a Sunday. (We gaijin were permitted to take up to three weeks leave a year—without pay.)*

However, you could sense the reach of authority from beyond the company boundaries. One night, as we were closing the late edition, one of the deskmen looked at some dry, statistic-laden piece we were publishing and snapped.

"Why are we putting this out? It doesn't mean anything," he said to me.

"Beats me," I replied.

"I want to get out and report, talk to real people about real issues," he continued.

"So why don't you?" I asked.

"I don't know. We just get pinned down," he said, and concluded with conviction: "It's the system."

The Japan Times *did report on real issues and real people. However, for nearly all of its government and business news, it had little choice but to be spoon-fed meaningless statistics by nameless government sources or corporate flaks. Japan has evolved an ingenious press club system that throws a muffling blanket over nearly all controversy. (The exception is politics, which provides an entertaining sideshow.) Every government agency, right down to the local police station, and every major company or business group has a "kisha club." Members are coddled with closed briefings (to the fury of foreign reporters, who have long been excluded), but the implicit bargain is that all reports will be limited to agreed-upon facts.*

The upshot is that many Japanese reporters know a great deal more than they are able to tell in print. Being ignorant of this in my early days at the JT, I was surprised to learn from Doi-san, a bright star on the desk, that the ruling Liberal Democrats frequently paid their bitter opponents, the Socialists, to act as go-betweens with the North Koreans. I found this hard to believe. I certainly hadn't read it in the Japan Times. *But in 1991 Doi-san was proved absolutely correct. Shin Kanemaru, the LDP "godfather" who kept millions in gold stashed under his floorboards, went hand in hand with Socialist leader Makoto Tanabe on a diplomatic foray into North Korea. There they dined with the Great Leader himself, Kim Il Sung, Korea's answer to Stalin. Kanemaru bungled the trip, promising more than Japan's bureaucrats were prepared to give. A year later, he fell from grace when a shady businessman confessed that he had wheeled a shopping cart stuffed with $4 million in Japanese banknotes into an underground garage to pay off Kanemaru for political favors. The businessman was backed by right-wing gangsters. But money politics holds ideology cheap. Some of that $4 million undoubtedly snaked its way through the political swamp into* *the clutches of North Korean commissars. After all, arranging a trip to Pyongyang costs money.*

Eventually, things came full circle. Kanemaru's fall toppled the ruling party itself, and the Socialists, blinking with astonishment, found themselves partners in a ruling coalition led by defectors from the LDP. Less than a year later, the Socialists walked out of that coalition and into a deal with the very Liberal Democrats who were ostensibly their bitter opponents. Together, they formed one of the strangest governments democracy has ever seen: a conservative cabinet with a Socialist face. And the Japanese press had, in some sense, been a silent witness to the corruption that made it all happen.

So are Japanese reporters lazy? Hardly. Many are ambitious and most are hardworking.[35] Important politicians like Kanemaru were followed around the clock by squads of reporters. The only thing comparable in America is the press corps that dogs a front-running presidential candidate. But unlike their American brethren, Japanese reporters tend to keep a lid on the juicy stuff until a press club—say, at the prosecutor's office—validates it.

Japanese reporters are reluctant to let go of the "kisha club" system because of the security it affords them. Nevertheless, the foreign press in Japan is battering away at it. The kisha club members were especially galled, for example, when T. R. Reid of the Washington Post *broke the news of Crown Prince Naruhito's engagement to Masako Owada. All the Japanese media had known about it for weeks, but had obeyed a government request to withhold the news until the Imperial Household Agency gave them the green light. David Butts, my boss at UPI, who went on to become Tokyo bureau chief of Bloomberg Business News, dealt the system another blow in the summer of 1993. After years of quietly seeking membership in the stock exchange press club, which like most press clubs had no provision to admit foreign members, David finally began a highly public series of protests inside the club. I accompanied him the day CNN came to film the scene. It was highly amusing to watch him shout, "We're all journalists! We're not supposed to restrict information!" at a club member who hid out of camera range behind a bookcase.*

However, the press club later showed that it was not amused: Its members voted to relax the rules, but in a demonstration that in Japan the nail that sticks up still gets hammered down, they admitted Bloomberg's chief rival, Reuters, but rejected Bloomberg itself.[36]

Of course, the press was not the only industry whose actions were influenced by the government. About the time I started working for the Japan Times, *Rumiko was being courted by Nippon Steel, one of Japan's biggest companies. Nippon Steel, once the centerpiece of Japan's industrial policy, was getting a little long in the tooth. What's more, it was under pressure from the bureaucracy to make some helpful gesture toward reducing trade friction with the United States. Demand for its steel was slipping, so it had to close down several sprawling old factories in Kitakyushu, on the northern tip of Japan's southernmost main isle. But Nippon Steel still had one of the country's largest private workforces—more than 60,000 people. The era of personnel "restructuring" had not quite arrived, so it needed to find new jobs for the thousands of workers who had been employed in the shuttered plants. The managers settled on a plan that, for a staid old company like Nippon Steel, was positively radical. They would convert an outdated foundry into a theme park called Space World. Going from manufacturing to service was a big leap, but theme parks were a*

growth industry at the time, thanks largely to government encouragement.

Since leisure was what Americans knew best, Nippon
Steel would go a step further: It would incorporate the
best of American amusement park know-how and technology. This would not only solve the problem of what
to do with the old factory, it would earn the company
brownie points with the government for reducing international trade friction.

That's where Rumiko came in. As a Japanese architect
with a U.S. graduate degree, she could help them deal
with the Americans and furnish designs appropriate to a
Japanese project. Normally a company like Nippon Steel
would be loath to hire a woman in her thirties for a professional job. The firm prided itself on having in-house
expertise of all sorts, even architects. The vast majority
of its employees were hired right after graduation and, if
male, would stay with them until retirement. (If female,
they would normally be nudged into marriage with a
suitable man, possibly from within the company, and
retired after five years of service.)

But the times they were a-changing, and Nippon Steel
was determined to keep up with them. When the need
arose for someone to deal with the Americans, they
turned to one of those newfangled headhunters. They
did not flinch when the man the headhunter produced
turned out to be a woman.

Engrossed in my own work, I had only the vaguest
idea of all this. One night, I returned from a shift at the
Japan Times to find Rumiko standing in the middle of
our living room/dining room/kitchen, looking disori-
ented and pale. A flush of anger coursed through me.
Some high school boys, realizing that I was away in the
evenings, had lately been harassing her, tapping on the
windows of our ground-floor "mansion" and making un-

speakable suggestions. Just a week ago I had switched worknights and staked out the corner. Sure enough, about 9:30 a couple of guys in black, Prussian-style school uniforms, no doubt on their way home from cram school, came sneaking up to our bedroom window and tapped on it. I caught them red-handed. Well, I almost *caught them. Cursing them out in fractured Japanese must have slowed me down. But at least I thought I had scared them off for good. Now I was not so sure.*

"What's happened?" I asked.

"They made me an offer," Rumiko replied. "I think I might accept."

Rumiko often says things that surprise me. Even after years of living with her, I'm amazed to find how rarely our thoughts move in parallel channels. At this juncture, however, I was shrewd enough to suspect that we were talking at cross-purposes. I requested details.

Rumiko sighed. As a Japanese, it really irritates her to have to spell out everything for me. She can't understand why I can't grasp the meaning from her . . . her whatever it is I'm supposed to grasp. The Japanese call it haragei, *"belly-talk." How you are supposed to read someone's belly, even on the remote chance that it is exposed, remains a mystery to me. I poured a couple of beers in hopes of loosening her tongue.*

Eventually, Rumiko enlightened me. Nippon Steel was now offering her a one-year contract at the salary equivalent to that of a man with ten years' service to the company. There probably wasn't another woman in the company who could command its equal.

This was clear but confounding. Rumiko had just launched a private practice, in partnership with some old friends. Their firm, Square Inc., was out of the shoals and spinning off a modest income for each partner. Becoming a partner in one's own firm represents an enor-

mous step in the career of an architect. What's more, although Square required hard work and plenty of it, Rumiko could adapt her hours to our schedule. I was disturbed by the idea of her working a nine-to-five job at Nippon Steel while I worked from early evening till late at night. But, large-souled creature that I am, I naturally said, "Go for it." After all, Nippon Steel's offer amounted to Big Money, something in the neighborhood of $60,000. It never occurred to me that they would get every yen's worth. Nine to five, indeed. Hah!

THE EMPIRE STRIKES BACK

Women have always been the throwaway element of Japanese labor. Talk of loyalty, benevolence, or paternalism—except in the arrangement of marriages—is quite out of place with female labor. As Japan began to industrialize late in the nineteenth century and labor fell into short supply, employers resorted to kidnapping young women from the countryside to work in their textile mills. There they labored fourteen hours a day in gloomy, airless factories under lock and key. Poor families often consented after the fact, especially when the factory paid the young woman's wages, small as they were, directly to her parents.[37]

Factory work for three to five years fit neatly into the transition from daughter to daughter-in-law. "Being young and from the still feudalistic rural areas of Japan, women in factories were not inclined to protest their conditions," says one scholar.[38] Submissiveness was pounded into females from the earliest age. "Girls must be gentle and graceful in all things," instructed a sixteenth-century textbook by Ekken Kaibara on the education of women.[39]

However, it wasn't mere etiquette that restrained women. Starting in 1889, the Japanese government passed a series of laws that banned women from attending rallies or participating in politics of any kind.[40] On the factory floor, observes another scholar:

> [R]apid turnover inhibited the creation and passing on of their own tradition of resistance to factory bosses. They did compose and pass on songs about mill life that clearly reflect their creation of a factory culture of anger, despair, yet hope for a better life, but until the 1920s the most common form of protest . . . was escape, not dispute.[41]

Female laborers, then, were docile and cheap. The only problem was that living under lock and key in the cold, cramped factories, they tended to die of tuberculosis.[42] Most inconvenient.

After the war, the Occupation authorities, aware of the vicious exploitation of female labor in the prewar days, wrote detailed protections for women into the labor laws—even as they guaranteed them equal rights under the constitution. Women were forbidden to work late at night, for example, and were entitled to days off for menstruation.

In the long run, however, such rules served mainly to disqualify women from career jobs at the best companies. The 1947 Labor Standards Law, says one scholar, "gave employers an excuse for their evident reluctance to promote women."[43] Help-wanted ads remained divided into men's and women's sections, and the jobs themselves contained a vast disparity in lifetime wages and security. Still, the role of women in the Japanese workforce did evolve. As administrative jobs expanded, many became O.L.'s—that is, "office ladies" who, stereotypically, poured tea and answered phones until they could be part- nered off to a suitable young salaryman.[44]

Jeannie Lo, a young American woman who took a leave from Harvard to spend some months as an O. L. at Brother Industries' Nagoya plant in 1986, says the O.L.'s main ambition was to make herself attractive enough to land a husband from within the company. This involved playing the *burikko*, the girlish innocent. Even though she might be sexually active, the successful O. L. had to present herself as a childish naïf to avoid threatening the male sense of superiority.[45] "Unfortunately," laments an- other social researcher, "many men continue to view women as not fully adult, an attitude that dominated the thinking of the old family system."[46] Or, as Jane Austen put it, "Imbecility in females is a great enhancement of their personal charms."[47]

O.L.'s have long been nicknamed "office flowers," a la- bel that betrays a deep contempt, as this extract from a Japanese report on the salaryman shows:

> The graying corporate warrior might view [female workers] as if they were colorful flowers in a vase. They serve a temporary use. But once they begin to fade, they should be replaced. "Nothing worse than a wilted flower hanging around the office," he might scoff with his drinking companions about a woman who chooses to continue work beyond the marriage- able age.[48]

The contempt went beyond words: Offices were rife with bottom-pinching, breast-fondling men, and, worse still, bosses who coerced sex from their female employ- ees. I interviewed a wide variety of women for a story on their experiences in the workplace, and whether they worked in a bar or a bank, the undertone of sexual harassment rang true.

In 1985, however, a trickle of change began to flow. An Equal Employment Opportunity Law was passed under great pressure from women's groups and the Socialist party, who argued that Japan would be an international pariah if it failed to do so by the end of the U.N. Decade of the Woman. The law banned most forms of discrimination, but as is so often true with Japanese laws affecting business, it provided no meaningful penalties for violations. However, market forces and the determination of women combined to open far more opportunities than lawmakers had envisioned.

A labor shortage, brought on by Japan's phenomenal economic growth and slow population rise, left companies little choice but to hire women for every sort of job. While the flow of men into the workforce leveled off, the number of women taking jobs jumped by as much as 5 percent a year. The labor laws that had helped employers keep women's wages down were now a hindrance. Starved for labor, companies appealed to the government to lift the limits on overtime for women.[49] At the beginning of the eighties, only one in three Japanese workers was a woman; by the end of the decade four in ten were.

For the first time women became cabdrivers and construction workers. Even the conservative Defense Academy had to open its doors to women in the face of dwindling male enrollments. Meanwhile, the female entrepreneurial spirit blossomed. The number of women heading companies jumped 8 percent in 1991 to 42,000.[50] Women burst into the professions as well. In 1992 one in five of those taking the national bar exam was a woman, up from one in seven the year before.[51] Two years later, for the first time a woman was named to Japan's Supreme Court.

As women poured into the workplace, a change came over them. Many no longer regarded work as a waystation on the path to marriage. However, none of this meant that Japanese business leaders were prepared to abandon sexism altogether. The mere thought of a woman supervising men causes much tooth-sucking and shuddering among Japanese businessmen. Despite the constitution, the equal opportunity law, and a huge rise in the number of women in the workforce over that decade, the fraction of women in managerial positions rose from 2.3 percent in 1981 to just 3.6 percent in 1991.[52] Many companies continued to devise "female executive" positions to make sure women managers only supervised women.[53] A 1990 government study found that just 13 percent of women felt they received equal treatment in the workplace.[54]

When the recession took hold, employers began to dump women by the hundreds of thousands, just as they had in the past. But this time was different. Even with recovery in sight, some of Japan's biggest corporations refused to hire women. In May 1994, the Labor Ministry found, unemployment among young men began to dip, but among young women it rose to a record high of 6.3 percent, more than double the overall unemployment rate. Clearly, "office flowers" had become too costly and even, at times, too dangerous a luxury to maintain.

Still, for many women the most discouraging aspect of Japanese companies was not job discrimination. It was the structure of work itself. As things stand, "women's jobs," combined with housekeeping, force married women to put in an hour and a half more work a day than their husbands.[55] The construct of the salaryman as a corporate warrior who never rests—who can be dispatched anywhere, anytime, for as long as the company wishes, and who must, if necessary, endure *karōshi*, "death by overwork"—makes it virtually impossible for a woman to cross the line into a "man's job." To do so, she would have to abandon all hope of marriage and children, for what husband could be expected to shoulder household responsibilities? Is it any wonder, then, that Japanese women lead the world in job dissatisfaction?[56]

FROM FUNHOUSE TO CHARNEL HOUSE

Soon after the Space World project got started, Rumiko hit the road. In characteristic Japanese style, Nippon Steel dispatched its employees to learn everything they could about amusement parks. Rumiko and several colleagues roamed the world in search of perfect leisure knowledge. One day they were examining the giant roller coaster at a mall in Edmonton, Canada, the next they were somewhere in Alabama. Rumiko quickly racked up enough miles to become a premier member of United Airline's frequent flyer club.

Even when she was back in Tokyo, Rumiko rarely got home before ten or eleven. But at least she did get home. The men in her office were frequently obliged either by the actual volume of work or by peer pressure to stay overnight at a nearby hotel.

As the pace picked up, her weekends vanished into a black hole of work. When I saw her at all, Rumiko looked drained. Her eyes were dull and her voice flat. She ground her teeth in her sleep.

I grew more and more frustrated with the situation. Finally, one Sunday afternoon, to Rumiko's great embarrassment, I called her at the office and insisted she come home. "Tell them you have an emergency at home!" I said. She didn't have to; they could guess. For a spouse

*to call the office on a matter less urgent than death was
unusual, and the anger in my voice must have tipped off
whoever had answered the phone. They let her leave.*

*Back home, I paced furiously until she arrived. What
was going on? I demanded to know. "Meetings," she replied wearily. Long, endlessly long meetings in which
everyone tried to figure out what everyone else was feeling without tipping their own hand. Politics—tense,
back-stabbing, power-play politics in which various
managers who had come to the project from different
backgrounds tried to line up factions against one another. All this had to be done without creating so much
as a ripple on the surface of the pool (harmony must be
preserved!), so naturally it took far more time than open
warfare would. And of course, work itself: The original
task had quickly doubled in scope and budget as ambitions grew, but the schedule had not. Only the hours
grew longer.*

*Despite my anger, it seemed there was nothing to be
done about the situation. Rumiko felt she was already
getting off light compared with the others in the office.
It was the Japanese version of the prisoner's dilemma: If
one left, the others suffered more. There was no overt
command to stay. But because responsibility lay undi-
vided with the group, everyone felt obliged to hang
around for the sake of the others. No one ever felt sure
that his day's work was done.*

*The next morning, Rumiko was out the door again be-
fore eight o'clock. I barely saw her again for a week, and
when I did she was little more than a sleepwalker.*

*I started to worry about her health, not to mention
the health of our marriage. One night, I decided to
voice my concerns. "Rumiko," I said in a voice intended to convey both reason and compassion, "you*

are young and strong, but you're not invulnerable, for Chrissakes. If things go on the way they are, who knows what . . ."

She exploded. I don't recall exactly what she said, through the tears and rage, but the gist of it was that I was only making things worse. She was under tremendous pressure and what she needed from me was support and practical help, not advice. My feelings were hurt, but it later struck me as bitter comedy that I was being asked to play the role of the "good wife" to her salaryman shtick. Not that I was ironing her chemises or anything. But she was telling me that I should be indulgent and supportive rather than critical and challenging.

I shrugged and got on with my own work. But the situation grew intolerable. Finally, we hit on a mutually agreeable solution: Have a baby!

We went to work with a will. If anything, life was even more exhausting now, but at least it had its fun moments. Finally, one of the little pregnancy testing strips turned blue: We were going to be parents. As it happened, this was too late to trim any time off Rumiko's contract, but it gave her a reason to lighten up her schedule somewhat in the later stages.

Rumiko was lucky. As a mother, she had no choice but to be present for the birth of her child. One of her colleagues at Nippon Steel was not so fortunate: When his wife gave birth to their first child, he was on assignment hundreds of miles away. Many weeks passed before he got to see his child. Another colleague of hers was a man eager to start a family. But to the rich amusement of everyone around him, he simply lacked sufficient opportunity for intimacy with his wife. It seemed that he always got home too late or too exhausted.

But the excesses of work proved tragically unfunny in

the end. Shortly before the project was completed, one of Rumiko's supervisors—a lean, hard-driven man in his forties—flew down to Kyushu to inspect the site yet once more. Shortly after arriving, he dropped dead in his tracks. It was plain to all that overwork had felled him. Nippon Steel might have a new vision of its business, but its corporate culture had hardly changed a whit.

BARE BONES

Incredibly, the label by which this system has come to be known is "human capitalism." It reflects the serious, thoughtful effort of economist Robert Ozaki, a naturalized American of Japanese origin, to offer the Japanese system as a model for the world. Ozaki rightly points out that the nineteenth-century British form of capitalism emphasized raw materials and machinery and took labor more or less for granted, whereas postwar Japan, having nothing else to rely on, made labor the primary element of its economic system.[57]

As a critique of Western capitalism, this is excellent. Certainly, America has long, dark stains on its economic record ranging from slavery to the days of the robber barons, when railroads would slash pay at every chance and strikers would be shot down by company goons, to the modern era of executives who are paid hundreds of millions to "downsize" a company by dumping its workers onto the streets. As an attempt to abstract the best of the Japanese management style, it may be admirable. But when Ozaki writes, for example, that "the humanistic firm is free of outsider influences, and its management and workers make decisions independently and autonomously, controlling their own destiny," he must be thinking of a Platonic ideal rather than a real Japanese company. No one familiar with the power of Japan's bureaucrats, the influence of its banks, or indeed the power that one firm exerts over another within the vertical and horizontal chains of organization that characterize Japanese business could speak of any of its parts as "controlling their own destiny." As for workers, the historical evidence leaves no doubt that the postwar Japanese management system came into being especially to prevent workers from taking control of their destinies.

So long as workers' motivation and business demands overlapped, the coercive power of companies remained largely hidden. But as Japan attained hyperwealth in the late eighties, employee discontent came out into the open. Unions, though still largely impotent, complained noisily about the abuse of their members. "The Japanese are clearly overworked," an official of Japan's largest trade union federation told the *New York Times* in 1992. "After all these years of prosperity . . . the system must respond to our demands for shorter hours."[58] Japanese management, ostensibly so responsive to workers, dug in its heels. The government set a target of 1,800 annual work hours by 1993; management said it could not possibly achieve it before 1996. Even that was too soon for most companies, so management began to talk vaguely of meeting the target around the turn of the century.[59] Ironically, the recession achieved what the government could not: In 1992 annual work hours fell nearly 3 percent to 1,957, the first time Japanese workers had ever logged less than 2,000 hours in a year.[60] This still meant that the Japanese were outworking everyone in the Western world. Even so, with the recession raging, second-tier companies begged the government not to force them to implement a forty-hour workweek mandated by law. Perversely, they claimed that slack demand made it impossible to change. Speaking on their behalf, the Tokyo Chamber of Commerce said "the new measures should be deferred as long as possible, given the present economic climate."[61]

But no power can any longer stave off change in Japan. Blue-chip companies have begun to retreat from lifetime employment with unseemly haste. Pioneer Electric Corporation, a leading Japanese electronics manufacturer, responded to the slump by firing thirty-five senior "lifetime" employees. Other companies followed suit. Public protest forced some companies to back away from layoffs, but they soon devised more subtle methods of getting rid of well-paid senior workers. The practice of *kata-tataki*, "shoulder-tapping," was enough of a hint for some. Those who clung to their jobs were baited and harassed, had their phones cut off, and found themselves transferred to remote sites. When they finally caved in, they were listed as having voluntarily resigned.[62]

Before long, it became clear that the bloodletting was not merely a response to a recession. The lifetime employment system had outlived its usefulness. Shrewd observers of the Japanese system had long ago noted that lifetime employment offered companies the opportunity to employ scads of young people at little expense. Starting wages were fixed below true value across whole industries, and workers endured them in return for security and promised raises. "It may be that the major economic benefit from internal labor markets [was that they] enabled large firms to minimize their wage bill by paying large numbers of young workers below their marginal productivity," scholar Robert Cole wrote in the late seventies.[63]

By 1993, with the proportion of workers fifty-five or older rising to 13 percent, that benefit had turned into a costly burden.[64] Nearly 40 percent of Japan's workforce had fifteen years or more of seniority.[65] This posed a grave problem: Under seniority-based wages, only a tiny fraction of those older workers could be expected to produce more than they earned. "Restructuring" set in with a vengeance. In addition to firing or farming out workers, companies laid plans to replace seniority-based wages with pay-for-performance, a cheaper path when so many workers are reaching middle age, but a violation of the principle under which they were hired.[66] Fortunately for management, Japan's "cultural" bias against contracts leaves workers little recourse.

It wasn't only the white-collar workforce that was affected. In 1992 unionized labor had to take its first cut in bonus pay in eighteen years.[67] Union credibility, never high, took a beating. After eighteen years as head of Sanyo Electric's company union, Takaharu Yamada told a Japanese newspaper that labor unions "have become mere mouthpieces for management."[68] Faith in the beneficence of the Japanese company withered. A government survey found that between 70 and 75 percent of young workers were prepared to change jobs if a better opportunity arose.[69]

In the space of a few years, the foundations of the much-lauded Japanese management system had cracked. The promise of lifetime employment was frayed, the seniority structure undermined, and the company union debunked. But there was a greater challenge facing the system: At long last, women were on the move.

YOU MUST BE JOKING, MR. MANDELA

With so much discontent in the air, something was bound to give. At the Japan Times, *I witnessed some of*

the changes firsthand. When I started working there in
1988, nearly all the Japanese employees had been in har-
ness for their entire careers. Indeed, one of the senior
executives had, according to Sophie, begun as a copyboy
at the age of fourteen.

But the freshman class of 1989 was a breed apart, as
the Japanese might say. I was invited to sit in on some
of the interviews during recruiting season. The new hires
impressed me from the start, especially the women, who
outnumbered the men that year. Bright and ambitious,
the class of '89 chafed at the traditional apprenticelike
tasks to which they were set. (Among these was to clip
and paste stories in file books. The young woman most
often stuck with this work was quickly nicknamed "the
Clipper" by her peers.) Editors, accustomed to barking
out orders in monosyllabic commands and seeing them
obeyed, found they were being challenged. To the as-
tonishment of everyone, especially us foreigners who
had bought the "harmony" line, shouting matches be-
gan to erupt on the domestic news desk.

It didn't take management long to notice that some-
thing peculiar was going on. One day Kuroishi-san came
over to share his thoughts. Shaking his head sadly, he
asked me in a low voice if I had noticed how difficult
some of the new employees were to handle. I allowed as
I had (though I didn't add that whatever their shortcom-
ings as journalists, and those could be grievous, I ad-
mired their spunk).

Kuroishi-san paused for one of those famous Japanese
silences and looked off into the middle distance. I knew
he was preparing to say something difficult. Did he
think it was the gaijins' fault? Was he going to blame
me somehow? Hell, my job had simply been to evaluate
their English; I hadn't been given any say in who got
hired. But no, he had a another theory.

"We hired too many women," he said with a quiet laugh. "Women these days are too strong."

Stunned, I lit on that most noncommittal of Japanese phrases: "Ah, sō desu ka?" ("Is that so?")

Kuroishi-san had a point. The new women were too strong to manage, at least in the accustomed way. One of them, a brash, self-proclaimed loudmouth with a sparkling sense of humor, made her mark at a press conference called by Nelson Mandela. The black South African leader was then visiting Japan to raise funds. Women reporters in Japan are expected to play a very different role from their male counterparts. They are mostly used on television, where they serve to add "charm" to the scene. The female interviewer often plays the naive stand-in for the viewer, asking questions in a tone of breathless admiration and drawing out explanations fit for the simpletons who are assumed to be watching. No woman is expected to ask hardball questions.

So when it came Kuwata-san's turn to ask Mandela a question, no one in the Japanese press would have been the least surprised if she had asked, "How do you like Japanese food, Mr. Mandela?" But they were flabbergasted when in her loud, clear voice she asked him why he hadn't criticized Japan's coddling of apartheid and why he hadn't stuck up more for the rights of women in his country.

Mandela himself, who had until then maintained that magnificent calm that characterized his long imprisonment, was taken aback. He broke into an embarrassed smile and, wagging a finger at her, replied that women today were so strong they could make their own case. The room erupted in laughter, nearly all of it male.

The Japan Times tried harder than many companies to adapt, but it too was a prisoner of the past. It could not *adjust quickly enough to the new realities. Ironically, the management had put great effort into altering relations with the gaijin staff. Whatever their intentions in hiring Philip, Kuroishi-san had seen to it that communication with the foreigners was better than ever, and ever more responsibility had devolved upon them. One foreigner, a Chinese-born permanent resident of Japan, had even been admitted, somewhat uneasily, to the ranks of the sei-sha-in, the "permanent employees."*

But there had been too little change in the employment conditions of the Japanese themselves. First the women, and then some of the men, began to quit in search of other jobs or lifestyles.

Yumiko, known to us gaijin as "the Admiral" for shattering the taboo against women reporters boarding Japanese naval vessels, went into the master's program at Columbia University's journalism school. Yuri went on to become a reporter with the Associated Press. Almost none of the departing women followed the traditional Japanese path of resigning to get married and raise children.

The Japan Times liberation movement did not stop there. Before long, a group of deskmen in their forties also made the leap. This clique of sixties graduates, many of whom dabbled in radical politics back then, had long since settled into the lifetime groove. But the upheavals of the eighties proved more unsettling than the politics of the sixties. Soon they were gone. The first one out the door was the deskman who had complained of "the system" preventing him from talking to any real people. Poor old Kuroishi-san was back to his old habit of doing double shifts just to fill the empty seats on the domestic desk.

Of course, the paper did not collapse. New staff were

hired, many of them women. Bit by bit, the company adjusted to the new situation.

Carl and Sophie, meanwhile, were steadily editing away. They had been there when I started and they were there when I left. By now, they had more seniority than many of the Japanese around them.

THE RACING CIRCUIT

The Japanese had many reasons for changing jobs, but in the main they sought jobs that would allow them a more livable life. This was especially true for women. A friend of Rumiko's whom I'll call Kazuko faces an arduous but not exceptional struggle to keep up her career and raise two small children. Every morning, she gets up before dawn, feeds and clothes the children, leaves the house by seven, and walks them to her car in a rented parking space ten minutes away. She drops off her son at the local nursery and then drives to the next township to another nursery for her daughter. (Like most Japanese nurseries, her local one has too few openings.) She returns to the parking lot near her house and, leaving the car, walks to the nearest train station. After a fifteen-minute ride on one train, she changes lines and rides another twenty minutes. At the terminus, she walks to another parking lot, where she keeps a second car, and then drives several miles to the campus where she teaches. In the evening, she makes the same journey in reverse, getting home by about seven. Because the children are always ravenous by this time, she quickly makes a couple of rice balls for them and then goes downstairs to pick up the groceries she has had delivered. At about eight, when dinner is ready, her husband comes home in the family's third

car, too late and too tired to be of much help. But there's
still laundry to be done and children to be bathed and put
to bed and who knows what else. A decade ago, three
cars in one family would have been considered an outrageous luxury in Japan. Now, for Kazuko and her husband,
it's a matter of survival.

Too many families are now enduring this kind of debilitating lifestyle for things to remain unchanged for long.
Mental health experts have begun to detect alarming
signs of stress in career women, ranging from ulcers to
psychosomatic blindness.[70] Either family or work must
give way. Yet attempts to discourage women from working have proven useless. When the recession hit, employers began to dump women by as many as 100,000 a
month. But rather than go off and become good wives
and wise mothers, young women streamed into public
employment agencies demanding work.[71] Polls showed
that married or not, women want the financial independence that work provides.[72] The government itself found
that the number who considered themselves economi-
cally independent shot up 10 percentage points between
1986 and 1991, to 59 percent.[73]

With unaccustomed confidence, women went on bat-
tling the status quo. Sexual harassment, shortened by the
Japanese to *sekuhara*, suddenly became a hot issue. At
first, women tried seeking redress within the company.
The first who complained was fired for making trouble.[74]
With scant hope of relief from the company itself, Japanese women have started taking their grievances to the
government. The Tokyo metropolitan authorities received just thirty sexual harassment complaints in 1988,
but by 1990 they were coming in at a clip of ten a
month.[75] Women also resorted to the courts. Kiyomi Kikuchi made news by stepping forward in 1992 to discuss
her suit against her former boss, who, she charged, had

tried to force kisses on her and coerce her into having sex with him at a motel.[76] Before suing—still an unusual step in Japan—she complained to the branch manager of the credit company where she worked, but he refused to act, and soon, she charged, her harasser was spreading malicious rumors about her sex life. Speaking at a symposium, Kikuchi said, "I felt I had to let companies know that women aren't always compelled to give in."[77]

That same year, for the first time ever, a Japanese court ruled in favor of a woman who sued her former employer for sexual harassment.[78] Meanwhile, nine women filed wage discrimination suits against Hitachi Corporation, the giant electronics and industrial equipment manufacturer. They claimed that Hitachi systematically underpaid them for as long as thirty years. Women at Kanematsu Corporation filed an administrative complaint when they learned that fifty-five-year-old women were being paid much less than twenty-six-year-old men.[79] Twenty-one women filed a grievance against Sumitomo Life Insurance Company on similar grounds.[80] And on and on it goes.

In the long run, women will not be denied. The recession may have given companies the upper hand for a while, but sooner or later they will be starved for labor again.[81] And although the curtailment of "office lady," "elevator girl," and other decorative positions may be painful for now, it should actually boost the status of women in the workplace. What's more, the labor shortage will be most acute in those jobs where women have always fared best. The days of Japan's explosive growth in domestic manufacturing are finished: High-skill, low-wage Asian competition has seen to that. But the service sector is bound to be highly dynamic as Japan shifts from mom-and-pop shops to large-scale retailing, and from mass production to leisure, health care, and other services.

Meanwhile, the tide of women's anger is rising. They have shown their clout in elections, they have demonstrated a will to fight in court, and some are forming their own unions beyond company walls. However, though they want to work, women are by no means prepared to step into the salaryman's shoes. As sociologist Sumiko Iwao observes:

> Men's lives in Japan today are confined and regimented by their jobs to an extreme; they are alienated from their households and deprived of time to engage in culturally enriching pursuits. This is not a model women think worthy of emulation. On the contrary, they think that happiness for both men and women would be better assured [if] women could fulfill fewer family duties and seek more responsibilities related to outside work, while men could slacken their work commitments and take on more family-involved responsibilities.[82]

Here we come to the most dramatic effect of women in the workplace: They are changing the attitudes of men.

BOWING OUT

My work for the Japan Times came, somewhat ironically, full circle in the end. In late 1989, the Associated Press called me to say they had an opening. I had long since given up on them. In spring I had interviewed there and had taken their dreaded three-hour exam, but nothing had come of it. Now Larry Thorson, the AP's director of Asian news, was offering me a job. Just a few months earlier Kuroishi-san had presented me with a terrific new contract that involved a lot more money

*and considerably more reporting. He had even given me
my own desk, something that few people in the crowded
newsroom could boast. I signed with enthusiasm. But
now the chance to get back into the American news
stream—and with the AP in particular—was like a siren
call to me. Kuroishi-san, as always, was sad but understanding. He released me from my contract and wished
me luck. I felt genuine regret at betraying Kuroishi-san's
trust, but was thrilled at the prospect of entering the big
leagues of American journalism. So what if the pay
stunk? This wasn't a job, it was a calling.*

*My work with the Associated Press was every bit
as gratifying as I'd hoped, but there was one great
problem: Not only was the monthly gross far less than
I'd been accustomed to, but I had now to pay both
U.S. and Japanese social security. Every day I worked
was costing me money. After five months of this, I
was feeling pretty strapped when my old friend David
Butts, who was now Tokyo bureau chief for United
Press International, offered me the job of correspondent. His offer combined glory with a handsome salary. I jumped ship again. Becoming a UPI correspondent brought me even headier journalistic experiences:
Within a month I was covering the Cambodian peace
talks that Japan sponsored, and within three months
I was leading the reportage on Japan's frozen-in-the-
headlights reaction to the Gulf crisis.*

*But not long after, the lights dimmed at UPI. The lat-
est in a long string of owners had gone bankrupt. With
only a trickle of subscriber fees coming in, our pay was
chopped by 35 percent. Suddenly, my pockets were painfully light once again. Back in '87, the weak U.S. dollar
had forced me into the arms of the Japan Times. Now
the weak U.S. economy was doing the same thing. I
called Carl and asked him to broach the subject with*

Kuroishi-san for me. A day later, he called back to say that things sounded favorable.

So, like the prodigal son, I turned up one afternoon at Kuroishi-san's desk to sheepishly inquire if I might possibly work one or two nights a week on the copy desk. Just as Carl predicted, Kuroishi-san welcomed me back. He asked how things were with me and, as always, cautioned me not to work too hard.

By now the Japan Times *had moved into spanking new quarters in a glitzy skyscraper erected by the auto-parts magnate who owned the paper. The copy desk was outfitted with the most advanced computer system available, running advanced American software of the type used at the* Washington Post *and other major papers. A couple of new TV monitors piped in CNN—in color! But the most striking difference was in the people. All but a handful of the deskmen I'd known were gone. On the copy desk, Philip had departed, and Kuroishi-san, reaffirming his better nature, had appointed Sophie the new chief. All of the feature staff had flown. Most of the bylines in the paper were unfamiliar to me. And not one of the class of '89 was anywhere to be seen.*

SAYONARA, MR. SALARYMAN

The example set by women has encouraged Japanese men to draw a line between work and private life. Young salarymen, says a Japanese report,

> . . . see the relative independence of the working women. They seem to go home when they want. And if they find the job boring and unappealing, they quit and find another job or work at a part-time job.

Some [young salarymen] begin doubting about working so hard.[83]

Single men want to get out and spend time with friends from outside the company, just as the women do. Married men—61 percent in one study—want to spend time off with their families.[84]

As social life increases in importance, the old attitudes about work fade. During the boom years, not only did young workers become notoriously unwilling to do work considered "dirty, dangerous, or difficult,"[85] they soured on all but the plummiest jobs. "My career" became the catchphrase of the new generation as permanent loyalty gave way to a job-hopping craze. Headhunting firms, such as the one that tapped my wife for Nippon Steel, flourished. Of the college graduates hired in the late eighties, nearly one in three had changed jobs by 1990, the Labor Ministry found.[86] A generation earlier, fewer than one in ten young workers had done so.[87]

Young people were emboldened by the knowledge that they were in demand. Some college graduates opted to skip the usual recruiting process and go *arubaito*. This term, from the German *Arbeit*, meaning "work," is akin to the German idea of *Gastarbeiter*, or "guest workers." In Germany it meant cheap foreign labor; in Japan it came to mean young mercenaries. Some *arubaito* would work nine months out of the year, quit, and travel abroad for three months on their earnings before returning to find another job. Commenting on the young transients, one study noted, "They feel they [have] little to lose by quitting their jobs and moving on to other opportunities."[88]

At the same time, older workers, who had always gone along to get along, began to resist. Some of the half-million *tanshin funin*—those unfortunate men and women who are posted to remote locations without their families—formed mutual support groups.[89] One of them, Tetsuji Sagawa, a middle-aged technical researcher with Japan Railways, sued over his forced transfer from Tokyo to the distant province of Miyazaki. He was not the first to do so (litigation in this area goes back to the mid-1960s), but with the case already in its fourth year, the Tokyo Lawyers Association weighed in for the first time with a brief that termed such transfers a violation of human rights.[90] Meanwhile, a poll of Tokyo workers found that nearly a third were prepared to refuse a transfer order from their employers, even though that might bump them off the promotion track.[91]

Families who lost their loved ones to overwork began to fight back in court. Honda Motor Company was slapped with a suit by a widow who alleged that Honda had dispatched her husband to Canada after he complained of chest pains from working too hard.[92] While juggling three assignments in four Canadian cities, he collapsed and died. Because he was overseas, the company life insurance policy was void. His widow went to court seeking $1 million in compensation.

Ordinary salarymen began to exhibit a subtle independence. Many chose to leave the office before their bosses, a breach of the unwritten rules of work. Some actually adopted a nine-to-six workday. "I don't think the Japanese are hardworking by nature," Takashi Hirano of Mitsubishi Corporation, one of the nine-to-sixers, told the Associated Press in 1992.[93] Still others followed their younger colleagues into the wide-open world of job-hopping.

The recession, it appears, has only strengthened workers' sense of autonomy. Company leaders have noticed the change. In his 1993 New Year's address, Naohiko Kumagai, president of the giant trading house Mitsui & Company, admonished:

Our company does not need any commentators. I'm afraid some people care too much about figures and play too safely to take decisive action. And others fail to make enough effort on their own and just blame systems and organizations when things go wrong.[94]

President Kumagai, you'll note, at once threatens dissenters and bewails the lack of initiative in his company. This contradiction reveals in miniature the great dilemma facing Japan: Companies can no longer afford to bind all their workers in a lifetime embrace, but keeping the productive ones will require satisfying their desire for autonomy, creativity, and free time. Even big companies will have to make work more attractive. Recognizing this, Honda has created a new personnel policy calling for the "active promotion of young people," even as it pares away 1,000 midlevel administrative jobs. The new policy, remarked the *Nikkei Weekly*, "has left older managers, who contributed to Honda's growth, wincing in pain."[95] Others, like Toyota, which long maintained a rigid corporate culture, are struggling to adopt "lifestyle-oriented" employee policies.

The need is urgent. As the noted labor expert Haruo Shimada observes, "Japanese industry's lead over U.S. industry, which at one time was widening, has been shrinking in recent years, while Asian manufacturers in countries that have attracted Japanese investments have been gaining competitive power."[96]

None of this means that Japanese companies will become pushovers. But the less dedication and loyalty they command, the more they will have to operate like their counterparts in the West. Already, Japanese companies are facing unaccustomed pressures from shareholders, who want more control, and Japanese consumers, who want cheaper goods and more accountability for defects. But above all, Japanese companies face a revolution in labor relations.

As the working couple becomes the norm, they are finding it impossible to sustain the kind of commitment demanded in the past. The age of the dogged Japanese salaryman is drawing to a close; the era of the skeptical, self-interested, family-oriented worker is at hand.

4

FOLLOW THE FLOATING WORLD

Half blinded and utterly naked, I groped my way through the hot, billowing fog toward a sliding door. What lay beyond I could not tell, but an overpowering urge to escape the scalding mist drove me on. I peered ahead. It was like a scene from the steam baths of a health club in hell. The tile floor was strewn with obstacles: buckets, plastic shampoo bottles, little wooden stools, even stray bars of soap. Voices echoed madly all about me. Just as I neared the exit, a naked man heaved into sight through the veil of steam. He squatted before a tap set close to the ground and glanced at me malevolently. Then he lathered himself with a small white towel until he seemed to dissolve in froth. Clutching my own small square of terry cloth, I maneuvered gingerly around him and stepped out into the wide world.

Immediately, a cold wind began to lash my bare, dripping limbs. But there was no going back. Before me stretched a vista of paradise. A craggy bluff, split here and there by a gnarled pine, tumbled down into the sea. The sun had just set and the moonless, indigo sky scintillated with a thousand million stars.

Not that I had the luxury of enjoying the view. Right in front of me, half a dozen men of the Japan Times *were lolling about in a volcanic hot spring. Standing cold and naked before your coworkers doesn't ordinarily inspire ease. Of course, this was no ordinary occasion. We were on a company trip, on assignment to relax and have fun. It wasn't quite working for me.*

The men were soaking in one of Japan's famed rotenburo, a "bath beneath the heavens." It did not look heavenly to me at that moment. I don't see very well without my glasses, and my imagination tends to fill in what my eyes fail to discern. A curtain of sulfurous vapor rose from the surface of the shallow, rocky pool. It took ghastly shapes before my eyes. The wind blew harder, and they vanished like souls carried off to hell. Still I waited, paralyzed by indecision. Was it better to perish slowly in the icy ocean breeze, or to boil to death in the volcanic pit before me?

Suddenly, a far deeper chill took hold of me. A voice from above called out my name. A familiar voice. A female voice. I looked up. There was Sophie, leading a brigade of young women from the Japan Times. *They were hooting and whistling like construction workers at a burlesque show. Of course, the hotel that operated this rotenburo did not intend to expose its guests to such ignominy. These enterprising young viragoes had managed to pry open a frosted window and now enjoyed a front-row view.*

I jumped into the pool. The water, whose virtues were lavishly praised on a framed certificate in the changing room, seemed to peel the skin off my feet. It couldn't have been more than one or two degrees below the boiling point, or so I thought. After all, hadn't it just come bubbling up from the lava pits under this rocky promontory? The whole Izu Peninsula was no more than a cork

*in a volcanic bottle; indeed, I could see the smoking
cone of Oshima Island's live volcano from where I
stood, hunched over with my arms wrapped around my
chest, picking up one foot then the other. Then I stepped
on a sharp bit of pumice and all of a sudden I was up to
my neck in the primordial soup. I felt I'd be done and
ready to serve in about six minutes.*

By now, all the men of the Japan Times *were smirking,
and some were laughing outright. A kindly young reporter, suppressing his mirth, explained: "Naff-san, you
are supposed to cover your private parts with the towel
when you come outside."*

*I had used the little scrap of terry cloth to wash my-
self, which was correct procedure, but as it turned out,
the thing was additionally expected to serve as towel
and fig leaf. (It's strange but true: If the water is hot
enough, you can actually dry yourself with a wet towel.)*

*What's more, young Sato informed me, you are sup-
posed to acclimate yourself to the hot water by pouring
bucketsful of the stuff over yourself from a pool in the
shower room. Of course, I thought bitterly. In Japan, there
is a* yarikata *for everything, even the elemental experience
of wading naked into a volcanic pit full of scalding water.*

*I brooded awhile. Then, to my surprise, I discovered
that I was feeling quite content. It was heavenly. My mus-
cles uncoiled like boa constrictors after mealtime. The
warmth got into my bones and set the marrow to tingling
pleasantly. The gurgle of volcanic water danced above the
far-off crash of the ocean waves. Overhead, the stars twin-
kled in a friendly, reassuring way. How much did a little
social faux pas weigh on the great scales of the universe?
they seemed to say. Less than a trifle.*

*There really is nothing like a soak in a hot springs
bath under the purpling sky to make you forget even the
most hideous of experiences. No doubt, that is why hot*

springs are such a popular choice for company trips. Looking back on it, I have to say that this trip was a turning point for me in my attitude toward the Japan Times. *It was also, to a small degree, pivotal for the company. It marked the first time that the foreigners had been invited en masse to join in a company trip. Sophie had wangled invitations for us.*

Despite the honor, only a handful of the twenty or more gaijin on staff had agreed to go. For one thing, the out-of-pocket expense was considerable: including rail fare, nearly $300 for a one-night stay. (Though the company gave its blessing for the trip, it was not willing to pick up the tab.) For another, just because the Japanese staff had agreed to let foreigners come along did not mean they were throwing the doors open altogether. When I asked whether my wife could join me, I was told politely but firmly that family members had no business joining a company trip. Rumiko was disappointed but not surprised. As it turned out, she had to work that weekend at Nippon Steel anyway, so I left with no qualms. Well, not many. It was a little unnerving to join in such an event without someone to whisper dos and don'ts in my ear.

We assembled bright and early on a railway platform at Tokyo Station. It was Saturday morning, and most of the staff had the day off.[1] Of the fifteen or so in the group it looked as if Sophie and I were going to be the only foreigners. However, shortly before the train pulled in, Allison, an American working on the features desk, came panting up the stairs. I was still fairly new to the staff and stood awkwardly by while everyone else chatted noisily. Considering the hour, they seemed awfully chipper. I soon learned why. One of the staff photographers, a man who normally paid absolutely no attention to the foreigners, strolled over and, beaming luridly, thrust his back-

pack at me. "Dōzo," he said. ("Help yourself!") I peered inside. The entire sack was filled with cans of beer.

"Ah, dōmo," I said apologetically, "mada kōhi o nonde inai." ("Excuse me, but I still haven't had my coffee.") He didn't seem to think much of my excuse, and our opinions of each other had fallen by the time he withdrew. Then I noticed that nearly all of the men and several of the women were indeed drinking beer. At eight-something in the morning! I was astonished. Of course, I was still a newcomer to Japan. Had I been in the country awhile longer, I would have known that the first thing most men do when they leave on a trip is drink. (That the women joined in just showed what a progressive company the Japan Times was.) Beer is the mildest form of indulgence; some start the journey with a belt of whiskey. So, to Japanese eyes there was nothing the least bit disrespectable about a group of sightseers guzzling beer on a public platform shortly after daybreak. It was simply, as I was to learn, the overture to a binge on an operatic scale.

I wandered down the platform to buy a drink from a vending machine. One of the great things about Japan is that you can buy almost anything from a vending machine: beer, whiskey, cigarettes, dirty comic books— though oddly enough, you cannot purchase a candy bar this way.[2] Still, you are never far from a machine that dispenses canned beverages, hot or cold. I opted for warm canned coffee. On reflection, I should have accepted the beer. The coffee tasted like oversweetened motor oil.

RUMBA, ANYONE?

Throughout Japanese history, a fun-loving spirit peeps out from behind the iron mask of discipline. Even the poorest of farming communities had an annual festival that fell little short of bacchanalian. There remains living proof of this. Come festival time, long lines of men flushed with drink and naked but for a loincloth snake their way through the streets bearing on their shoulders an ornate portable shrine all aglitter in gold, chanting and swaying to the beat of giant *taiko* drums. At some festivals they splash each other with buckets of water, at others they brandish giant wooden phalluses, and in one they reach such a frenzy that they beat anyone in range with their fists.

Farmers could hardly be condemned for such excesses. Being too poor and too busy to consider entertainment during the remainder of the year, they traditionally put all their saturnalian energies into the annual festival. If they drank too much sake, well, it was the one time a year when they could afford to do so.

The urban mercantile classes of the Edo period had more time on their hands, and a burning desire to use it for pleasure. Under the Tokugawa shoguns, merchants were the lowest order of society, but through their enterprise they soon had the most money, and they spent it creating costly entertainments. Foremost among these stood kabuki, which, though undeniably a refined and highly formal art, was then considered a vulgar entertainment, not to be compared with the ancient Noh plays of the imperial court.

"The culture of the townspeople," says historian G. B. Sansom, "was essentially the culture of a prosperous bourgeoisie devoted to amusement."[3]

At the turn of the eighteenth century, the merchants of Edo, as Tokyo was then known, created what they called "the Floating World," a dreamy escape from harsh reality. "This," Sansom declares,

is the world of fugitive pleasures, of theaters and restaurants, wrestling booths and houses of assigna-
tion, with their permanent population of actors,
dancers, singers, storytellers, jesters, courtesans,
bath-girls, and itinerant purveyors, among whom
mingled the profligate sons of rich merchants, disso-
lute samurai, and naughty apprentices.[4]

The samurai of the day, though they might have indulged in the gaudy entertainments of the Floating
World, sternly disapproved of it. Indeed, historian Richard Storry observes that "During this age the urban civilization of Yedo [Edo] and Osaka was unusually brilliant;
and correspondingly there was, so everybody said, a de-
cline in the old samurai virtues of hardihood, loyalty, and
martial excellence."[5] But they needn't have worried. The
Genroku Age, as this period was known, soon burned itself out. Inevitably, the Spartan mentality of the samurai
reasserted itself.

All the same, the desire for fun has remained a glowing
coal in the Japanese psyche. Hidehiko Sekizawa, executive director of the Hakuhodo Institute of Life and Living,
told me he believes the fun-loving and frivolous Edo
spirit is reviving. He went on to make a striking comparison:

SEKIZAWA: "It might be strange, but actually speaking,
Japanese people are like Latin people."
NAFF: "People of Latin America?"
SEKIZAWA: "Or French or Italian or Spanish. They
want to enjoy their daily lives."[6]

Today, no foreigner thinks of the Japanese as party animals. The idea of comparing them with, say, Brazilians,
would strike most Westerners as absurd. But before we

write off the Japanese as a bunch of workaholic stiffs, maybe we should ask ourselves: Do they despise leisure, or have they just been deprived of it?

Ten years after the war, desperate poverty quickly gave way to unheard-of affluence as the whole nation seemed to leap into the ranks of the middle class. To be able to purchase the "Three S's"—a *senpūki* (electric fan), a *sentakki* (washing machine), and a *suihanki* (rice cooker)— became in the late 1950s a mark of attainment to which everyone aspired. By the mid-sixties, acquisitive ambitions had turned to the "Three C's": car, air conditioner, and color TV.[7]

But using wealth to attain leisure was another matter altogether. Postwar business culture scooped up leisure and put it to work. "In Japan after World War II," writes a Japanese author, "'work' was regarded as a virtue and 'play' as a vice because of the national mood that the country's economy must be expanded to reach the world level. It was the duty of every Japanese to work hard, and those who spent time in leisure pursuits were regarded as lazy."[8]

The typical salaryman found that leisure had been made part of his job. The company paid for much of his drinking, golfing, and even, in some cases, whoring, but it deprived him of choice. It set up company recreational facilities and organized company sports teams. It even organized trips for his days off at Golden Week in late spring.[9]

"There is something different about Japanese leisure— something that sets it apart from Western leisure," a semiofficial Japanese publication says. "Somewhere along the way, the sense of freedom and better living is lost."[10]

This may strike some as a fairly trivial matter: After all, a typical salaryman would select his friends from among his colleagues anyway, so why should it be regarded as an imposition to be expected to go out and drink with them, especially if the company was willing to foot the bill? And who could object to the purpose?: Don't American companies invest in team-building "retreats" led by smarmy, overpaid consultants? Surely these are less pleasant and productive than a weekly binge with one's coworkers.

Perhaps. But as we'll see, the sum of company efforts to build solidarity deprived leisure of its essence: If play is the egoistic child's way of learning the limits of its world (you can't pull the cat's tail without getting scratched), then surely leisure is the adult's way of exploring the frontiers of identity. I may know that I am a Mitsubishi man, for example, but only through free exploration can I discover that I also am a jazz lover, a hang-gliding enthusiast, or a devotee of French cinema. It's not as though the Japanese are uninterested in exploratory leisure. The Japanese are, by and large, an intensely curious people, and a powerful strain of self-improvement runs through them. They have, for example, produced an outsize number of acclaimed classical musicians, of whom the Boston Symphony's conductor, Seiji Ozawa, is perhaps the best known. Interestingly, though, in creative fields many of Japan's brightest stars are women: Maestro Ozawa aside, Japan's most renowned musician is perhaps the violin prodigy known as Midori. And it's not just in classical music. Virtually the only bands able to rise above the wretched cupidity of most Japanese pop to achieve international popularity have been composed of hard-driving women.

"[A] lot of the Japanese punk bands are female," Joe Rhea, a Harvard social researcher, told a Japanese magazine in 1991. "That's something unique about Japanese punk."[11]

Why? There are, of course, talented and accomplished Japanese men, and many try to cultivate a hobby. But the vast majority have little or no opportunity for true self-exploration. From early childhood, they are molded for the career track. College provides some time to dance off the straight and narrow, but once inducted into a company, a man finds the jig's up. It's not just work, but the social demands of work, that eat up his time. "Every weekend," says the *Nikkei Weekly*,

> many of Tokyo's white collar workers rise early for work. But they don't wear business suits, and they don't go to the office. Instead, they don't company baseball or soccer uniforms [and head for] matches with their firm's clients, intra-company baseball games and other corporate-sponsored sports events in which firms tacitly require the participation of all employees.[12]

The article goes on to say that both working women and the wives of men who are required to spend their time off in company events have begun to protest this intrusion into their lives.

THE BARE NECESSITIES

The Japan Times, *as I say, did not feel it had the wherewithal to pay for our trip, so we decided to take a local down to Umigahara, even though this made it a four-hour trip on a standing-room-only train. The decision proved unwise. As soon as we got on the train, a toothless old man with a mouth like a carp decided, in the interests of international understanding, to strike up a conversation with the foreign women. He was a seago-*

ing fisherman, it turned out. He told us this, but we could have guessed from the odor. A grizzled old character with a squinty eye and a squashed nose, he was unshaven, unkempt, and seemingly unshakable. To move away from him in the packed car was impossible; we'd be lucky if we could get off at our destination. Sophie, imperturbable as always, traded pleasantries with him in Japanese while keeping a running commentary in English for our benefit along the lines of "Oh gawd, how did we get stuck with this jerk?" After a bit of chat, our new neighbor grew quite friendly toward us. He produced a pack of Larks, which he offered all around. We declined, pointing out that this was a No Smoking car. This caused him to chortle loudly. "Daijōbu," he cackled, with a wave of his hand. ("It's okay.")

He seemed to feel that the No Smoking sign was just a formality placed there to show the world that Japan was in the forefront of health regulations. To my disgust, he lit up and blew a vast cloud of fish-flavored smoke over us.

I relate this not because it was typical of train rides in Japan, nor to suggest anything at all about the Japanese. The world is full of boors who force their conversation on you. No, I mention this so you will understand that by the time we reached Umigahara, four hours later, I felt nauseated and highly dubious about the whole notion of a company trip. It would be fair to say that I was prepared to be a severe critic of Japan's entire company-trip system. So it was remarkable that within twenty-four hours my feelings would completely swing around. For the moment, however, the only thing that prevented me from catching the next train home was the thought of another four hours standing alongside the likes of our Popeye the Sailor Man.

My mood did not improve when we stepped outside

*the station. A craggy little perch above the darkling sea,
Umigahara steams and hisses like a dragon with a hang-
nail. That, of course, is its big attraction: When you ease
into a heated pool there, you can pretend—or in my
case, believe—that the water comes to you directly from
the hellish magma pits that underlie the entire peninsula (and country, for that matter, though at safer depth
in some places). Of course, I didn't know these things
when I made my grand entrance into the rotenburo. I
recalled seeing, a little way up the line, a charming
monument erected in the late nineteenth century by
way of an apology to one of the first foreign visitors to
the area. This man—an English gentleman, it seems—
was taking his little dog for a stroll through the town.
He paused momentarily to admire the view and allow
the hound to relieve itself against a rock, when suddenly
a geyser erupted from below, lofting the poor dog high
into the air and returning him to earth lifeless and
scalded to the bone.*

*These days, most hotels take the sensible precaution
of penning up the geysers and storing their water, but
it seems to me they do a good job of reproducing the
original hazards.*

*A minibus from the hotel met us at the station. I was
glad to get away from the caged-up geyser that seethed
angrily just behind us. But looking over Umigahara,
where countless hotels and souvenir shops cling precari-
ously to the mountainside cliffs that slope down into
the sea, I had a feeling that my queasy stomach was in
for more distress. And I was right: Our hotel happened
to be on the far side of town, nearest the ocean.*

*My stomach rumbled mutinously as the jitney
lurched along switchback roads that led up and down
the steep hills. The place, so far as I could see, abounded*

in ramshackle little wooden houses and shops wedged
between old concrete hotels with rust stains running
down their sides. Not encouraging. However, when we
arrived at our hotel, it proved to be a gleaming palace of
marble and tinted glass. I didn't have long to consider
it, though. A platoon of neatly pinafored young women
and bellboys in creased uniforms rushed out to greet us,
followed by a man in a swallow-tailed morning suit. Evidently the manager. There was a great caterwauling of
"Irasshaimase!" ("Welcome!"), and as the young women
bowed decorously, the bellboys made off with our bags.
Inside the lobby, we formed a semicircle around the
manager while he explained the attractions of his establishment. The pride of the place was something called
the Amazon Bath—a sort of miniature biosphere like
the one in Arizona, only better, because it had bubbling
hot springs, pools of icy-cold water, and even its own
caverns, bats not included.

Clearly, this hotel was a product of the new prosperity. I began to appreciate why it cost $200 a night to stay
here. But that was before I saw the sleeping arrangements. There were more than a dozen of us, so I figured
we would be paired off in rooms. To my astonishment,
however, we were led upstairs to two adjacent rooms,
one for all the women, the other for all the men. The
floor of our room could have accommodated a largish
Persian carpet, but the fringe would have turned up
against the walls. There was no carpet, however. It was
lined with tatami mats, and bare of all furniture except
a large, low table in the middle and a small television
perched on a small safe in the corner. The bathroom was
down the hall. I could not believe that all seven of us
guys were expected to bunk down in here. But being the
only gaijin in the bunch, I held my peace. Nobody likes
a complaining American. Imitating the others, I sat

down on the floor and struggled to get my knees under the table.

COMPANY LOVES MISERY

There are actually two distinct kinds of leisure in the company world: *settai*, the entertainment of clients, politicians, or others important to the business, and *tsukiai*, socializing with bosses, colleagues, and subordinates.

Settai requires that company representatives spend a great deal of time and money incurring or repaying the obligation of people who can do the company some good. These outings need not have an agenda; often they serve just to procure goodwill. In 1989 alone, Japanese businesses shelled out over $30 billion for entertainment, more than the nation spent on its defense.[13] In some industries, such as construction, up to a third of income would be spent on entertaining those who could help the firm obtain new contracts.[14]

Westerners who did business in Japan during the eighties know the extravagant heights business entertainment reached: the Ginza "hostess bars" where it cost $500 for three or four men to sit down and let a pretty young college student in a leather miniskirt pour their whiskey and light their cigarettes; the restaurants so exclusive they have no nameplate on the door, where dinner and entertainment by a witty geisha for the same group of company men brings a bill of $3,000; the posh golf clubs that provide helicopter service to and from the links and charge as much as the fancy restaurants do.

What they may not know is how the participants in these orgies of ostentation felt. When entertaining a client, supplier, or politician, a host can never really relax.

"Japanese businessmen are not so very pleased to entertain every night," Takehiko Yamaguchi, a former trading company executive, told me.

Robert Collins, an American businessman and author of long standing in Tokyo, put it to me more bluntly: "You go home sick and show up the next day at work complaining, 'God, I hate to stay out till three in the morning.' But you've got to do it."

Without this constant massaging of personal relations, everyone said, business would dry up. As it happened, the reverse was true: When the speculative bubble burst at the end of the eighties and corporations had to tighten their expenditures, the first thing to be axed was the expense account. One by one, the lights in the Ginza bars and restaurants began to wink out.

Of course, not all corporate entertainment went to promote external business relations and not all of it went bust in the recession. A substantial amount of time and effort was devoted to employee relations. Every manager from section chief on up was expected to use part of his expense account to take his subordinates out drinking.

This *tsukiai*, or socializing, plays a vital role within the company, and not quite the one many outsiders naively imagine. Large Japanese companies are political battlefields where, in the absence of clear job descriptions or standards for promotion, a man's hopes for advancement to an executive position turn largely on his ability to attract loyal retainers. This works both ways. An ambitious junior must learn the inclinations and desires of those on whose coattails he hopes to ascend. As the sagacious Asia-watcher Ian Buruma notes, "The unfortunate salaryman's chances of success do indeed depend to a large extent on his or her capacity for fawning, dissembling, and attending to the boss's whims."[15] *Tsukiai* provides the means. Through after-hours drinking, paid for by the boss, secrets are revealed, favors promised, and mutual obligations incurred. This, to return briefly to the feudal metaphor, may be called the bonding of lords and vassals, and the chapel where vows are taken is the small, murky *nomiya* (literally, the "drinking house") where men go for *tsukiai* after work.

To refuse to join in these rituals on any grounds is to risk the wrath of the group. Nobody likes a loner. Hiroaki Kono, director of the National Institute on Alcoholism, told the *Los Angeles Times* that to be branded *tsukiai ga warui*—"no good at socializing"—was "the most fearful thing that can be said about a person in Japan."[16]

And there is a practical side of it as well. Wives, as I noted earlier, generally manage the household finances in Japan, doling out an allowance to their husbands for basic needs and amusements. Inevitably, men regard what they receive as too little, and indeed the cost of drinking and eating and singing karaoke songs can easily run to 10,000 yen (nearly $100) in an evening. So it falls to the men with expense accounts to lighten the burden. In this way, as the Leisure Development Center of Japan observes, "Drinking has become part of their work."[17] Indeed, many of those who have expense accounts go out drinking virtually every weeknight.[18]

In addition to serving political and practical ends, *tsukiai* feeds a part of the Japanese psyche that psychiatrist Takeo Doi describes as *amae*. This translates as "dependence," but connotes something more, something like an infant's need for a mother's unconditional love and indulgence.[19] Because such feelings of dependence can be so intense, he says, the Japanese feel great anxiety about casual kindnesses or confidences, which may turn into lifelong obligations. Therefore, Doi says, they only feel truly at ease within their "private circle."[20] For men, this "private circle" of mutual dependence aptly describes the stable, long-term relationships that are constructed in the company world. But it turns out that this arrangement carries a heavy price. "In such a world," says Doi, "there is no freedom and independence of the individual in the strict sense of the word."[21] Freedom, Doi concludes, requires more than self-consciousness. A person needs to be able to interact outside the cozy little group:

> "Freedom of the individual" does not mean that the individual is free in himself, as he is; freedom is only acquired through the fact of participation in another group originally unrelated to the group to which he belongs.[22]

This is precisely the freedom that the company system of leisure denies.

MORNING BECOMES HER

As I scrunched my knees under the low table, it began to dawn on me that we men were going to have some sort of meeting. I wished Kuroishi-san were there to explain things to me. I missed his tired, kindly face. It occurred to me that he was probably manning the desk so that these guys could be here. The deskmen on this trip had pretty much ignored me so far, and I didn't know many of the reporters. Just then there was a knock, and the maid came in, shuffling her way across the tatami *and showering us with greetings. I call her a maid, but she was more likely a grandmother. Wrapped in an austere kimono, with her hair done up behind her in traditional fashion, she looked like a living artifact of a lost age.*

Several younger assistants shuffled in after her and

began pouring green tea and passing out bean-paste cookies for the traditional welcome. The chief maid, her wrinkled face agape in a plaster smile, began a speech in the most eloquent and convolutedly polite language I had ever heard. At that moment, Sato, the young fellow who was later to instruct me on the etiquette of outdoor bathing, picked up a swatter and smacked a fly on the table. "Hah!" grunted the man next to him, peering at the speck on the table. "Shinda." ("He's dead.") The chief maid, angered by the interruption but unwilling to abandon her decorum, had a look. "Onakunari ni narimashita, ne!" she agreed. ("He's dead.")[23] Having thus proved that in Japanese anything worth saying is worth embroidering with fustian courtesy, she resumed her lecture.

I couldn't entirely follow what was being said, but I gathered that she was laying out choices and asking our preferences. It didn't matter. Nakamura-san, our cherubic chief, spoke for the group. My mind wandered. I tried to reconcile my expectations with what I saw. In some ways, this hotel was far more luxurious than my customary digs. Certainly, it was clad in enough marble to make a party of stonemasons from Carrara feel right at home. On the other hand, I couldn't quite wrap myself around the notion that all us guys were going to go to the mattresses in this one bare room, like a Mafia cell during a police crackdown. As I puzzled over this, an incident in Botchan, *a much-beloved novel by Soseki Natsume, came back to me.*

In Botchan, *the eponymous hero leaves Tokyo to start life as a schoolteacher. Arriving in the small town where he is to take up his post, he checks into a hotel:*

> *I had been told that you should give a tip when out traveling; that you would never be welcome,*

*without giving a money present on your putting in
at a hotel. That I was put into a small dark room
could only be accounted for by the fact that I had
given them no tip; that I had on shabby clothes,
and was carrying old carpet bags and a cheap umbrella. "They have assumingly looked down upon
me, these detestable rustics! They shall know how
they should behave toward their guests. They shall
have a great surprise by being given an enormous
tip."* [24]

*Having slapped down five yen, a sixth of his monthly
salary, Botchan finds an amazing change when he returns to the inn:*

> *I had scarcely entered the gate when the hostess
> at the counter came out quickly and welcomed me
> with sweet words, bowing so very low that her head
> almost reached the floor. Taking off my shoes, I
> went in and was shown into a room by the maid;
> she said it had just been evacuated. It was a fifteen-
> mat front room upstairs with a large fine tokonoma
> [recessed altar].* [25]

*"A tip!" I thought. "That's where we went wrong."
But it was a cold triumph of the intellect. We had failed
to tip and there was nothing I could do about it. If a
sixth of one's salary was the going rate, I had neither the
cash nor the nerve to remedy the situation. Suddenly,
Nakamura-san yanked me out of my literary reverie.
"Naff-san," he said. "What time do you want to eat
breakfast?" Sunday breakfast was the farthest thing
from my mind just then, but being on the spot, I thought
I'd better aim at a middling late hour.
  "How about nine?" I said.
  I noticed several bemused smiles on the faces around*

me. Nakamura-san translated my suggestion. The maid
burst out laughing in a grandmotherly way. Again, I
couldn't follow everything she said, but boiled down, the
brutal fact remained that at 6:30 in the morning the
hotel staff was going to remove our futons, and we had
little choice but to stumble down to breakfast as well as
we might. In no event would breakfast be served after
eight.

I began to reconsider a tip, but evidently those were
the unshakable rules of the house. This seemed to me a
peculiar notion of satisfying the customer. However, it
proved to be typical. Even rational, one might argue. In
a country where group trips have long been the norm,
hotels endeavor to spare their guests the agony of reaching a group consensus on every detail by simply min-
imizing their choices. Can't decide what to have for
dinner? Not to worry, the hotel serves identical meals to
everyone, and all at the same time, too. Not sure what
time to get up? The hotel takes care of that for you, too.
That all this standardization makes life simpler for the
hotel is purely coincidental.

It was a great relief when the greeting ritual came to
an end. Downing my bitter cup of green tea, I rushed off
in search of Sophie. She was just coming out of her room,
where a similar conference had been under way.
"Sophie, what the hell is going on?" I yelled. "Are we
really expected to cram into these two rooms? I don't
even think you can fit seven futons in ours."

"Don't worry, they'll take the table out," she said. I
found this a mighty slender reed of comfort.

"But why?" I persisted. "For twenty-five thousand yen
a night, why can't we have our own separate rooms?"

Sophie looked at me as she might have regarded a dull
child. "Look, kiddo, this is a dantai ryokō. A group trip.
We're building solidarity. What kind of togetherness

would we have if everyone trundled off to their own
room after dinner?"
I gave up. Trundling back to join the men, I accepted
a beer and began a daylong slide into glad numbness.

THE PEACE THAT PASSETH
UNDERSTANDING

Many Americans have a deep ambivalence about alcohol,
stretching back to our Puritan roots and branching
through temperance societies and Prohibition. Not so the
Japanese. In my early days in Japan, I was frequently
stunned to be asked by someone I had just met, "Do you
drink a lot?" But the question carried no stigma. As a
Japanese columnist put it: "In Japan, the drunkard's Eden,
you may drink like a baboon and not lose an iota of re-
spectability in the eyes of the people."[26]
Alcohol, in the form of sake, has a religious sanction.
It is the drink you marry by, the drink your Shinto priest
employs at a ground-breaking ceremony, the drink you
celebrate victory with, the drink you leave at the grave of
a loved one. Of course, Buddhism, the other religion to
which most Japanese concurrently subscribe, frowns on
alcohol. But as the late religious studies scholar Keiichi
Yanagawa observed,

> "[P]eople have long since ceased to be conscious
> of it as a prohibition. There are indeed many Bud-
> dhist priests who are very fond of drinking."[27]

In any case, alcohol's secular role outweighs all religious considerations. It's not how much the Japanese
drink as how freely. Alcohol practically fuels recreational
activity. I have sometimes thought that even Papa

Hemingway would have recoiled in horror from some of the drinking activities of the Japanese. When I climbed Mount Fuji in the summer of 1988, what little breath I had left was taken away in astonishment at the sight of the brisk booze trade conducted along its slope. At every way station from base to summit, Japanese hikers paused to down a can of beer or jar of sake. Why they didn't fall down the mountain is a mystery to me. Personally, halfway up the 12,000-foot peak, I would have traded away a six-pack of St. Pauli's for a small canister of oxygen.

OUT OF EDEN

After a long soak in the rotenburo, *I dressed in the blue-and-white cotton robe that the hotel provided to each guest, shoved my feet into the hotel slippers, and went to join the others for dinner.*

I should pause to note a curious aspect of this: There is a persistent belief in the Japanese hospitality industry that in footwear, one size fits all. Anyone who has seen Japan's Olympic volleyball team knows that there are Japanese who could stand nose-to-nose with an NBA center. They are others who could ride the bus for free in many American cities. Their feet tend to vary in size correspondingly. But in this, as in every other hotel and inn I stayed at in Japan, the proprietors always issued guests identical slippers. In my case, though I am not especially tall, I have enormous feet. The heel of the slipper fitted neatly into my arch—neatly, that is, if it was intended to be a torture device. I considered going barefoot, but I felt curiously reluctant to stand out from the group. It wasn't that I feared retribution or anything. But I hadn't really been accepted by this group so far, and that made me uneasy. Of course, it wasn't as if I were going to spend the rest of my life with these people or anything, but still . . . In nameless agony, I hobbled off to dinner.

The Japan Times gang had gathered in a private banquet room for dinner. It was a largish tatami room. One of the best things about tatami is that you are not allowed to walk on it in slippers. I spent a luxurious moment waggling my bare toes against the tightly woven straw and looking around. Recalling the room that my father-in-law had engaged for our first meeting, I guessed this private hall was part of the routine of a group trip. Here we would be able to perform all the rituals of solidarity without feeling silly in front of strangers. But what might they be? I wondered. At the front of the room was a kind of stage area. Hulking ominously in the middle of it was a karaoke machine.[28]

My heart sank. Would I be forced, once again, to sing "My Way"? Averting my gaze from the dread device, I looked for a place to sit. There were two rows of low tables, with cushions on the floor for the guests to lower themselves upon. Each setting had a lacquered tray with dinner already laid out. Fortunately, there was a spot open next to Sophie. I filled it. She was carrying on a voluble conversation with the Nakster, our desk chief, who was seated at the far end of the table. Before me were what seemed like dozens of tiny dishes, most of them complete mysteries to me. I did recognize the small slices of raw fish banked against a mound of grated turnip as sashimi. There were also some strips of gleaming white squid, curled into the form of a nest, and a salted minnow on a skewer, next to what was either the smallest lobster or the largest shrimp I had ever encountered. A rather dark, tough morsel stuffed into a shell turned out to be roasted sea slug. M-m-m-m.

I did not inquire what the other items on my tray might have been. It has been my experience that you can enjoy Japanese food a lot more if you don't ask. There was a multicolored brick of what I supposed to be fish paste, and a small porcelain pot filled with a custardlike substance. Japanese food is nothing if not a feast for the eyes. Still, I was just a little irritated to sit down to a cold meal. After Sophie's lack of radiant sympathy for my complaints about the room, I didn't want to harp on it, but I couldn't help grumbling to myself: $200 and not even a hot entrée!

Just then a swarm of kimono-clad ladies scuffled into the room bearing huge tubs of steaming rice, hot bowls of miso soup, tall bottles of beer, and delicate porcelain flasks of warm sake. I immediately cheered up and was about to pour myself a beer when Sachiko-san, a beautiful, willowy reporter whom I had only just met that morning, slipped in beside me and filled my glass. I was not alone in receiving this favor. All the women in the room were filling the glasses of the men around them. This was just one more of those gracious if sexist Japanese customs that have come down through the ages. It began as a ritual but soon melted into good companionship all around, as everyone poured for everyone else. Cynical as I might have been about the idea of building solidarity on a company trip, there really was something endearing about this habit, especially as it kept up throughout the meal.

Finally, when the meal wore down to the last grains of rice, people began making toasts. Nakamura-san, bashful and hesitant but still the leader, offered the first one, and several others, mostly good-humored, followed. To my great relief, that was all. No karaoke, no inspirational speeches. Dinner broke up and the real business of the trip began: It was back to the rooms for heavy drinking and even heavier complaining about work. I could not follow what was being said, but the more whiskey that the men threw back, the louder their voices became. I started to wonder where I was going to sleep if a fight broke out.

But to my surprise, the group whose solidarity we had been building all day soon divided along generational lines. The younger Japanese, bored with the shoptalk, headed down to the Amazon Bath. I followed, along with Sophie, Allison, and Carl, who had arrived at dinner after putting in an early shift at the paper that day.

Before long, we were all soaking together in the hot pool, with only tiny cotton towels to preserve our modesty. The setting could only be called surreal. The Amazon Bath was like a rain forest under glass. The light was murky, dim, and uncertain. Huge palm leaves cast deep shadows. Waterfalls crashed down tiny pumic mountains and churned up the pools. Bird calls echoed under the glass.

Perhaps it was the primordial surroundings, or perhaps it was the knowledge that konyoku, *"mixed bathing," is an honorable tradition in Japan. But what had earlier seemed a traumatic break with convention now seemed perfectly natural. The nervous jokes soon died away. We sat in a steaming pool, watching the lights play off its surface, listening to the strange bird calls. It seemed that the younger breed of* Japan Times *Japanese was of a contemplative cast of mind. No shoptalk for them. Just a quiet soak in the innocence of a reconstructed Eden.*

Or so I thought. But soon it was out of the bath and off to the next adventure. Within a few minutes, we had left paradise and were in a dark, cavernous den, gyrating like tortured souls under the black lights and mirrored ball of a disco. A thunderous sound system rattled our innards.

I'm no anthropologist, but on reflection, the move to the disco strikes me as significant. The essence of the traditional company trip is to deepen solidarity. But the disco, that inferno of Western pop culture, prevents all but the most primitive communication. Shake yer booty. This was pure fun.

The DJ kept his two turntables in constant motion, assuring that the beat never faltered and the roar never faded. We, however, did. Shortly after midnight we made our way back upstairs. I was about to say goodnight to Sophie when something caught my attention. The disco had left me somewhat deafened but I hadn't lost so much of my hearing as to miss the uproar coming from "my" room.

The older guys had been punishing the whiskey all the while, and they were now venting their opinions louder than ever. I couldn't really tell what it was all about. I only knew that it was going to be impossible to sleep in there for some time to come. Fortunately, Sophie was feeling more compassionate by now. After checking to see that all was well in her quarters, she invited me to come in.

The futons had been laid out, and a game of cards was going on in the middle of the room. Sophie joined right in. I saw at once that I was not the first man to seek refuge in there. Several of the young Japanese men had fled the commotion next door. They saw no percentage in getting involved. Besides, they could easily keep up with everything that was being said from here; it came rumbling through the walls. Sato-san was there, dealing out cards to the women with a broad smile on his foxy face. The Admiral, that admirable woman, sat by a lamp reading a book. But some, like me, just wanted to get to sleep. I watched as one fellow, a freshly minted college graduate whose buckteeth and cowlick had earned him the nickname "Dennis the Menace," calmly removed his glasses, slipped into one of the futons, and went to sleep. Since we were all wearing cotton yukata *robes furnished by the hotel, there was no need to change. "Oh, well," I thought, as I too crept into a futon that had been intended for one of the female cardsharps in the center of the room. "When in Rome . . ."*

SLIP, SLIP, SLIDIN' AWAY

To say just how many alcoholics there are in Japan is virtually impossible. The Ministry of Health and Welfare puts the number at a mere 22,000, but in a nation of 124 million in which a majority drink, this is preposterous. A 1985 Ministry study found that 11.9 percent of men were "problem drinkers," along with 1.7 percent of women.[29] This translates into 8.4 million alcohol abusers. Anecdotal evidence suggests the problem may be even bigger. Nearly three-quarters of all respondents to the inevitable government survey said they felt they drank too much.

Indeed, the per capita consumption rate has climbed 50 percent since 1965, amounting to twenty-two gallons of alcoholic drink per year. Three-quarters of that is beer, but the average Japanese adult manages to put away more than four gallons of sake and nearly a gallon of whiskey as well. What's more, the proportion of Japanese who drink continues to climb, having passed 60 percent recently. In 1968 the figure was just 44 percent. Eight out of ten men drink in Japan, up from seven in 1968, but the most spectacular

change has been in the habits of women: In 1968 only one
out of five Japanese women drank or, at any rate, admitted
to drinking; now well over half do.[30]

The Japanese are not by any means the world's heaviest
drinkers—Americans down nearly twice as much beer,
and the French outdrink everyone in the West. But many
Japanese are poorly constituted for drinking, a difficulty
they put down to a lack of certain enzymes that help digest
alcohol. As a result, the smallest amount of alcohol, often
just half a glass of beer, has a dramatic effect on such
people: Their faces become flushed and their breathing labored. A few more drinks and they act like freshmen at the
end of their first frat party. Such is the power of alcohol
over them that I have watched a senior vice president of
one of Japan's largest banks, attended by two "hostess
girls," do a somersault over a low couch in a bar. But there
is another force that has an even more powerful effect.

The Japanese have been called the world's most amiable
drunks, and, though I have met my share of disagreeable
ones, I am inclined to agree. However, it is a mark not of
their inborn amiability but of the power of social pressure
to compel them to behave with *enryo*, "self-restraint." You
may have been led to believe that while drinking, the Japanese drop all inhibitions and let it all hang out, like the
banker barrel-rolling over the couch. But such behavior is
positively straitlaced compared with the past. The Japanese, as much as anyone, are stirred to aggression when
drunk.

In the mid-nineteenth century, before the samurai were
disarmed, the results were often bloody. Algernon Mitford,
later Lord Redesdale, forebear of the literary Mitford sisters and one of the first British diplomats posted to Japan,
wrote of how his sleep in the Shinagawa district of Tokyo
was shattered from time to time by horrible screams. The
cause became clear at first light:

More than once, riding through that sinister and ill-famed quarter at early dawn, we would come upon bloody traces of the night's debauch. Under the heady fumes of the hot sake, men's blood would boil. . . . An angry word, a fierce dispute, a cry of hatred, a flash of cold steel—and a headless body would be spouting blood upon the mats.[31]

Such barroom brawls are virtually extinct. Only *yakuza* gangsters keep up the samurai tradition of bloodying one another. The modern samurai salaryman finds that Japan's unwritten code of behavior requires him to remain nonviolent and mostly amiable even when drunk. As I learned on the *Japan Times* trip, company men may roar but they don't come to blows.

If men of business control their deeds even while drunk, may they not control their words as well? It seems to me the corporate culture sets limits on what a man may do or say in the company of his fellows, even when he is intoxicated. The power relations among them, which after all are presumed to be for life, form a complex and sensitive web. Unless he is a fool, a salaryman does not truly expose his weaknesses or fully bare his heart. He may rant and rave, but there remains an invisible hand on his shoulder restraining him. If he is clever, he will use drinking as cover to ingratiate, scheme, manipulate, intimidate, or otherwise improve his standing.

You may wonder how I could possibly know such things. After all, you might say, the presence of a foreigner in a drinking circle would inevitably bring some measure of reserve into the proceedings. I agree. However, the evidence that Japanese men do not entirely unbind themselves in the company of their fellows lies wholly in the public domain.

To glimpse a Japanese salaryman truly stripped of his

dignity and inhibition, you must observe him, as I have done countless times, catching the last train home. After the long hours in a damp, smoky bar swigging beer, chatting amiably, and taking turns at warbling into a cordless mike, the fresh air often takes a terrible toll. Somehow, the salaryman learns to time his alcoholic poisoning so that he is able to stumble merrily to the train station, arm in arm with his comrades-in-labor, singing some dimly remembered college song and looking as if he hasn't a care in the world. But the moment he goes through the gate to his own train, where he stands among strangers, the last picket of inhibition topples.

Every night of the week, as midnight approaches, the train platforms become spattered with the vomit of salarymen who had one too many. The station attendants keep buckets of sawdust handy to minimize the hazard of slipping. Racing to catch the last train on my way home from a night shift at the *Japan Times*, I learned to treat the platform as if it were a minefield with the danger zones marked in sawdust.

Still, I always looked gratefully upon the ones who vomited on the platform. They are public-spirited citizens of the first whiskey-and-water, compared with those who don't get it out of their systems until they are aboard the train. Even late-night trains tend to be packed. Once someone near you starts to heave, there is often little you can do except turn away and hope he aims for your shoes.

Many salarymen are lulled by the swaying of the train into a kind of coma. They slide to the floor and sprawl there as peaceful as the dead. When the train pulls into a station, boarding passengers step carefully over their spread-eagled limbs. Occasionally, though, one of these drunks remains erect, and then you learn how much aggression has been held back. In a train car full of strangers, he feels free to let go at the top of his lungs, showering those around him with vile abuse.

The men who pass out on the platform benches—the ones who slide to the floor in their own vomit, the ones who rave and moan all the way home—are not considered alcoholics: They are respectable employees of major corporations.

At last, though, it has begun to dawn on the authorities that something may be going wrong. A survey of 7,000 high school students found that 14 percent of the boys and a nearly identical 13 percent of the girls were already alcohol abusers.[32] A team of Japanese physicians produced research showing that alcohol abuse eats up 7 percent of Japan's medical expenditures, and that in 1987 the social costs—in lost productivity, etc.—amounted to 2 percent of Japan's gross national product, or roughly a $45 billion expense. They concluded:

> Alcohol abuse is a problem that greatly affects our society, not only in terms of health but also socially and economically. . . . Public health intervention urgently needs to be administered in order to reduce alcohol-related health and social problems.[33]

This kind of message is filtering through to the public. By 1991, *the Nihon Keizai Shimbun*, Japan's leading business daily, ran a story titled "Alcoholism: Firms Sober Up to Problem."[34]

THE PARTY'S OVER

The next morning, as promised, the hotel staff came barging in bright and early to remove the futons. This

*naturally entailed bundling us out of them. I staggered
down the hall to the bathroom, blinking in the dawn's
early light. In spite of being rousted at this early hour, I
was feeling good. The invigorating effects of the bath
were apparently long-lasting, and besides, the whole
thing had been such an adventure. A strange thought entered my head: It hadn't yet been twenty-four hours, but
I really was feeling a kind of solidarity with these
people. You can't go through experiences like pouring
each other's beer and bathing together without feeling
friendlier than you were before. I felt particularly close
to Sato-san, who had, since being kind enough to inform
me of my error in the* rotenburo, *had rather opened up
to me. He was, I now knew, a man yearning to quit his
job in business features and go to America, possibly to
get an M.B.A. and go into a more fulfilling line of work.
How often did a foreigner get to glimpse the heart's
dreams of a Japanese man? On the other hand, what was
the point of building solidarity with someone who was
planning to quit the company?*

*I was pondering this as I brushed my teeth in the com-
munal bathroom when a ghastly image appeared in the
mirror. I turned around. It was Okuma-san, one of the
traditionalists who had led the roaring faction the night
before. I stared. I don't think I'd ever seen quite that
shade of green before, except possibly on the coroner's
slab at the hospital where I'd once been a volunteer.
Okuma-san stumbled toward me and made an effort at
getting me in focus. He grinned wolfishly and croaked
"Osu," short for "Ohayō gozaimasu," or "Good morning." It sounded as though he had been gargling Drāno.
Far from having a hangover, though, he was still dead
drunk. Whiskey was practically streaming out of his
pores. He hadn't slept at all, I suspected.*

After a quick breakfast of rice, fish, seaweed, and raw

egg (at which, in hair-of-the-dog fashion, several of the men drank beer), we packed up and headed out. The train back to Tokyo was slightly less crowded than the outbound one had been. There were no free seats, of course, but there was plenty of standing room. Several of the men from the roaring faction lay down on the floor and went to sleep.

As we zipped along, I reflected that the trip had probably been as great a success for those guys as it had been for us. (By now, the younger Japanese and the gaijin had bonded into a single unit in my mind.) We had packed as much fun and adventure into twenty-four hours as we could. We had, in an entirely innocent way, shed our inhibitions and enjoyed each other's company. They, on the other hand, had used the same time to work out a year's worth of frustrations, bitterness, and rage. Now they smiled contentedly in their sleep on the floor while the train whisked us back to Tokyo and the routine of work.

CAN YOU FIGHT TWENTY-FOUR HOURS A DAY?

As the pace and pressure of work increased in the eighties, companies gave more attention to relieving the stress of their employees. However, the sincerity of the effort was open to question: "Corporate Japan has recognized the existence of the problem [of overwork] and devised a battery of high-tech and ingenious solutions to stress, other, that is, than what might be thought the obvious—reduction in working hours, decentralization of population, and provision of facilities for cheap relaxation in natural surroundings," writes critic Gavan McCormack.[35] Many of these solutions verged on the bizarre: immersion tanks filled with warm water and soft music, scents

injected into the air to replicate ocean breezes, and—the
old standby—sex tours of Southeast Asia which, in an
irrational response to the AIDS epidemic, began to focus
on child prostitutes.

The pharmaceutical industry saw a bonanza in the
making, and set its chemists working overtime to produce new stimulant products to perk up the exhausted
salaryman. Soon concoctions whose chief active ingredi-
ents were caffeine and a variant of nicotine were being
marketed under the charming rubric of "health drinks."[36]
A TV commercial for one teased the viewer with the
playful slogan: "Businessman, can you fight twenty-four
hours a day?"

When official Japan roused itself to examine overwork,
it too regarded the problem as a business opportunity.
The 1987 Law for the Development of Comprehensive
Resort Areas touched off a boom in resorts, theme parks,
and golf courses. So frenzied were the efforts to cash in
on the "leisure boom" that in a short time fully 15 percent of the land in Hyogo Prefecture, adjacent to Osaka,
Japan's second-largest city, was slated for development
into golf courses. Two years after the passage of the law,
100 theme parks were on the drawing boards or under
construction—in a country the size of California.[37] Space
World, the project my wife worked on, was a sterling example a great and humorless irony: To fulfill the government's vision of a more "leisure-oriented Japan,"
thousands of people were being worked to the brink of
death. Some, like Rumiko's supervisor, actually fell over
the precipice.

Despite the passage of the "Resort Law," and the government's official "vision" of a more leisurely lifestyle
for the Japanese, most men remained confined within the
orbit of work, occasionally whooshing home like stray
comets in the late watches of the night.

BREAKING AWAY

Koji Tanaka broke the taboo. He may not have been the
first in the country. He may not even have changed any
minds at his company. But his decision to drop out of
the drinking game changed his life.

After graduating from Keio University in 1980, he
joined a large electronics company. For the next ten
years, his life went along quite normal lines for a promising salaryman: He rotated through several posts and
was then sent overseas to get an M.B.A. degree at an
American university, which is where I first met him. On
returning, he married and settled into an overseas mar-
keting analysis position in the firm's communications
equipment division. But his wife, who also worked, began to wonder aloud why she had to spend the evenings
alone at home, doing chores or watching television,
while he was out with the guys from the office.

At first, this seemed to him like silly carping. What
did she want to do, join the boys at the bar? That was
unthinkable. No wife joins her husband in company socializing.[38] Indeed, no woman would want to.[39] She
should have a baby; that would satisfy her, he thought.
But Koji, a quiet man given to prismatic thinking, began
to consider what she had said from another angle. Why
should he spend all his evenings with his office mates?
They were not his only friends; in fact, they were not his
real friends at all. Koji was no teetotaler, but the nightly
bouts of drinking had lost their charm. After spending
all day together, there wasn't much of interest to say at
night. So they joked and sang. He joked, too, but that
was just to get along. Koji was cerebral—a reader, a
thinker—what the Japanese call interi, short for "intellectual." His wife, a teacher, shared his love of Japanese
history and literature. His office mates, well, frankly,

they were lightweights. What's more, they distrusted him for having studied overseas, even though he believed he was far more faithful to the traditions of Japan than they, with their love of Scotch whiskey and American slang, would ever be. Increasingly, Koji thought, the after-hours camaraderie seemed forced.

Long after the crisis had passed, Koji sat across from me on the straw-matted floor of his traditional Japanese home, sipping green tea from a lacquered cup. The house actually belonged to his parents, who occupied the northern half of it. It sat in a small grove of bamboo, which screened out the sights and much of the noise of modern Tokyo, a few yards beyond. I couldn't help thinking that, except for my presence, it was like a scene from one of those novels by Natsume, the author of **Botchan** whom Koji had introduced to me by pulling a 1,000-yen note from his wallet and showing me the novelist's likeness engraved upon it. That was Koji's smug way of indicating that Japan respected its cultural heroes.[40] Now, however, his mind was on other things.

"Frustration is extremely high among salarymen," he told me. I nodded sympathetically, trying as always to conceal my own frustration at sitting cross-legged on the floor.

"Of course," he continued, "you can relieve stress in various ways. But even if a Japanese man wants to play tennis or take a vacation, he can't do it. The easiest way is to drink."

He went on to tell me how at last he had taken a stand. One summer night, he refused to go out drinking and went straight home instead. He didn't give any excuse, just said good-night and left. The next day, he found he had been ostracized.

"By acting as an individual and going home," he said

gravely, pausing to sip his tea, "I came to be known as an 'unusual person.' Everyone talked about me."
He bore the stigma in quiet dignity for several months. But at last the coldness on all sides began to disrupt his work. He felt he might even be fired, if they could find an excuse. Instead, Koji quit and started a business of his own, together with some friends. Friends who had nothing to do with the company. Friends for whom business, even their own business, was a thing to be set in balance with the rest of life.

THE OLD SONG AND STANCE

As it happened, Koji was just a little ahead of his time. The company's psychological grip on the employee—the instilled sense of *amae*, or dependence, to use Doi's useful term—is slipping. One evening in 1993, I met up with a midlevel manager at a large Japanese company for drinks. It was my turn to treat, so when the bill came I attempted to collar it and found myself practically in a wrestling match with my acquaintance. After much back and forth, I finally realized that there was something more to his pleading than mere politeness.

Then, with an embarrassed smile, he explained: His young subordinates refused to go out drinking with him. This astonished me. It wasn't as though he had a bad personality; on the contrary, he was a man of considerable charm. But these young pups just didn't want to go out with their boss. They reckoned they could have more fun going to a pool hall with their own friends or whatever it was that appealed to them in their off-hours.

"They make too much money!" my friend said disgustedly. "Anyway, I have to turn in some expenses or I

will be laughed at by my superiors. They will think I
don't know how to be a manager. So, please . . ."

Much as it pained me to do it, I let him pay. How could
I refuse?

My friend the manager was not alone in his predica-
ment. Although the old ways have by no means died out,
there is an unmistakable tapering off of tradition. In a
study of generational differences among salarymen, the
Hakuhodo Institute of Life and Living found that a large
majority of young workers they surveyed were not both-
ered by the idea of leaving work before their bosses.[41] And
while most recognize the strategic importance of going
out drinking with their bosses, in practice young salarymen go out twice as often with peers than with their
bosses. Their elders, by contrast, tend to socialize with
their superiors more often than with their equals or subordinates.[42]

Those old mainstays of garrison morale, the company
song and calisthenics, elicit derisive laughs from young
salarymen these days. I know: In 1991 National Public
Radio asked me to do a story on the subject. The only
company I could find where people still knew the words
to the song was Matsushita, and there it was mentioned
with a smirk, even though that firm had recently watered
down the words to make them less provocative and, well,
less embarrassing than the old lyrics, which included
lines such as, "Doing our best to increase production,"
and "Grow, industry, grow, grow, grow!"[43]

Company trips like the one I took with the *Japan
Times* have also lost their luster. For all that I enjoyed
myself, had I been compelled to go on that trip every year,
my attitude would have been very different indeed.
Sapped of the vital ingredient of choice, the thing would
have turned to ashes and gall. So when I read that two-
thirds of young workers feel they are coerced to partici-

pate in official company trips, I wasn't astonished to learn than a third oppose having them at all.[44]

For young Japanese, leisure has little to do with business. Their aim in leisure is to socialize with friends, according to a 1989 survey by the semiofficial Leisure Development Center.[45] Only 9 percent of respondents thought its purpose was to contribute to work. Those who sought their sense of worth entirely in their work amounted to less than 3 percent.

These are not merely sentiments of how things ought to be. Despite the paternalism of the company, young workers are more inclined than ever to spend their free time with people unrelated to work. In a study on Japanese work habits, Keio University economist Yoko Sano found dissatisfaction with traditional company life sharply on the rise among young workers. More than half of those she surveyed had friends outside their work circle, while less than a fifth spent much time off socializing with their company superiors. "It is evident," Sano concluded, "that the number of those who want to spend days off particularly with friends outside of their companies is increasing."[46]

Some have begun to express their sense of autonomy by inverting one of the most powerful and ubiquitous symbols of membership in Japan: the business card. For years, it has been an article of faith that in any meeting between two strangers, a business card tells everything the two need to know about each other's status: which organization they belong to and what rank they hold within it. But now, some young people have started to have personal cards printed for use outside company hours.[47] These cards, some of which bear extravagant designs, express their individuality in ways the traditional *meishi*, or business card, never could. I have one of these personal cards in my file. It is lime-green, imprinted with a florid script, and bears the drawing of a fish. It positively trumpets individuality.

SNOW WHITE AND THE TOP TEN HUNKS

When I was in Japan in the summer of 1992 doing a radio documentary on changing lifestyles, I revisited Tokyo Disneyland. Despite the recession, it was packed. As crowds formed to watch Disney on Parade, I approached two young women and asked if I could interview them. They were somewhat reluctant, and I assumed they felt shy to speak with a foreigner, especially one bearing a microphone. But it turned out that wasn't it at all. Once I assured them that my report would be broadcast only in America, they were happy to talk. It seemed they were playing hooky from their jobs. And not, apparently, for the first time. With an embarrassed giggle, one of them confessed to me that this was her twentieth visit to Tokyo Disneyland.

Returning to Tokyo proper, I discovered that other women were seeking a different kind of fantasy than the one offered by Disney. In Kabuki-cho, a sort of red-light zone in Tokyo's trendy Shinjuku district, I attempted to enter a burlesque theater for women. Kabuki-cho is a warren of dark lanes and alleys, some lit only by aka-chōchin, the red paper lanterns that hang outside old-fashioned stalls and shops, and others ablaze in lurid neon signs. The area is home to dozens of yakuza gangs, who control the more dubious entertainments offered there. These range from pachinko parlors, where salarymen gamble their allowances on pinball games for cash prizes, to sex theaters and bawdy houses. There are also movie theaters, batting cages, drugstores, fortune-tellers, and a huge 1950s-style Mr. Donut shop, but it's

the sex business that really draws the crowds. In front
of each stands a gangster, typically dressed in a white
suit, black tie, and dark glasses, and serving as barker
and bouncer all in one.

As I may have mentioned, I'm not particularly brave.
Gangsters make me nervous. What's worse, reporters
make gangsters nervous, a thing never to be encouraged.
The mobster outside the women's sex show looked particularly jumpy. It's possible he found his assignment a
little embarrassing. After all, he had to stand in front of
a large poster advertising the "Gal's Best Ten," a lineup
of hunky Japanese beefcake decorated only with strategi-
cally placed tassels and stars. Or it could be that he
hadn't beaten up anyone in a long time and was getting
itchy? There was no way to tell. Nevertheless, I screwed
my courage to the sticking place and, with microphone
in one hand and calling card in the other, approached
the gentleman in a genial yet purposeful manner, the
way I imagined Mike Wallace would have done.

It worked. He seemed utterly astonished. After I had
explained myself twice, he took my card and asked me
as politely as a British butler to kindly wait a moment
while he went to see the boss. He disappeared down a
narrow, gaudily decorated stairwell that apparently led
to what was literally an underground theater. I could
hear an announcer bellowing through a loudspeaker and
peals of feminine laughter and applause. I was aching to
go down and see—not who was performing; that didn't
interest me—but who was watching. Middle-aged
housewives with curly perms and thick arms? Wasp-
waisted O.L.'s with flowing tresses and pink lipstick? Department store clerks still in their uniforms? I could not
guess. Alas, I was fated never to know.

At long last, the barker/bouncer/butler returned with
the boss and one or two aides in tow. The boss was a

smooth, supple-looking fellow. His hair was heavily greased, and combed straight back. He was dressed in smart evening clothes, but the way they hung on him suggested a powerful frame within. I tried my Mike Wallace act again, with emphasis on the genial. The boss studied my card thoughtfully for a moment and then spoke.

Both my hopes and fears proved unjustified. I should have known. Of course this guy wasn't going to let me in on his own responsibility. As a remember of the respected American media, I might be able to visit on another night, he said, but there were procedures to be followed. I would have to apply to the district boss, and then if he approved my request I would have to arrive at the theater at 6 P.M., an hour before the first show of the night, and stay throughout. Instantly, I realized what was going on. The better class of Japanese gangster is known for his etiquette. In exactly the manner a Japanese bureaucrat or PR man would use, he was rejecting my request by setting difficult conditions. If I met these, no doubt others would arise. But of course, he would never presume to say no. That would be rude.

OF CHERRY BLOSSOMS AND YELLOW CABS

Japanese women have begun to slip into traditionally male bastions such as *rakugo*, the ancient art of humorous storytelling, and every sort of up-to-date pastime as well. In the summer of 1993, Yukiko Gyoba became a sort of Jackie Robinson of her sex.[48] The fifteen-year-old daughter of a Little League coach tried out for her high school team and won a spot in the lineup. The team's coach simply said he could find no justification for turning her down. With Yukiko aboard, the team got into the preliminary round of the national championships. But there Yukiko could only watch from the bleachers. The All Japan High School Baseball League prohibits girls from participating in official games.

Once out of high school, many young women took a daring and experimental path. If the girlish *burikko* persona had been constructed to please men, the strange new *oyaji* gal arose purely for self-delight. This female incarnation of machismo—whose nickname translates roughly as "like-yer-old-man gal"—shocked many people. In place of the cute 'n' cuddly young Japanese woman, swarms of *oyaji* gals elbowed their way to the bar to throw back shots of neat scotch, shouldered their way into the track to bet on the horses, and—much to the disgust of businessmen—crowded up the links. Where male golfers took their inspiration from "Jumbo" Ozaki, women idolized Ayako Okamoto, whose international ranking was better than that of any male Japanese golfer.

But the most controversial of women's activities proved to be something that appeared quite innocuous: tourism. In 1993, 12 million Japanese, most of them tourists, went overseas. A decade earlier, the outflow of Japanese was just 3 million a year, and most of those were businessmen. Two decades before that, travelers needed official permission to go abroad and were severely limited in the amount of yen they could exchange. The restrictions, intended to protect Japan's foreign exchange reserves, led to those picturesque groups of Japanese shuffling forty or fifty strong behind a tour leader with a flag and a bullhorn who rushed them from sight to sight, pausing only long enough to allow their camera shutters to click.

Nowadays, young Japanese women—rich, confident, and adventurous—travel when they please and where they please.[49] To understand how this could be controver-

sial, you have to look at it from the Japanese man's point
of view. Men do not feel quite so much at liberty. It's one
thing to leave the office at six. But it requires a lot of
courage, even recklessness, for a salaryman to take all
his personal vacation time. A few companies have begun
publicly urging their employees to take vacations, but
career-minded men remain skeptical. They remember
the attitude that officially prevailed until recently. This
was captured by an American researcher who spent time
working in a Tokyo tool and die firm:

> When workers took their full vacation days or re-
> fused to work overtime because they had personal
> business, managers labeled them *wagamama*. It was
> a particularly harsh criticism—*wagamama* trans-
> lates as "selfish." It symbolizes letting the collective
> community down to indulge your own personal in-
> terests. . . . [A] willingness to take your full vacation
> days is seen by the company as an act of disloy-
> alty. . . . The higher the number of vacation days you
> use, the greater the tendency to see you as disloyal
> and the lower will be your annual performance ap-
> praisal.[50]

In recent years, the Japanese government has taken to
claiming a loss of control over big business. But in the
matter of leisure, at least, despite a great deal of propaganda about shorter working hours, the government
leads by notoriously bad example.

One disgruntled member of the ruling bureaucracy
broke the code of silence to publish an account of what
he called "inhumane, inefficient, and anachronistic"
working conditions. Masao Miyamoto, a U.S.-trained
psychiatrist, says that when he requested two weeks of
vacation time (out of the twenty-three days' leave to

which he was nominally entitled) for a trip to Europe, his superiors at the Ministry of Health and Welfare bawled him out, saying, among other things, that he ought to be too busy to think of taking a vacation.

Outraged, Miyamoto, who had joined the Ministry after thirteen years of practicing and teaching in the United States, penned a stinging indictment of the bureaucracy—which became a best-selling book called *Oyakusho no okite,* or simply "Government Office Rules." For his impudence, Miyamoto was transferred to the docks and put in charge of the quarantine section at Yokohama.

In an interview with the *Japan Times,* Miyamoto outlined what the government regards as proper uses of leisure time:

> Athletic meetings, cherry blossom–viewing parties, and annual office trips are all intended to reinforce sameness. Government workers share the grand illusion that those who belong to the same organization should look alike. But this is only possible when you give up your private life, and I will not give that up.[51]

Few men are as bold as Miyamoto, but the relative freedom women enjoy in matters of leisure causes widespread resentment and envy among men. And this has led to the great "Yellow Cab" brouhaha.

I first became aware of the alleged promiscuity of Japanese women abroad when Shintaro Ishihara, novelist, politician, and author of *The Japan That Can Say No,* mentioned in an interview rumors that Japanese women were flying to Guam to sleep with black GIs. Ishihara is old enough to remember when the rape or seduction of Japanese women by black GIs was a favorite theme of

leftist filmmakers and novelists in the wake of the Occupation. I took this to be just another expression of Ishihara's peculiar blustering insecurity.[52] But to my surprise,
the theme soon reemerged in a new guise: the "Yellow
Cab girl." Japanese women who traveled to New York, it
was said, were snidely referred to by American studs on
the make as "Yellow Cab girls," because you could hop
on and take a ride. The term gained wide currency in a
book by that name. Written by a Japanese writer (female,
incidentally), it purported to reveal the sleazy secrets of
Japanese women living in New York and Los Angeles.
This became a hot topic for TV talk shows and tabloid-
style magazines. A lengthy debate over the origin of the
phrase ensued in, among other forums, the *Japan Times*.
Tokyo resident Philip Cunningham wrote:

> The term *Yellow Cab* as used to refer to sexually
> active Japanese women abroad reminds me of other
> peculiarly Japanese usages of the English language
> such as *Christmas cake* or *old miss* for a single
> woman beyond the marriage age, or *Bobby-ko* or
> *Hammer-ko* for a woman dating a black man. The
> popular usage of *Yellow Cab* in Japanese books is
> particularly odious because it sneakily and disingen-
> uously attributes to native English speakers a novel
> form of *Japan-bashing* (itself a Japanese term as far
> as I can tell), while pressuring young Japanese
> women to avoid foreigners.[53]

The controversy finally died down after some of the
women who had purportedly been subjects of the case
study wrote to the Japanese press to denounce the book
as a fraud. There was never much doubt in my mind that
the "Yellow Cab girl" was a Japanese invention. It
seemed so improbable as American slang. Among other

things, you have to pay to ride a cab, and no one was suggesting that rich Japanese women were prostituting themselves. If anything, they were simply having for free the kind of overseas sexual adventure that countless Japanese men had paid for handsomely. But where the men got away without any opprobrium whatsoever, the women were tagged with a vicious label. What's more, there is little doubt in my mind that the number of young Japanese women daring enough to engage in sexual liaisons with strangers in strange lands was slight indeed. Of the 3.3 million Japanese who annually visit the United States, a third or more of whom are women, the author of *Yellow Cab* "documented" the experiences of eleven.[54]

The whole "Yellow Cab" affair comes to this: Certain Japanese traditionalists are attempting to rein in women by sexual slander. Thanks to them, Japan can proudly add to its claims of uniqueness: It has created the only society in which women are at once more oppressed and more at liberty than men.

LADY OF SPAIN

Fusako, a perfectly ordinary secretary with wire-rimmed glasses and a slight gap in her front teeth, was part of a circle that met each Wednesday evening at the Asahi beer hall in Shinjuku. For a time, until work consumed my leisure, I used to join her and three or four friends for a few beers and an idea of what ordinary office workers wanted out of life. Fusako and her friends were taking after-work English lessons, to be followed invariably by after-class drinks. One of their circle was married to an American who worked for Honda, and the others, who were single, spent a lot of time discussing the advantages and drawbacks of marrying a foreigner. The Honda husband often had to work late, and so I was frequently the only example at hand of the article in question. To my embarrassment, the women used to have lengthy debates about my qualifications, breaking off now and then to pepper me with questions: "Do you get up before your wife?" Fusako would ask. "Yes, sometimes," I'd say, and she would round triumphantly on her friends, as if to say "See, I told you!" Michiko, a small, pixielike friend of Fusako's who wore an ornate ring on every finger, aimed a threatening tankard of beer at me and asked, "Do you have girlfriends?"

I hesitated. This is a tough question for a man to answer. His ego gets in the way. But truth won out. "No, not at all," I replied at last. Michiko grinned smugly at her companions.

As I say, this kind of scrutiny embarrassed me intensely. Reporters rarely field questions about their personal lives (though this would probably be a healthy exercise to institute before the next U.S. presidential election). However, I considered it a fair exchange for the insight I was gaining about them. After some weeks, I thought I knew them pretty well. Michiko was a hot pepper: quick-witted, tart-tongued, and restless. Already in the time I had known her, she had changed jobs. Although she liked earning money, she didn't care a hoot about her job outside working hours. And although she liked the independence her earnings provided, her big goal was to land a good husband, someone who would make a good living and leave her plenty of elbow room to have fun.

Fusako, by comparison, was subdued. With her tame clothes and quiet manner, she reminded me of a librarian. Perhaps, too, the impression formed because she was a reader. I remember being startled to find that she was reading Don Quixote—*in English, a thing I myself had never done. To be sure, it was an abridged version, but still . . .*

One week when I dropped in on the circle, Fusako, normally a mainstay, was gone. No one, not even Michiko, seemed to know where she was. The next week, however, she reappeared, tanned and showing off her gap-toothed grin more than ever. She had gone to Spain for a week, she announced. I was floored. "By yourself?" I asked incredulously. "Oh, yes," she said casually, and drew out a packet of photos of herself in an orange grove in Seville, in front of the Prado in Madrid, and so on.

Of course, Spain was not terra incognita, and Fusako was no born adventurer. But for a shy, bookish Japanese secretary, the adventure was about as improbable as Coronado's search for the Lost City of Gold.

For Sayuri, on the other hand, Spain would have been far too ordinary. Before she came to work at the Japan Times, she had already spent months in the Amazon rain forest, on an international habitat project. The daughter of a well-to-do family of sake brewers, she was highly educated and cosmopolitan. Unlike most Japanese, she understood the American sense of humor. In newsroom banter she could give as good as she got. Although she tried to suppress her brassiness in dealing with the deskmen, it was clear from the start that she irritated them. Her voice, for instance. It wasn't pitched high and silvery the way a working girl's should be. In fact, it wasn't girlish at all. She sounded downright womanly. And then there was her laugh: She never covered her mouth and giggled. Hers was more of a ho-ho-ho than a tee-hee-hee. Though she sounded refreshingly natural to us Americans, she was evidently a great annoyance to the older Japanese men. It probably did not help that she had the body of a female athlete: graceful but strong, obviously strong. The deskmen frequently *lost their tempers with her, bellowing at point-blank range over some small failure to follow directions.*

Under these circumstances, I suppose it was inevitable that she would leave the Japan Times. *Certainly the news that she was quitting came as no surprise to me. What astonished me, however, was word of her new plans. She had signed up to participate in an international expedition of women to ski across the Antarctic to the South Pole. The last time I set eyes on her was by pure chance at Narita Airport, when I was on my way back to the United States with my family. She spotted me and rushed over to say good-bye. I asked where she was headed. "Oh, I'm going to Switzerland," she said nonchalantly, "to train in the Alps for my expedition."*

I don't know whether the expedition ever came off, but if it did, I feel certain that Sayuri was right there in the pack, schussing along over the crackling snow and dreaming up some bold new quest.

THE GOOD, THE BAD, AND THE SILLY

Young Japanese are scurrying down all sorts of avenues in their search for identity. The use of illegal drugs in Japan, especially amphetamines and tranquilizers—"uppers" and "downers," as they are often known—appears to be rising fast. Glue-sniffing is common in certain pockets of society. Even cocaine is catching on. In 1992 seizures of contraband drugs shot up by 70 percent. In the first six months of 1993, Japanese police seized 1,120 pounds of marijuana, considerably more than the annual total for any previous year.[55] Of course, the amounts are trivial by American standards, but they are rapidly climbing.

In Matsumoto, a small, quiet city in central Japan, I

emerged from the train station and noticed some people handing out leaflets to children. Intrigued, I approached them and asked for one. After some evident reluctance, they handed me a copy. It was an antidrug leaflet with a familiar-sounding English slogan on its cover: "No, Absolutely No!" (rendered as *"Dame. Zettai."* in Japanese). Published by the Drug Abuse Prevention Center of Tokyo, the brochure shows young people how illicit drugs reach Japan. As with most educational pamphlets in Japan, cartoons figure prominently in this one. There are cute little bad guys in dark glasses and wild-eyed addicts sniffing glue.

For the more sophisticated reader, however, it offers graphs and charts that show, among other things, that cocaine seizures in Japan shot up from less than a pound in 1988 to more than 150 pounds in 1990. I was at once pleased and disheartened by this pamphlet. After hearing so much about how Japanese children were too well bred to fall prey to drugs the way decadent American youth had, it pleased me to think some Japanese were prepared to acknowledge the universality of the drug menace. On the other hand, it pained me to think that illegal drugs were spreading so fast in Japan that this kind of effort had to be mounted even in an old-fashioned town like Matsumoto.

· · ·

Japan's famous moral relativism—its emphasis on specific rules rather than general principles—means that as pleasures proliferate, the rules lag behind. There are gaps in Japan's moral and social proprieties that often shock Americans. Take pornography, for example. In a country where language remains heavily regimented, there is nothing approaching a consensus on the question of what is or is not appropriate visual discourse.[56] To put it bluntly, nobody says "fuck," but you can hardly avoid seeing the act depicted in the magazines read on commuter trains.

The rule is simple, so simple as to make a mockery of censorship: no explicit depiction of genitals or pubic hair. Comic artists have therefore devised ingenious ways to mask the genitals in ways that allow the viewer to see what he wants to see. Some make the penis into a living creature, with eyes and arms, a bit like the Chinese mushrooms in Disney's *Fantasia*. So when is a phallus not a phallus? This is the question police must decide, and they take it quite seriously. Investigators on porno detail spend countless hours screening videos and thumbing through magazines in search of penises, pubic hair peeking out from behind the shaded area of the film, or drawings that are a little too suggestive of labia. But they let go by the most hair-raising depictions of rape, mutilation, child molestation, bondage, necrophilia, and —what do you call it when bodily waste becomes a sexual plaything?

These products are not confined to the back shelf of a pervert's emporium. They are ubiquitous, the everyday fare of train-commuting salarymen, college students (male and female), and, increasingly, children. A government study showed that 64 percent of male junior high school students admitted to having read porno comics, along with about half of junior high girls.[57] In high school, the rate jumps to more than 85 percent.

I don't believe in censorship or in a simple cause-and-effect link between pornography and sexual behavior, but considerable evidence exists that the rules—not morals, but rules—governing the sexual behavior of Japanese youth are crumbling. In 1993, for example, police discovered that girls from some of Tokyo's most elite high schools had agreed to pose in adult videos and to sell their underwear to a porno producer, who was arrested for using minors in his productions.[58] In all, police questioned ninety high school girls who allegedly performed naked in porno videos for 50,000 yen each—just under $500.

It is a great irony that one of the most highly refined cultures in the world should, in its contemporary form, so often wallow in bad taste. Even allowing a wide latitude for moral relativism, I find it odd that Japan bans the depiction of genitals, which for centuries appeared in celebrated Japanese erotic art, but lets pass any sort of sexual horror or outrage without the flicker of an official eyelid. Cartoon magazines for junior high school boys offer up images that make *Mad* magazine look like a Golden Book reader: pictures of mothers composed of feces, boys breaking wind in the faces of their fathers, hydra-penised monsters committing multiple rape of schoolgirls, and other grotesque fantasies of juvenile aggression.[59]

Please don't imagine that I am equating mere sex with tackiness. In fact, sex is the least of the aesthetic depredations practiced in Japan. At a small Japanese guest house I visited, a video player was provided in the lounge for guests, along with a collection of tapes. One of those that happened to be playing when I walked in was called *Za Shocks!* It consisted entirely of disaster footage, with the emphasis on people dying horrible deaths. I only watched for a moment, but I can still see in my mind's eye footage shot in an African village along the route of the notorious Paris-Dakar motor rally. Barefoot villagers line both sides of the dusty road as cars bounce along at high speed. Suddenly, one of the drivers loses control and his car smashes into a group of boys standing on the side of the road. Bodies fly into the air; others are crushed under the wheels. As if this were not bad enough, the filmmakers ran the same footage over again in slow motion.

What gave the proprietors of that inn the idea that this was appropriate stuff to offer their guests? Well, possibly they got the idea from the local video store, whose shelves are stocked with quantities of such material. Like the porno videos, these are rarely sequestered from children in the shops. Apparently, there is a big market for the stuff. In 1993 an enterprising video producer announced a new entry in his *Death File* series: scenes of mangled corpses from the civil war in the former Yugoslavia. He promised the public footage of rotting bodies, gouged-out eyes, and split skulls. "The concept is to appeal to curiosity," Koji Yamashita, the producer, told the *Mainichi* newspaper in the summer of 1993. "We Japanese have a difficult time understanding ethnic and religious killing." Ah, of course, an educational video.

Many social activities were also morally, culturally, or environmentally questionable. Young lovers stirred the outrage of their elders by their passionate kissing in public.[60] On the beaches, teenagers roared around the bays on jet skis, while in tranquil mountains swarms of skiers, climbers, and hang gliders vied for space on the crowded peaks. In the cities, gangs called *bōsōzoku*, "wild tribes," gathered in their hundreds to hot-rod about in souped-up jalopies and motorcycles. Young women began to drink alcoholic beverages concocted especially for them with provocative names like "Fuzzy Navel Peachtree Fizz." Young men began indulging in mascara and makeup, applied at salons with names like "Men's Esthétique." And how's this for cultural ambiguity: I once stumbled across a gathering of no less than twenty Japanese Elvis impersonators—male and female—in a park.

Fortunately, there are innocent pleasures as well: In 1990 the All Japan Hula Association formed to meet the needs of 10,000 hula hoop enthusiasts.[61] Cycling began to overtake golf in popularity.[62] Young women took to body building like never before, as an aerobics and weight-training craze swept the nation.[63] Angling, the thinking man's solitary sport since the days of Izaak Walton, gained 30 million adherents in Japan.[64]

Of course, all that exploration cost money. Not content merely to spend what they earned, young people began to use revolving credit with wild abandon. The pent-up demand for fun was greater than any government planner could have anticipated. In 1990 alone, the number of credit cards in circulation jumped 20 percent. The average young urban "posh boy" or "body-con girl" carried six of them at a time. As the economy soured, many of these young people went bankrupt, some with spectacular debts. In 1992 more than 35,000 Japanese filed for bankruptcy, exceeding the old record by more than 10,000 cases. The *Los Angeles Times* reported on one O.L. who managed to run up $236,000 in debt on no less than thirty-three credit cards.[65]

Then, just as suddenly, a change in attitude swept the nation. As the recession dragged on, the boom in consumerism suddenly swung around, as the Japanese tacked from extravagance to asceticism. A book called *The Philosophy of Honest Poverty* hit Japan's best-seller list in the fall of 1992 and remained on top for most of the next year.[66] At about the same time, interest in Edo-period culture revived.[67] Attendance at the kabuki theaters picked up and sales of traditional music recordings grew. Young women began to study Japanese dance out of interest rather than to enhance their worth in the marriage market.

At a glance, the Japanese might appear to be reverting

to form, but this is not quite so. Form used to require
sacrifice for the benefit of the nation. More particularly,
in the past the government encouraged people to minimize their consumption and maximize savings so that
all available resources might be directed at exporting. So
explicit was this goal that in the fifties the Bank of Japan
set up branches in public schools to teach children the
virtues of saving their allowances. By 1993, however, Japan had come to rely on its domestic consumers to pull
the nation out of its slump. But just when consumerism
became patriotic, people weren't buying. Or, to be more
accurate, they were buying in an unaccustomed way: Department stores were out, discount houses were in. High-
priced Japanese goods were out, less-expensive imports
were in. Maine's L. L. Bean swept Japan with booming
sales in the midst of that country's worst retail recession
on record.[68] When a discount clothing store opened in
Tokyo in the fall of 1993, 500 men lined up on the sidewalk before 7 A.M. for marked-down suits.[69]

Meanwhile, angry shoppers inundated a consumers'
group hot line with complaints about stores that had not
lowered their prices in line with the yen's rising value.[70]
Just a few years earlier, Japanese trade negotiators were assuring Western countries that the Japanese consumer
never looks at price but only considers quality and brand
name.

All this is not meant to suggest that Japanese society
is lapsing into chaos. However one might feel about any
particular activity, it remains true that there is less antisocial behavior in Japan than in any other industrialized
society. Japanese youth are, by comparison to Western
young people, positively obeisant to authority. However,
many Japanese tastes and mores have dissolved into con-
fusion. Once clearly defined and circumscribed, they are
being trampled underfoot as young people mill about in

an aimless and unbounded search for identity. But each new step carries them farther in the direction of freedom.

BASKETBALL JONES

The effort to shape Japanese youth has long relied heavily on sports. Sumo, kendō (Japanese fencing), and other traditional Japanese sports are all regarded as excellent ways to instill discipline and appreciation of traditional values. Even baseball, the great American pastime, has served more to produce good Japanese than great ball-players in Japan. Coaches there emphasize sameness, routine, teamwork and sacrifice. One American critic writes:

> *Talent might help, but* konjō *(guts) is the key. Players here practice till they drop, thus proving they have* konjō. *Management truly believes that if their team—which is deeply mired in last place— would just practice twenty-two hours a day instead of twenty, they would win the pennant.*[71]

The Japanese have perfected their version of the sport, which they call kanri yakyū, *or "managed baseball," by eliminating the jarring unpredictability that so bedevils the American game.*[72] *Thus, in Japanese baseball, when a man reaches first with no outs, the next batter, though he be the home-run king of Japan, will bunt. You can bet the house on it.*

Even the fans of baseball are conditioned in a way that strikes the first-time observer as scary and the seasoned fan as merely tedious. When their team is up to bat, the fans, led by whistle-toting marshals, rise to chant the same cheer over and over while beating

together plastic cones used as megaphones. In the upper
bleachers, trumpet players keep the tune of the chant
with ear-splitting accuracy, over and over and over
again.[73] Fortunately, when their team is in the field, the
fans sit down, so an aficionado only has to miss half the
game. But with the other team's fans in full throat, there
is no hope of the kind of baseball chat that American
fans revel in. I have enjoyed myself at Japanese baseball
games, but my lasting impression of the experience is a
dull throb between the temples.

In 1993, however, a radical new development swept
the Japanese sports world: Japan's amateur soccer federation turned pro, touching off a nationwide craze for the
sport. Fans mobbed the small town of Kashima, several
hours from Tokyo, to watch a team with the improbable
name of the Antlers take on rivals such as the Nagoya
Grampus Eight and the Yomiuri Verdy. After the first season, the town announced plans to build a new stadium to double the 15,000-seat capacity of the old one.

The J-League, as the soccer federation is known, introduced totally new behavior on and off the field. Instead of
all looking alike, players reveled in their differences.
Some had long hair, others were cropped. On-field personalities shone, inspired by Brazilian and European stars
who were brought over to salt the mine. After goals, Japanese players burst with emotion, hugging teammates and
at times crying with joy. By contrast, the sumo wrestler
remains stone-faced in victory or defeat.

In the soccer stands, there was little of the regimented
cheering that marks (or, in my view, mars) Japanese
baseball. Soccer fans paint their faces in gaudy colors,
bare their chests, and yell themselves hoarse in a constant, throaty, primeval roar, accented by thousands of
"cheer horns."

With the rise of soccer, youngsters are turning away

from baseball in droves. The opening-day game between the Yomiuri Verdy and the Yokohama Marinos drew a 32.4 percent share of the television audience, nearly double what pro baseball games normally drew in the same time slot.[74] *Fred Varcoe, a* Japan Times *sports editor who writes frequently on soccer, told me, "You look around at a pro baseball game these days and all you see is salarymen. You look at the crowd at a J-League game and you see the future." Indeed, the fall in attendance at pro baseball games in Japan was so alarming that its owners began talking in 1993 of reorganizing its leagues to try to pump new life into the game.*

Soccer may be just the beginning. One fine day in Tokyo, as I was walking, I gradually became aware of a familiar rhythm. Dush, dush, dush, swish. I rounded a corner and there it was: a basketball, being dribbled on a concrete driveway by a boy of about twelve. Dush, dush, dush. He dribbled, stopped, and heaved. Swish! The ball snapped smartly through the bottom of the net.

The boy saw me and smiled. I smiled back and looked inquiringly at the ball. He tossed it to me, and I took a long jump shot. By luck it went in, and our game was under way. Twenty minutes later, winded and sweaty in my street clothes but thoroughly pleased, I stopped to chat with him.

His name, it turned out, was Tadashi, and he was actually thirteen, a junior high student. "How do you find time to play?" I asked him. "Don't you have to go to cram school?"

"Nah," said Tadashi, tossing the ball back into the hoop. "All my friends go to juku, *but it's not for me. Too much study is no good. That's what I think."*

"How did you get interested in basketball?" I asked him.

"Oh, I watch the NBA all the time on satellite TV,"
he told me. "I'm a fan of the Chicago Bulls. Michael
Jordan!" he added, and offered me his imitation of a Jor-
dan monster dunk, which came about two feet short of
the mark. I wished him luck and went on.

Is it possible that by the time Tadashi grows up there
could be a Japanese player in the NBA? Why not? If kids
like Tadashi can be inspired watching the likes of Mi-
chael Jordan play, eating McJordan hamburgers at Mc-
Donald's, and attending McNBA games at the Tokyo
Dome indoor stadium once a year, I see no reason why
some of them should not grow up to be pro material.
And even if they don't, they will have discovered yet an-
other new identity. Not sumo, with its Shinto mystique
and arduous apprenticeships, not Japanese baseball with
its martial overtones, not golf with its business luster,
but basketball, on whose courts a boy can grow up to be
a hot-dogging, wagamama jock.

5

THE DEAD TREE
GIVES NO SHELTER[1]

As the eighties wound down, our lives took a momentous turn. Rumiko had served out her time at Nippon Steel in an ever-swelling state. Now that she had retired into full-time maternity, her pregnancy became the focal point of our lives. We began to search for a place for her to give birth. This proved surprisingly difficult. We first went to a large public hospital for an obstetric exam. Upwards of 200 pregnant women sprawled on chairs and benches in the boxcar of a waiting room. It seemed to me we could not possibly meet the doctor that day. However, I was mistaken. The hospital had a system. A few minutes after we arrived, ten women filed out of the examining room, and a doughty nurse bellowed ten more names. A few minutes passed and the procedure was repeated. In little more than an hour, Rumiko's group was called.

I do not know if the doctor actually wore roller skates. Rumiko was in stirrups at the time, and he whizzed by so fast she didn't have a chance to raise herself up and look. She did glimpse a scowl on his face when she shot a question at him in passing. By and large, the Japanese

*doctor does not like to be questioned. "O-isha-san" is,
typically, a busy man. He examines, he prescribes in accordance with Ministry guidelines, and he moves on. Of
course, I cannot claim to have seen such a thing. I was
not present. How could a husband possibly accompany
his wife with nine other female patients in the room?
When Rumiko asked, the nurse had rebuked her. "Men
are dirty," she snapped. Whether this referred to our
spiritual or our physical condition was never made
clear.*

*After that episode, we began calling around to other
hospitals. If anything, they sounded worse. Nearly every
place where we inquired forbade fathers to be present
for the birth and kept the baby isolated in a nursery for
several days afterward. Few had any time for the notion
of natural childbirth; some required the mother to
undergo anesthesia as a matter of course.[2] One hospital
even required all women to give birth by induced labor
on a fixed schedule. This, I supposed, was an offshoot of
the just-in-time inventory method that made Toyota so
successful. True, Japan led the world in preventing infant
mortality, but evidently it did so by virtually mechaniz-
ing the process of birth.*

*Shocked and dispirited, we hired a consultant to help
us find a more suitable hospital. Higashi Fuchu Byōin
turned out to be just that. Patients were called one by
one, and the doctors spent considerable time with each.
They accepted questions and even allowed fathers to be
present throughout. It may not be entirely coincidental
that the chief doctor had done some of his medical
training in America.*

*Like most Japanese hospitals, it was a small, for-profit
institution run as a family business for at least two generations. But unlike most, it had a policy of administer-
ing the minimum amount of drugs necessary and of*

actually encouraging natural processes in childbirth. We
began Lamaze training on weekends at the hospital
with half a dozen other couples who were expecting at
about the same time. The crucial task for Rumiko was
to learn to say "Hee, hee, hoo!" in a firm and ringing
voice while she exhaled. As partner, I had little more to
do than the ringside manager who massages his fighter's
shoulders between rounds and tells him, "Come on,
slugger, yer doin' great!" But it felt good having even
that role to play. And I was pleased to see there were
Japanese husbands alongside me who felt the same way.

Ironically, I would be the one to drop out. As
Rumiko's due date approached, the doctor told us that
she had a pelvic problem that would probably require
her to deliver by cesarean. My enthusiasm for Lamaze
instantly wilted. Rumiko wanted to go on, just in case
she was able to deliver naturally, but I persuaded her
that there was no point. And, as it happened, I was right.

On May 2, 1989, Rumiko was wheeled into the deliv-
ery room, conscious and calm, with a spinal sedative
numbing the lower half of her body. I followed, camera
in hand, numb with excitement. A half-curtain spared
Rumiko the gory sight that was about to follow. The
doctor drew his scalpel across the half-moon of her
belly, opening a bright crimson gash across it.

"Daijōbu ka na?" the doctor asked. "Are you all
right?"

"I'm okay," Rumiko replied.

"No, not you. I'm worried about your husband," he
said.

I felt myself sway. Grinning weakly, I said I'd be fine.
But just to be sure, I leaned against the wall. In another
moment, the only miracle I'd ever witnessed occurred:
A head emerged from my wife's belly. Our daughter
was born.

THE CRUMBLING PYRAMID

The birth of any child is a miracle, of course, but one that grows increasingly scarce in Japan. Rumiko's grandmother was one of twelve children. Rumiko's mother was one of two and had two. Rumiko gave birth to her first child at the age of thirty-four, and at most she will have one more.

To see this pattern writ large in Japan, one need not look at generations. A few years will do. The number of children per Japanese mother was believed by some to be 2.17 on average in 1987, roughly the same as a decade before and just about the rate needed to maintain a stable population.[3] But in reality, the number had plummeted to 1.8, and by the end of the decade it was down to 1.57. A couple of years later, in 1992, it had slipped to 1.53. That year, a panicky Ministry of Health and Welfare reaffirmed its ban on oral contraceptives, offering the cynical excuse that legalization might add to the spread of AIDS.[4] If keeping contraception difficult was meant to boost the birthrate, the strategy failed. Undeterred by the high failure rate of Japanese condoms, women went on having abortions (thirty-seven for every 100 births) to limit their family size.[5] More important, young women put off marriage and childbirth until their thirties.[6] The birthrate continued to tick downward, hitting 1.50 children per mother in 1993 and 1.46 in 1994.

And so, Japan's population pyramid totters ominously on a narrowing base. The number of Japanese children fifteen or younger is falling by more than half a million a year. Already, the proportion of children in Japanese society has slipped below 17 percent.[7] That is one of the lowest proportions in the world, and certainly the fastest falling. The day when the elderly will exceed the young is drawing near. Meanwhile, social security and pension benefits have been growing rapidly as the traditional family mechanisms for taking care of the old are being stretched beyond the limit.

All these trends represent a direct threat to Japan's economic health. They are in many ways an inversion of the conditions that brought Japan to prosperity. One of the overlooked sources of Japan's economic miracle has been its comparatively youthful population: Since the end of World War II, the great majority of the Japanese have been of working age. In contrast, Britain and most other Western European nations have turned steadily grayer since World War II, until at last they found themselves with roughly 15 percent of their populations aged sixty-five or older. The United States, too, has been steadily graying, though it trails the Europeans with 12.5 percent of its people in the over-sixty-five bracket.[8]

Compared with these, Japan has been a fountain of youth. In 1960 the elderly amounted to 6 percent of Japan's population.[9] A decade later, this proportion had barely budged, reaching just 7 percent. Not only was Japan carrying an almost negligible defense burden, by virtue of its modest social security benefits and sparse claimants, its economy could race ahead unimpeded by the two largest drags on Western treasuries.

Suddenly, though, Japan has raced from the back of the pack to become the most rapidly aging nation on earth.[10] During the 1980s, as the birthrate plunged, the proportion of elderly in Japan's population shot up, surpassing 12 percent before the decade was out. It has since rocketed by the United States and is on course to match Sweden, currently the leader at just over 16 percent, before the end of the century.[11] By the year 2020, the Japanese government projects that more than 25 percent of its people will be over sixty-five. In the United States, by contrast, the number of elderly will creep up by just a

few percentage points to 16.6 percent in 2020, according
to U.S. Census projections, while 25 percent of Americans will be under eighteen.[12]

That will put Japan in a unique situation. The populations of most advanced industrial nations have more or
less stabilized. As the Organization for Economic Cooperation and Development said in a 1990 report:

> During the next fifteen to twenty years many
> OECD countries will enjoy a respite from the pres-
> sures of demographic aging. . . . Japan is an im-
> portant exception to this general pattern. Japan is
> already facing an aging process which is causing im-
> mediate and serious problems.[13]

Of course, having a large population of elderly is not
necessarily a bad thing. It can offer some advantages, not
least of which is a lower crime rate. But crime doesn't
menace Japan the way it does Western societies, whereas
the whirlwind of population change in Japan threatens to
be far more disruptive than the gradual graying of the
West. Japan cannot convert schools and colleges into
nursing homes and hospitals with a snap of the fingers.
Still less can it transform teachers into nurses and
doctors.

No peacetime society has ever faced the challenge of
operating under such rapidly changing conditions.
Makoto Atoh, director of population policy studies for
the Ministry of Health and Welfare, is understandably
perplexed. I went to interview him for National Public
Radio in the summer of 1992. With his squared-off, phar-
aonic beard, he looks more like a scholar than a bureaucrat. Atoh, who indeed holds a doctorate in public health
from the University of Michigan, described Japan's population pyramid with a furrowed brow. He worries that,

in addition to an explosion in the number of elderly, the extremely low birthrate will mean a plunge of as much as 25 percent in Japan's population within a single generation. When I asked what all this would mean for Japan, his face contorted into a smile of pain.

"Honestly speaking, nobody knows," he said. "We [can't] imagine how difficult [are] the problems we face in 2020."

NEW YEAR'S RESOLUTION

There is a deep tranquility in the Japanese New Year. Work stops for three days. Traffic thins. A hush falls over the entire nation, except, of course, in the vicinity of Tokyo Disneyland. At the Hirata household, all was calm, all was bright. We had just rounded back from Christmas with my parents in Philadelphia in time for New Year's in Tokyo. Maya, now a lusty-lunged eight-month-old, made it an exceptionally exhausting trip. But, as always, we spent New Year's Eve sweeping out imaginary cobwebs, plumping cushions, and generally sprucing up an already spotless house, and, as always, I found myself revived by this work. Perching on a stool to dust a tall bookshelf, or helping Rumiko's father to shift a heavy storage case in the kitchen, worked off a smidgen of the vast indebtedness I felt toward my too-kind in-laws. Besides, it got my blood moving again.

After a late supper, we settled in the cozy living room around the gas heater to watch the annual musical contest between men and women on NHK. I glanced over at Mr. Hirata. He was sitting on the couch, contentedly smoking a cigarette. In the coming year he intended to wrap up his career and retire. Already, at sixty-four, he was several years past his company's retirement age. As a manager, he had the privilege of staying on, and he had exercised it partly because he wanted to see his youngest daughter settled before he quit.

But Megumi was back now after a year of studying English at the University of Pennsylvania. She had gone there intending to complete college in the United States. But the better her English got, the more she fell into the American lifestyle. She wasn't getting herself hooked on drugs or anything like that. Megumi didn't even drink. But like so many young Japanese who come to America, she was intoxicated by freedom. Before long, she was off on a Caribbean vacation. In a year, she was back in Tokyo, her ambitions trampled in the sand.

Her parents were flummoxed. They simply didn't know what to do. Here was their daughter, in her mid-twenties with no career and no prospects. Her grandmother had an answer: Marry her to some young man. But of all people, Ichio and Tatsuko would be the last to force marriage upon their daughter. Indeed, they seemed reluctant to push her in any direction.

Megumi had her own answer. She began working in a succession of clothing boutiques. She had a talent for sales, it seemed. Her commissions were good. But each time she changed jobs, they worried. Meanwhile, she acquired a boyfriend—a nice, chubby stockbroker who had hopes of settling down and raising a family. In short, he was a father-in-law's dream. But Megumi had an answer to that as well: no. She refused even to entertain the idea of marrying at that point in her life.

On this New Year's Eve, however, Ichio seemed to have reconciled himself to her puzzling, headstrong, yet not quite independent ways. As she sat at his feet, playing with her big marmalade cat, I saw him smile indulgently at her. The cat, who was being made to waltz on his hind legs, yowled mournfully. Papa, as everyone

called him, broke into a silvery laugh. Under the thatch
of white hair, his craggy face looked at peace. Beside
him was a plastic case filled with English language tapes
and instruction manuals. At last he was thinking about
himself: He would retire and then travel abroad, first to
America, and then who knew where else? The yen was
strong, and he had money in the bank. The world was
his oyster. Little did we know that it was about to
snap shut.

OF SILVER AND GOLD

With the start of the new decade, public alarm over the
prospect of an aging, shrinking population began to show
up in Japanese government surveys. Despite an inescap-
able sense that Japan is overcrowded, in 1990 fewer than
one in ten said they regarded the country's falling fertility
as desirable.[14] A year later, another government survey
found a rising tide of anxiety about the aging of society.
For the first time, a majority expressed fear not just for
society but for their own welfare as they grew old.[15]

This was ironic, for at the same moment, the nation
was celebrating one of its greatest postwar achievements:
In 1947, at the time of the Allied occupation of Japan,
life expectancy there was just fifty years; since then, the
Japanese have become the longest-lived people in the
world. Prosperity, attentiveness to hygiene, and a healthy
diet have combined to push the average Japanese life span
to seventy-six years for men and eighty-two years for
women. That is nearly four years longer than the life expectancy of Americans. Moreover, it is worth recalling
that in the same period the Japanese have secured the
world's lowest infant mortality rate.

The Japanese are rightfully proud of these accomplishments. On August 1, 1992, all Japan celebrated when an adorable pair of identical twin sisters with the delightful names of Gin-san and Kin-san (Silver and Gold) reached their one hundredth birthday. The public frenzy rivaled that over a royal wedding. Kin-san and Gin-san were everywhere. Their cherubic, wrinkled faces peered out from every newspaper and television set, wreathed in toothless grins. Radio stations constantly broadcast their voices. Their faces were printed on posters, placards, and even on the telephone cards the Japanese use to make calls at pay phones.

Celebrity brought a new lifestyle to the sisters. They were escorted everywhere in limousines. A television network paid to have them whisked around the country on a bullet train so they could sample local specialties and give their opinions on live television. (After slurping down some noodles in their hometown of Nagoya, they gave the inevitable verdict: "Delicious!")

Aside from their longevity—and their good-natured compliance with the public demands made on them— Kin-san and Gin-san seemed a rather unremarkable pair. They were simply fortunate to have been in the vanguard, for by all indications they will soon be still more unre- markable. Already, Japan claims the world's largest pro- portion, if not outright number, of centenarians. As of September 1993, authorities counted 4,802 Japanese who were 100 years old or more.[16] The figure was up 16 per- cent from a year earlier. Like Kin-san and Gin-san, most were women. All this suggests that Japan is in for a sec- ond kind of inversion: Not only will those over sixty-five soon outnumber those under sixteen, but the super-old will begin to outstrip the merely aged.[17] Who will care for them? As we'll see, the traditional answer—their children—will not serve.

.   .   .

Japan's burgeoning population of old people is a testament to the hardiness of its prewar generation. These are the ones who suffered through the privations of war and the Herculean task of rebuilding afterward. But the causes of its shrinking supply of children are, as I have suggested, rooted in the growth-at-all-costs policy Japan developed after the war. To be sure, many factors come into play, not least of them education and urbanization. Still, it was bureau-industrial policy that made women entirely responsible for raising children, that removed the father from the home, that overcentralized the country and forced families to live in ever-smaller dwellings, and that created so arduous and costly an education system.[18] Polls show that women want to have more children, but the older ones feel they can't afford to, and the younger ones balk at the enormous burdens that come with the role of motherhood.[19] In short, the unintended effect of Japan's postwar economic policies has been to raise the toll of childbearing beyond many women's willingness to pay.

Of course, most Japanese women eventually do marry and have one or two children. But it will take more than that to maintain the population. Even postponing these steps into one's thirties and trying to maintain a career, as more are doing, raises complications. For much of this century, a woman's life was predictably phased: She would work, then quit to marry and raise children. During this period, even though she owed duties to her mother-in-law, she could generally count on help from her in raising the children. Later in life, she might return to work part-time but would certainly give priority to caring for the elderly members of her family. Now, however, the phases are oscillating wildly. Instead of receiving help with child rearing, many mothers find that the grandmothers of the family are working or caring for the

great-grandmothers. "In the past," says Japanese writer
Noriko Okifuji, whose own mother cared for her child
while she labored at her career, "grandmothers, who
could not work even if they wanted to, were supportive of
their working daughters. Lifestyles have now changed and
grandmothers and daughters have to face up to this."[20]

Indeed, the numbers of working women in their fifties
and early sixties have risen faster than any other category
in recent years.[21] Some women must attend simultane-
ously to the old and the young, even while they try to
keep up their jobs. Far from being complementary, each
role competes for the mother's attention, and each aggra-
vates her sense that her husband doesn't do his fair share.
The results, as we'll see, can be tragic: Some people grow
old secure in the knowledge that their children will look
after them, only to find themselves cast out in their dot-
age. But the implications for Japan as a whole are even
graver. The inability of women to fulfill all the roles demanded of them requires from Japan not reform but
transformation. It is, in many senses, a life-and-death
challenge.

RIDING THE ROLLER COASTER

*The new decade brought anxieties to me as well. I had
just left the familiar and congenial newsroom of the Japan Times for a berth in the Tokyo bureau of the Associated Press. As the new kid on the block, I was assigned
to cover Tokyo's stock market several days a week. For
years, this had been about as exciting as the community
calendar. Ever since its momentary plunge in the 1987
global crash, the market had ticked upward with plod-
ding regularity, so much so that it had become the*

world's richest market. But the moment I took the reins, the market went wild. One day it would swerve off a cliff and lose more than 1,000 points in a headlong plunge; the next day it would hurtle back. As days turned into months, however, the unmistakable trend was downward. By the time the first azalea buds unfurled, the mighty stock market had lost a quarter of its value and was on course to lose half before the year was out.

The AP normally turned out four stories a day on the Tokyo financial markets. Now the business desk in New York called incessantly, demanding sidebars, analyses, and, on especially volatile days, hour-by-hour accounts of trading. Knowing that literally trillions of dollars were at stake, I became engrossed in the work. It was a Big Story: There was real fear that a financial meltdown in Japan might cripple the world economy. At first, terror of making a mistake nearly overwhelmed me. My understanding of Japan, its language, and its markets remained imperfect, to put it mildly, and the combination of tight deadlines and a wild market kept the possibility of a spectacular error grimly near. But gradually, I caught on and gained confidence. Exciting jargon, like "dead-cat bounce," began to play on my lips.[22] What's more, though I made minor mistakes here and there, I was earning some of that gruff acknowledgment that passes for praise in one of the world's premier newsgathering agencies. It thrilled me.

I gave little thought to what was going on in my real life. Rumiko told me that her father was bedded down with a cold, and I planned to drop by and take him something, but somehow I hadn't. The office, the trains I rode to work, the very walls of our apartment came to look translucent and airy, as if I might reach out and pass my hand right through them. Only the news

seemed real. In my sleep, a noise like the clatter of an
old-fashioned teletype machine went constantly
through my head. I was obsessed.

Then, at last, reality swooped in and seized me in its
talons. It was late evening. I had just arrived and was
slurping down some Japanese noodles when the phone
rang. Rumiko answered. I could tell immediately from
her rough speech that it was family. Her tone, however,
seemed unusually strained. She sounded angry. Maya
woke up and began to bawl.

When I came back into the living room with Maya,
Rumiko was putting on her coat. "That was my sis," she
said tersely. "My mother is away at a conference, and
my father says he's feeling worse. I'll be back in a
while."

When she returned, an hour later, Rumiko looked
grim. "What is it?" I asked.

"I think he just wants attention," she said irritably.
"He's feeling sorry for himself because my mother went
away while he was sick."

Somehow, I was not relieved. She knew her father better than I did, of course, but this didn't sound quite
right. Papa had a farmer's indifference to pain. And he
was tough. I had once known him to drive all night from
Tokyo to his hometown on the Sea of Japan, then turn
around and drive back the next day, with only two
hours' rest. When we hiked in the mountains, his lame
leg must have troubled him, but he would not let me
carry his heavy camera bag, even when I tried to tug it
away from him. I had heard him complain about food,
about traffic, even about me, but never about pain or
illness. So I worried. And I thought Rumiko did, too.
Late that night, she unfolded a bit: "You know what he
told my sis? He said, 'This may be the end.'"

POLICY, POLICY, WHO'S GOT THE POLICY?

I don't mean to suggest that Japan is complacent about the aging problem. On the contrary, it is brimming with plans. Indeed, the aging question has reshaped Japan's entire social policy framework. The postwar development of Japan's pension and social security systems is too big a tangle to unravel here. However, a few points are worth noting.

In the past, the elderly were a peripheral concern; the government's main social policy objectives were to secure a healthy, educated, and compliant workforce. The welfare authorities put much effort into public health measures for mothers and children.[23] As Rumiko and I learned shortly after the birth of our daughter, every new mother in Japan gets a home visit from a social worker and free immunizations for her baby. True, the elderly ranked higher among welfare officials than the much-despised poor and handicapped, but recipients were so few and the benefits so low that they caused little drain.[24] In 1965, for example, with Japan's economy booming, the standard social security payment to retired couples was *nearly tripled*, but it still amounted to a measly 10,000 yen a month (then the equivalent of $28).[25] Granted, living standards in Japan were far lower at the time, but this was still less than a third of the average monthly Japanese wage. Japan could conceivably have paid out more; at the time, social security consumed just 6 percent of national income, but, believing the family could cope with its old, the government concentrated on economic growth.[26] Company pensions were no better: By tradition, they took the form of a modest lump-sum payment on retirement, which, in large companies, took place at age fifty-five.[27] Not surprisingly, most aged Japanese relied mainly on their children for support.[28]

Since then, public and private pensions have greatly improved. By the mid-eighties, Japan was spending roughly $200 billion a year in social security programs, equivalent to 14.6 percent of its national income.[29] The average social security payment to elderly couples rose to 195,000 yen (about $1,400) a month and was indexed for inflation.[30] Japan became the only country to set as a goal for its social security system to replace 68 percent of average male wages.[31] Meanwhile, private pensions in Japan drew nearer to Western ones in scope of coverage and benefits paid.[32] With that kind of support, and a lifetime savings rate of 20 percent, 85 percent of elderly Japanese reported little or no economic hardship in their lives during the 1980s.[33]

All the same, these programs were so new that neither the private nor the public sector had yet felt the pinch. As recently as 1988, only 9 percent of Japanese sixty-five or over were actually receiving monthly private pension benefits. (Most had been given a lump sum on retirement.)[34] This figure will change dramatically as people with vested annuity benefits retire.

Many experts have termed Japan's public pension system overcomplex and, in view of growing life spans, overgenerous. Unless trimmed, warned the OECD report, "these structurally high benefit levels would result in the loss of equity between the working generation and the retired generation, would increase contributions, and would thus impose a heavy burden on the generation supporting the system."[35]

As a result of reforms in the eighties, the system has been improved, but difficult adjustments lie ahead. Benefits will have to be scaled back to keep them at the already generous 68 percent rate. Worse, an intractable problem lies in the changing population structure: Unless the retirement age is redefined, early in the next century less than half of all Japanese will be of working age (twenty to fifty-nine).[36] The Ministry of Health and Welfare projects that the seven workers who were supporting each retiree in the eighties will dwindle to fewer than four by the turn of the century, and barely more than two by 2025.[37] In America, by contrast, there will still be 3.5 workers per retiree.[38] Weighed down by extraordinary social security costs, working-age Japanese may compound the problem by having still fewer children.

Foreseeing a tidal wave of demands on the treasury, the Takeshita government in 1989 broke its promise and instituted a 3 percent national sales tax to fund care for the elderly. The Ministry of Health and Welfare devised what it called a "Golden Plan" for the elderly. The plan calls for building 5,000 new nursing homes and 10,000 new outreach offices for the elderly, as well as tripling to 100,000 the number of nursing aides who call on the elderly in their homes. It is an ambitious plan but may be hard to fulfill, and inadequate even then. For one thing, recruiting young people to be nursing aides has proven difficult. And without a rise in the sales tax rate, the Finance Ministry says, there won't be enough money to care for the elderly.

The plan has to be ambitious because Japan is starting its run for high ground from a long way back. As late as 1986, its outlays for social security, as a proportion of national income, were roughly half those of European states such as Germany, France, and Great Britain, and also trailed those of the United States.[39] Even in the nineties, Japanese gerontologist Daisaku Maeda remarks, "Although respect for the elderly is still considered one of the essential virtues, social services for the elderly, which

are indispensable for their well-being, are much less developed than those in the developed countries of the
West."[40]

That Japan has barely begun to prepare for vast numbers of elderly citizens is plain even to the casual observer. Many elderly people, naturally enough, have
limited mobility. Yet to move through Japan's public
transportation system requires a vigorous athleticism:
It abounds in staircases, gates, fast-moving crowds, and
obstacles of every other kind. Most Japanese rail stations have only primitive arrangements for those whose
mobility is impaired: Not infrequently, the wheelchair-
bound must depend on a strong platform attendant to
carry them up and down stairs. To board most buses requires a good leap from ground level. Aural traffic signals
for the blind are common, but few sidewalks or buildings have ramps. Toilets for the handicapped are virtually unknown outside hospitals. Still, such things
are trifles compared with the problems they encounter
at their destination. For if there's one place elderly Japanese go more often than another, it is to the hospital,
and what they find there is truly dismaying.

HOSPITAL BOUND

*The day after Rumiko visited her father, he checked into
a large, university-affiliated hospital and began undergoing a battery of high-tech tests. A few days later, we
visited. The hospital managed somehow to be at once
vast and cramped. Narrow, ill-lit hallways twisted
through its bowels. Hollow-eyed patients in bathrobes
sat in little alcoves, smoking cigarettes. Doctors strode
past, managing like busy waiters to avoid everyone's eye.*

Papa was in a ward room with three other patients. The walls were a numbing shade of hospital green and the floor had been waxed so many times it squeaked underfoot. The furnishings were ancient and depressing. Papa's massive, railed bed, seemingly made of industrial piping, occupied most of the space allotted to him. From a U-shaped rail over the bed hung a curtain that afforded all the privacy he was allowed. A tiny bedside table was cluttered with medical paraphernalia. While Rumiko and her mother greeted him, I stepped outside the curtain to fetch one of the metal stools provided for visitors. A ventilator along the wall clanged mournfully. Above it were three large windows whose usefulness was almost completely obviated by the heavy wire grill that covered them. It looked very much like a prison.

But for all that, Papa did not look so bad. He sat up in bed and joked with us. He asked about my work, and was alarmed to hear that I had ridden my bike to the hospital. I told him that I had always biked to work in the States, and that riding in traffic was nothing new to me, but he remained anxious. Being a member of the first generation to own automobiles, Papa firmly believed in their use. He was one of the few Tokyo residents who spurned the trains and commuted to work in his own car, and though his lame leg gave him ample reason to do so, I had always felt that he actually enjoyed city driving. Since I had refused his strenuous efforts to buy me a car, the least I could do, he felt, was to take taxis. But, as always when I behaved strangely in his eyes, he gave it a moment's further thought and then his face crinkled in silvery laughter. That settled, he began to play with Maya, letting her grip his forefinger in her tiny hand.

I was relieved, and yet I thought I detected a shadow across his beaming face. He looked haggard and his color was grayish. But perhaps I was just rattled by his presence in these grim surroundings. He was just sixty-four. He hadn't even retired yet. It was far too early to dwell on the end.

Rumiko and her mother asked him how he was being treated. I noticed a sort of artificial quality in their voices. They spoke a little louder and a little more deliberately than usual. It puzzled me.

"Papa," Rumiko said, "did the doctors tell you when you can leave?"

Her father, still playing with the baby, said no, they still wanted to do more tests on him, but they thought it was some kind of intestinal disorder and that it shouldn't be too difficult to clear up. He complained about the tests. They kept pricking him with needles and X-raying him and turning him upside down.

I thought of my own experience of working in a hospital as a volunteer orderly many years before. My duties had consisted mainly of wheeling listless patients back and forth between their beds and the labs. I knew that in a big university hospital, with its whiz-bang equipment, eager young doctors could test a person half to death just to get machine-made proof of the obvious. I hoped they weren't doing a lot of unnecessary tests on Papa. If he did have an intestinal bug, surely the thing to do was get on with treatment.

At that point, a nurse came in with his dinner. She was almost painfully bright in her starched white uniform and Florence Nightingale cap. Her studied cheerfulness carried with it a surprising weight of authority. She was almost like a schoolteacher addressing first-graders. Tatsuko bowed repeatedly and thanked her with what seemed to me extravagant politeness. But I had not even begun to catch on to the politics of the Japanese hospital.

Taking some silent cue, we made our departure. As we left, everyone told Papa, "Gambatte ne," a highly variable phrase that in this instance meant "Hang in there." I glanced back to give him an encouraging nod, but I was the one encouraged. Eating his dinner, he looked very much the tough, durable man I had always thought him to be.

HEALTH NUTS

Japanese hospitals and clinics are under siege. Every morning, elderly patients struggle in by the millions. They fill the waiting rooms and line the halls. They rock slowly on wooden benches or smoke feverishly in the vestibules. They wait for hours for a few minutes with a tired, tense, and overworked physician.

There are just over 200,000 doctors in Japan.[41] That works out to a little more than 1.6 doctors per 1,000 population, far below the 2.3 doctors per 1,000 people in the United States and the average of 2.2 found in advanced industrialized countries.[42] But Japan's doctors make up for their relative scarcity in zeal: They lead all major countries in the number of patients they see. American doctors may seem quite busy, but Japanese physicians see 2.4 times as many patients a day.[43] Why so many visits to the doctor?

There may be some cultural differences at work. Elderly patients in Japan are especially inclined to make frequent visits to the doctor.[44] But the fundamental reason is economic. Supply and demand aside, physicians operating in Tokyo and other high-cost urban centers (where most of the doctors and patients are) labor at a disadvantage. As one study notes:

The fee-for-service system operates under a mi-
nutely defined price schedule set by the government. All providers are paid exactly the same
amount, inclusive of physician's fees, for the
same service regardless of the physician's expertise
or the facility's characteristics or geographical
location.[45]

To make up for this inequity, self-employed urban doctors have developed two strategies. The first is to work
excessively long hours and encourage frequent patient
visits. What the American physician treats in a single
visit may require three or four visits in Japan, each one
chargeable to the medical insurer. Thus, even in private
clinics, crowded waiting rooms and hurried encounters
with the doctor are the rule.

The second is to massively overprescribe. It is an unfortunate quirk of Japan that doctors dispense the medicines they prescribe. Profit motivates the doctor to
overprescribe; tradition induces the patient to unques-
tioningly follow his orders. Japanese patients typically
spend more than twice as much as Americans for pre-
scription drugs.[46] In all, one-third of Japan's medical expenditures go for prescribed drugs.[47] This amounts to big
money, making up as much as half of a doctor's income.
In 1990 alone, Japanese doctors pocketed an estimated
1.3 trillion yen ($10 billion) from what investigators
deemed to be unneeded prescriptions.[48]

Japanese medicines generally come in waxed-paper
packets without descriptions, warnings, or any information other than when to take them. A patient has virtually no way of knowing what he is taking. Fortunately,
the Japanese get less for their money. Doses are lower, so
as to minimize side effects, and more than a few prescrip-

tion drugs are mere "stomach settlers" and other virtual placebos. Nevertheless, problems do occur. Antibiotics are so wildly overprescribed—Japan leads the world in their use—that deadly new drug-resistant bacteria infest some hospitals.[49] Elderly patients are especially over-medicated: On average, they take several different pre-scription medicines at any given time, resulting in frequent drug interaction problems.[50] I made it a rule to throw away any medicine whose purpose I could not guess. Foolish, perhaps, but I survived. In 1993 fourteen elderly people died and more than twenty others were made seri-ously ill when a Ministry-approved antiviral medication was prescribed along with a cancer-fighting drug.[51]

I met many personable and highly competent doctors in Japan during my time there, some of whom prescribed no more than three drugs per visit. But I could not help be-ing frightened by how overworked they were. Seeing pa-tient after patient, perhaps twenty or more an hour in seemingly endless shifts, how could they humanly avoid making mistakes?

A friend of ours was a doctor who, lacking his own practice, worked in a large hospital. Although he was al-ready in his late thirties and the father of two children, he worked a schedule that would have daunted an ener-getic resident fresh out of medical school. In addition to frequent round-the-clock stretches at the hospital for his salary, he was compelled to do a couple of shifts most weekends at a local clinic related to the hospital *for free.* This was not punishment for some misdeed, but appar-ently part of the regular employment practices of the hos-pital. Once in a long while, when he had a free Sunday afternoon, we would get our families together for some fun, but he nearly always slipped away after the first hour to snooze. If that's how Japan keeps its medical costs down, I thought, give me good old Blue Cross/Blue Shield any day.

Though they lack a profit motive, Japanese nurses work as least as hard as doctors and, if anything, are in shorter supply. Since 1985, nurses' hours have been climbing inexorably. By 1991, they were working a forty-three hour workweek, plus ten and a half hours of overtime.[52] Worse yet, they faced a constantly rotating schedule that included an average of nine night shifts a month.[53]

Their workload is appalling. Japanese nurses have to care for three times as many patients on average as their American counterparts.[54] Compounding the shortage is the fact that Japanese nurses are woefully underpaid: A thirty-five-year-old nurse receives an average of 268,000 yen a month ($1,985), 15 percent less than a vocational school teacher of the same age.[55] So it comes as no surprise that recruitment of new nurses to ease the shortage has fared poorly.

Since 1990, nurses and other medical personnel have been staging annual one-day strikes in an attempt to reduce this burden. So far the strikes have proven futile. Japan refuses to admit foreign nurses, as some other countries have done, and would probably face serious problems integrating them into the Japanese medical system if it did.

Things are nearly as stressful on the patient's side. The Japanese may have great respect for *o-isha-san* (the honorable doctor) and for *kangofu-san* (the nurse), but there are emerging signs of discontent with the health-care system. In a six-nation study conducted by the Harvard Community Health Plan, only 16 percent of Japanese respondents were satisfied with the quality of their health care—far fewer than those in the United States, Canada, Britain, Sweden, and Germany, where between 45 and 55 percent of respondents expressed satisfaction.[56] But it appears that quality is not so much the problem as access. The waiting, often in cramped, uncomfortable areas, is especially tough on older patients, who are its most frequent users.

Of course, this may be regarded as a bit ungrateful. After all, the postwar Japanese health-care system has contributed much to the country's low infant mortality rate and somewhat to its world-beating longevity. Public health measures have practically wiped out tuberculosis, which used to be one of the top three killers in Japan.[57] True, quality problems remain, especially in the private practices handed down from father to son. (Entry to medical school by bribery is common practice for sons who are not quite up to scratch.)[58] The pell-mell rush to turn out more doctors (5,000 a year currently) may, in view of the shrinking base of youth, compound those problems in future. But the dictates of the Health Ministry, which circumscribe the physician's actions, keep most patients alive if somewhat woozy from drugs. And the system is relatively cheap: Japan's overall health bills amounted to just 6.8 percent of GNP in 1990, little more than half the U.S. proportion.[59] That works out to 175,000 yen ($1,300) per person in 1991—again, half the U.S. cost.[60]

Nevertheless, Japan led all major countries in real growth of per capita medical spending between 1970 and 1990, and though the rises slowed in the eighties, Japan's health expenditures are starting to mount rapidly as the proportion of its elderly grows.[61] That's because the elderly not only use the medical system more, but they have more costly ailments: chronic degenerative diseases such as cancer, and circulatory ailments that require expensive, high-tech treatments such as dialysis.[62] Japan's per capita medical costs for the elderly are more than four times the average patient's.[63] Already, the elderly soak up a third of the nation's medical expenditures.[64] How will Japan finance their medical care, as well as their social security?

But from a humane point of view, there is a more important question: How will a medical system that keeps doctors and nurses on the brink of exhaustion function at all when the proportion of elderly rises to a quarter of the population?

VOW OF SILENCE

I rode my bike home from the hospital. Rumiko, her mother, sister, and Maya took a cab. When I arrived at the house, they were deep in discussion. This was puzzling, but I patiently entertained Maya until they were done. Then Rumiko took me aside. Her eyes had narrowed in dull, defiant anger.

"He has cancer," she said flatly. "It's in several places. They are going to do radiation therapy, but the doctors are not hopeful."

"What!" I cried, feeling the blood drain from my face. "But he said they told him it was just an intestinal flare-up."

"That's right," Rumiko said, the defiance in her eyes glowing a bit stronger.

"But that's outrageous! How can they lie to him!"

"Look, you have to understand," Rumiko told me firmly. "That's the way it's done in Japan. The doctors think that if they tell him, he will collapse." She paused. "We have decided not to tell him either."

I stared at her with disbelief. In my most morbid fantasies, I have sometimes wondered how I would spend

*my last days if I knew I had a fatal disease. Many varia-
tions had played through my head: sailing around the
world, writing that great novel I'd always known lay
within me, settling scores with everyone who had ever
wronged me. I have even fantasized about blasting off
into space to wander among the stars. But never in all
my imaginings had it occurred to me that I might be
condemned without being told. That everyone would
pity me as I drifted along toward my doom still worrying
about next year's tax return, or pondering whether to invest my retirement fund in stocks or bonds. It was just
too monstrous to conceive.*

*"I know my father," Rumiko insisted. "He wouldn't be
able to deal with it. He has been feeling sorry for himself
until now, but since they told him it's not serious, he
feels much better."*

*That was true enough. And I was well aware that the
Japanese have a far stronger belief in the power of the
mind over the body than we Westerners do. I was even
vaguely aware that Japanese doctors usually spare their
patients bad news, especially news of cancer. Still, it
seemed outrageous to provide Papa with a false sense of
security. It would soon betray him, I said to myself, and
when he realized he'd been lied to, he was bound to
feel worse.*

*"What about the choices that will have to be made?"
I persisted. "If radiation doesn't work, chemotherapy
might be next. Are you going to put him through that
without telling him?"*

*"I don't know. We'll have to wait and see." Her eyes
were blazing now, and I realized that she was angry with
me for forcing her to defend her family's decision. Finally, I backed down and shut up. But not for good. I
could not let such a momentous—and to my mind,
wrongheaded—decision go unchallenged.*

Papa went through radiation therapy with no apparent benefit. The doctors concluded that his cancer had probably begun in his lungs, spread from there to his pancreas, and was now hacking its way through his spinal column and vitals. The situation was beyond all hope. At best, he had months to live. Throughout the weeks of radiation therapy, the doctors had continued to tell him that he was being tested, though it was incredible to me that anyone could believe such a thing. Now they stopped all treatment. This must have been a giveaway, for he was growing weaker, but whatever suspicions Papa may have had, he kept to himself. And we, his family, filled the silence with empty chatter.

DEATH'S SMOKING SCYTHE

My father-in-law's cancer was almost certainly touched off by his heavy smoking. Like most men of his generation, he regarded smoking as a privilege, a symbol of Japan's postwar prosperity. The habit existed in Japan before the war but was largely confined to the well off.

By the time Japan joined the club of wealthy nations in the mid-sixties, some 80 percent of Japanese men smoked. After three decades of tepid effort by the government to discourage smoking, Japanese men remain the heaviest smokers in the advanced world.[65] Even now, more than 60 percent of them smoke. There is little to discourage them from the habit. Nearly half of Japanese doctors smoke, a fact that has earned them a rebuke from the director of the World Health Organization, who is himself a Japanese.[66] Only 250 out of some 90,000 restaurants and bars in Tokyo have adopted partial or total bans on smoking.[67] The few establishments that have no-smoking sections don't seem to understand their purpose: In a Westernish "family" restaurant I visited in Tokyo with my asthmatic daughter, the no-smoking section consisted of a table in the center of the room, surrounded by fully occupied smokers' tables. Had this been an experiment on secondhand smoking, a team of scientists could not have better positioned us to sample everyone else's smoke. I called over the waiter and explained that we did not request a no-smoking table to discourage ourselves from bad habits, but to avoid breathing other people's smoke. He sucked his teeth thoughtfully and with profuse apologies informed us that it was a *shikata ga nai*—"nothing can be done"—kind of situation.

Why have official efforts to discourage smoking been so halfhearted?[68] The answer lies partly in cigarette taxes, from which the government derives a healthy revenue, and partly in the political clout of Japan Tobacco, which until recently was a government-run monopoly controlling the production and distribution of all tobacco products in Japan. As a privatized industry, it remains well connected and dominant. Thanks to Japan Tobacco, the warning labels on cigarette packs in Japan advise smokers not to smoke "too much." (As if by practicing a little *enryo* [restraint], smokers could remain safe.) Thanks to Japan Tobacco, a quarter-million corner tobacconist's shops are scattered throughout Japan, in addition to the countless cigarette vending machines accessible to children. And thanks to Japan Tobacco, the television airwaves are saturated with emotion-laden nighttime commercials for cigarettes, many of which are aimed at the only potential growth market left: young women.[69]

Fortunately, the proportion of women smokers appears to have leveled off at just over 13 percent.[70] Meanwhile, cancer is starting to exact a terrible toll on male smokers. "Of particular concern," says one report, "is the rising incidence of cancers associated with smoking, especially among males. In the seventy-five-and-over group, Japan has a higher death rate for cancers of the trachea, lung, and bronchus than do France or Sweden."[71] It's not easy to beat a Frenchman at vice—wine, women, and Gauloise cigarettes are his birthright—but the Japanese male appears to have done it. Add it all up and what you find is startling. While life expectancy for women in Japan is rising, men are slipping behind. Japanese women presently outlive their men by six years; now the gender divide is expanding as cancer begins to shear off the men who lived it up in salaryman style after the war. Already, cancer leads all killers in Japan and strikes down three men for every two women.[72]

Meanwhile, among Japanese women, the incidence of cancer is actually decreasing, probably because of a broad reduction in carcinogenic food intake.[73] Thus, in 1992, while the life expectancy for Japanese women rose yet again, to 82.22 years, that for men dropped slightly to 76.09.[74] Some experts predict that male life expectancy will rebound, but they may not be taking full account of the cancer threat. To the Ministry of Health and Welfare, however, the price of the salaryman lifestyle has at last become clear: It forecasts that nearly 70 percent of Japanese women now alive will live past their eightieth year, but says only 48 percent of Japanese men will make it that far.[75]

With all that cancer going around, you might expect the Japanese to have developed sophisticated social mechanisms for dealing with it. In fact, the opposite is true. An altogether primitive taboo lingers around the topic of cancer. The disease is traditionally regarded as "a polluting force leading inexorably to death," which is itself a taboo subject.[76] The behavior of my family was, it turned out, quite typical. Researchers have found that Japanese family members not only cooperate with doctors in withholding news of cancer from the patient, but suppress all expressions of concern.[77] Thus, the brittle, cheery conversations that dominated our visits to my father-in-law in the hospital. Little or no genuine emotion could be expressed, for to do so would be to acknowledge concern, and that might deflate the patient's spirits.

Naturally, there is a cultural argument to justify this practice. The importance of maintaining a strong *ki*, the Japanese concept of "spirit" or "life force," is often invoked as a reason to spare a patient bad news. I don't deny the significance of *ki*. Certainly, there is good evidence that the mind plays an important role in healing. That the mind does so when the patient can only suspect the nature of his condition seems more dubious. But one thing is clear. In an age when many cancers can be cured if promptly detected and treated, most Japanese want to be told if they have one. A government survey of 31,000 people found 58 percent would prefer to be told if they had cancer, compared with just 19 percent who would not.[78] In an experiment conducted at the National Cancer Center in Tokyo, a doctor told 110 patients the true nature of their conditions and later surveyed them to learn their reactions. Most said they preferred to know the truth, and fully 88 percent said they were soon able to recover from the shock of being told they had cancer and come to terms with the disease.[79] A quarter said they were relieved to have confirmation of what had merely been dark suspicions in their minds. This touches a point that other studies have raised: The charade that conceals cancer often requires the patient's cooperation. He cannot ask his doctor or his family a blunt question, for he

knows the pain it will cause them, even as they lie. So
he pretends to believe their reassurances and tries to ignore the screams of his body.

The novelist Shusaku Endo has written, among his
many wonderful stories, one about a middle-aged man
who, after three years as a cancer patient in a hospital,
asks his wife to buy him a mynah bird.[80] Visitors come
and go, chattering inanely of his imminent recovery,
while the bird remains his constant but strangely silent
companion. As the man is wheeled off for an operation
to remove his cancerous ribs, he whispers to the bird, his
only true confidant, "I want to live!" In the end, the mynah dies and he survives. The story is dense with meanings, not least of them a rich Christian symbolism, but
for me, having observed Papa hospitalized for many
months, it was enough to understand the desire for a
companion with whom he could freely communicate.

THE KNIVES WITHIN

*We continued to visit once or twice a week, but since
we could not discuss what concerned us most, as the
months passed our visits became more tense and artificial. Damming up such portentous information was
completely alien to me. I simply could not easily imagine the feelings of people for whom it was the wisest and
most natural course. Still, I knew the strain must be
enormous. And it would have been difficult in any case.
What can you say to the dying? How can you hope to
understand their rage?*

*I never had an easy time communicating with my
father-in-law, across the gulf of language, history, and
culture that divided us. Now I found it nearly impossi-*

ble. Rumiko and her mother and sister kept up a brave chatter, but to my ears it rang false, and it seemed to me that Papa paid less and less attention. One bit of real news that they shared with him was that Clay-san was changing jobs again—I had decided to leave the AP and become a correspondent for UPI. If there was one piece of information I was not eager for Papa to have, this was it: To a man who valued stability and perseverance, all my job-hopping might well look like flightiness. He hadn't much liked my switch to the AP, and that had been only months ago. But this time he just shrugged and told me to do my best.

Papa had always been thin. Now he grew skeletal. When he reached out an arm, bones and cords were all you could see. The flesh beneath his skin seemed to have melted away. His face had a high sheen. He had stopped shaving, and a little white beard grew on his chin, giving him the appearance of a storybook Oriental sage. But his heavy-lidded eyes were not at peace. They seemed to burn with anger.

It was not only the loss of freedom, or of cigarettes— he had been compelled to give up smoking at last—or of any other creature comfort that made him distant or irritable. His mind was turning inward, to the disease that was attacking him with a thousand knives and to the life he would soon be departing.

He had every right to turn away from us, I felt. No one around him—not the doctors, nor the nurses, nor his own family—would tell him what was happening. He was alone, facing the sternest challenge of his life. In that conspiracy of silence, what choice had he but to turn inward and listen to the counsel of his body and spirit? The only person who seemed to really cheer him up was Maya. Held aloft, she would reach out to him with a forefinger extended, and he would raise his bony forefinger and touch hers. They giggled together.

During this period, from time to time I tried to talk to Rumiko about reconsidering the doctors' advice. Generally, she sloughed me off. But now I had to speak my mind. Spring was here. The cherry trees were blossoming. Perhaps if he knew his condition, he would want to be taken out to see them. After all, what risk does a dying man run? Perhaps he would want to come home. Dying at home would be far more pleasant and dignified than dying in a ward that offered barely more privacy than the waiting room at Union Station.

I had been too cowardly to raise my concerns directly with Rumiko's mother or sister. The fear of saying something unforgivable simply overpowered me. Communication in Rumiko's family was rarely explicit, particularly on sensitive topics. I had not forgotten that she had never actually told her parents that we lived together until our wedding day, and even then, she just showed them our apartment. To raise an issue, so it seemed, was to risk everything.

But, in facing Rumiko, my conscience outweighed my fears. We sat on the **tatami** floor of our bedroom, leaning against opposite walls. I spoke awkwardly. I was trying to sound sympathetic rather than argumentative. I was also trying not to wake the baby. But evidently my case was failing. Rumiko faced me with lips pursed, arms crossed, and her dark eyes blazing. Feeling desperate, I said, "Look, I'm not trying to impose my will on your family. I'm just asking you to raise these questions. Talk to them. The doctor is doing what is easiest for himself. The worst thing will be if you just let him make the decision for you. You have to think about what is best for your father."

Rumiko stared at me for a moment and then shot

back: "Of course we are thinking about what is best for my father. We are thinking about it all the time. You don't know him as well as we do. For you, it would be easy to tell him. But it might make things worse."

I backed off, unconvinced but unable to see a way forward. A few days later, however, Rumiko and her family did take steps to make things better. Papa would not come home, but at least he would move to more congenial surroundings. On a bright May morning, Rumiko, her mother, her sister, and I all went to the hospital together. It was one of those false summer days that steal up on Tokyo before the cool, damp rainy season sets in. The air was warm and sweet. Schoolboys were playing baseball in a sandlot across the street. In Papa's room the windows had been opened. We could hear the clang of the aluminum bats and soft rustle of the blossoming magnolias in the courtyard.

Papa looked haggard. He no longer had any feeling below the waist. A catheter bag had been attached to him to prevent his wetting the bed. Walking was impossible. Above the waist, however, his feelings were all too acute. His cancer had been torturing him. Despite the regular massages he received from the nurses, the months of prostration in bed had caused sore spots to form on his body. Today, however, everything would change.

Rumiko's mother called to him.

"Papa. We're going to move to another hospital. You will be more comfortable there."

He nodded in acknowledgment, but seemed not much to care. I was glad she was doing this for him, but I still felt guilty he had not been told what was really going on. How much had he guessed? I wondered. White-coated attendants came in with a litter and gingerly hoisted him onto it. He was covered to the chin with a sheet and strapped down, like a partially exposed corpse. The nurses turned out in the hall to bow; with hands folded neatly below their waists, they wished him well. Rumiko and her mother thanked them profusely, bowing low with every step. Feeling dazed, I just mumbled "sorry" and nodded as I went. Strangely, a camera crew was in the hall, but they turned out to have nothing to do with us. Someone famous was checking in. The attendants wheeled the litter past them and out into the semicircular drive. There an ambulance stood waiting. As the litter was chuted inside, its wheels folded up like the carriage of a jetliner. The neat machinery of death.

We scooted in alongside Papa, and the attendant slammed the door behind us. As the ambulance pulled away, Papa raised his head and peered out toward the sandlot where the boys were playing. Then he looked searchingly at me. There was sheer terror in his eyes. I'm not clairvoyant. I'm not even particularly sensitive, but at that moment I seemed to read his mind with absolute clarity. He realized he was being taken away to die and wanted to know how long he had left. But he could not bring himself to ask. Until that moment, I suppose, he had clung to a sliver of hope that the doctors would find a way to turn the fatal tide. At least there had been a routine to his suffering. Now he looked like an innocent man being led to a firing squad. But he wasn't going to die just yet. In fact, he was on his way to the only retirement he would ever have.

CROSSING THE BAR[81]

One of the many canards about Japan is that Japanese men retire at the age of fifty-five. The impression it gives—of men stepping down from years of hard labor to

put on flowery shirts and hit the golf course—bends the
truth out of recognition. Until recently, it was true that
men in large companies were forced to relinquish their
positions at fifty-five, but that hardly meant the end of
their careers. A comparative study notes:

> Japan's mandatory retirement policies represent
> perhaps an extreme among the practices of industri-
> alized nations. . . . However, the mandatory retire-
> ment rules in Japan did not usually mean that these
> former employees would stop working; rather, it was
> a managerial device by which the privileged status
> of an employee . . . was brought to a formal end after
> many years of uninterrupted employment, often
> called lifetime employment.[82]

The reasons for this system are sometimes cast in lofty
cultural terms, but they are better explained by economics. A Japanese scholar observes:

> By age fifty or fifty-five, the employee's salary is
> often much higher than his productivity. Most
> employers want to replace overcompensated older
> workers with low-cost younger personnel.[83]

For the worker, what typically follows "lifetime" employment is retirement employment, at lower wages and
without security. In 1988 about 67 percent of Japanese
men in their early sixties held jobs, as did 55 percent of
those in their late sixties.[84] This was more than double
the rate of postretirement work in the United States.
Some employers rehire the employee they have just
forced to retire, on a temporary contract at a reduced salary.[85] Others place retired workers in jobs at affiliated
firms. Some employees are simply pensioned off with a

lump sum. Thus, the "retirement" system is anything
but that. Seen from afar, it resembles a redistribution of
labor down the slope of a stepped pyramid. At the top,
bureaucrats from Japan's powerful ministries retire into
cushy jobs at the companies they used to regulate. What
we term a revolving door is known there, somewhat
wryly, as *amakudari*, or "descent from heaven." Top executives often step into "advisory" positions with the
same company. At the next rung, executives "retire" into
jobs with affiliated firms and suppliers. This system not
only saves companies money, it goes a long way to explain the strength of *keiretsu* corporate groups whose
exclusionary dealings U.S. businesses find so noxious.[86]
In a country where business decisions hinge on personal
relations, to distribute loyal personnel throughout the
system clearly serves corporate interests. When Texas
oilman and investor T. Boone Pickens tried to claim a
spot on the board of Koito Corporation, Toyota's chief
supplier of headlights, he met with implacable resistance. Never mind that Pickens had become the firm's
largest shareholder, management's hearts remained loyal
to the company they had started out with: Toyota.

At the lowest wrung, some of the most arduous and
unpleasant jobs in society, such as cabdriving and toilet
cleaning, are performed in large part by elderly "retirees."
The motivation for this kind of postretirement employment is plain. True, the Japanese genuinely embrace the
work ethic. And, true, men who have known nothing but
hard work their whole lives may feel terror at the prospect of giving it up. "Many Japanese face a void in their
later years," observes the *Nikkei* newspaper. "For men,
the tradition of devoting their lives to their companies
limits contact with their communities and their families."[87] But at least four out of ten old men work to make

ends meet.[88] "Japanese people are not *born* hard work-ers," notes the *Japan Labor Bulletin*. "Surveys show that the desire for work derives to a certain degree from the economic needs."[89] As if to prove the point, as the bene-fits paid by social security and pensions rise, the percent-age of old men who work is steadily dropping.

At the same time, a wonderful unfurling is taking place in the vanguard. Japanese men who have accumu-lated enough savings and pension benefits to feel secure are actually retiring to devote themselves to leisure, self-development, and genuine social activity, untainted by the demands of commerce. They are joining recreational clubs and taking classes ranging from cooking to ball-room dancing. They are traveling. They are volunteering their help for social service agencies. One newly retired man even offered to sweep the streets of his community as a way to get involved in it after so many years of being absorbed in company life.[90] To put it baldly, the Japanese are doing the things that retired people everywhere do. This marks an enormous change of consciousness. Less than a decade ago, retired Japanese—those who were be-yond working—rarely ventured beyond the confines of home, except to visit the doctor. One comparative survey in the early eighties found the participation rate of re-tired Japanese in social gatherings was just 6 percent, as against 68 percent in America.[91]

This change has not been absorbed by those who run Japan. "Elderly Could Help Solve Labor Shortage," says the headline over a column in a Japanese newspaper.[92] "Some business leaders are even arguing that retirement benefits should be reduced to encourage people to keep working at advanced ages in an effort to solve the labor shortage," it says. The government comes at the problem from a different angle: It wants to solve the aging problem by pushing the retirement age up to seventy. Already, most companies have, at the insistence of the government, raised the age of retirement to sixty.

The idea of cutting retirement benefits to any marked degree is likely to face tremendous political resistance, since the pool of beneficiaries and soon-to-be beneficiaries is so large. On the other hand, business will only consider raising the retirement age past sixty after it has abolished the seniority-based wage scale (which served it so well when most Japanese were young). And some companies, facing losses in the recession, have actually lowered their mandatory retirement ages once again.[93] Meanwhile, true retirement is just catching on in Japan. In years to come, millions of Japanese with strong pensions, flush savings, and good health will voluntarily withdraw their services from the labor market to pursue leisure interests. Those other millions, like my unfortunate father-in-law, whose lifestyle has doomed them, will never make it to seventy. They will cost Japanese society dearly by their loss.

THE FINAL CURTAIN

We moved Papa to a Seventh-Day Adventist hospital. It may seem an odd choice for a Buddhist family, but as I soon realized, they could not have chosen a better place. Since Tatsuko, despite her daily attention to her husband, was still working full-time with her staff in her home, she could not have returned him there. On the other hand, to have left him at the university hospital would have been a waste of medical facilities and an assault on his human dignity. And despite all the deception and high-tech manhandling she had allowed him to endure while some hope remained, songenshi, *"a* death with dignity," was what Tatsuko most wanted for her husband now.

Like most Japanese, then, he would die in a hospital, but at least this one was closer to being a hospice than most.[94] The Seventh-Day Adventists gave him no jolts of radiation. Instead, he received massive doses of loving attention. Doctors would speak in a soft and comforting way, unlike the often abrupt and mechanical physicians we had met elsewhere. Nurses would come in to mop his brow with a cool cloth. Staff and volunteers would gather in the hall to sing hymns to the patients.

However, he still was in a ward room swathed in beige curtains. After a few days, Tatsuko had her husband moved into a private room. It cost a fortune—nearly $200 a day for the room itself—but it was a supreme kindness. At last, Papa had a measure of privacy and a window he could look out of. He seemed more at peace for a while.

Then, like a black mist rising, the disease engulfed him. He spent much of the day writhing in agony, screaming and clutching at the monsters within. When these fits passed, he'd look about in a daze and mumble. By now it was summer. As these half-lucid moments became fewer and fewer, I felt sure the end was near. At last, he lost awareness of anyone around him—indeed, of anything but his pain. He would reach out a clawlike hand, then throw his arm across his face as if to ward off a blow. At other times, he would suddenly sit up and scream, the cords of his neck as taut as piano wire. The hospital staff gently suggested moving him back to the ward room.

So there he lay, surrounded by beige curtains. One bag, suspended on a pole above his head, dripped sustenance into his body through a tube stuck into his arm. Another bag, slung under his bed, collected waste from

*a tube in his groin. Between them, his existence seemed
no more than a stream of agony. Tatsuko, a lifelong Buddhist, took to visiting the Christian chapel next door.*

*Then, as summer tilted toward fall, a small miracle
occurred. One afternoon, we all came to visit, bringing
Maya with us. She had begun to rebel against these visits, and I had some misgivings about bringing her. Was
it right to expose a small child to such a horrifying spec-
tacle? But thinking it might truly be the last time, I persuaded Maya to go in. Papa was in deep slumber.
Suddenly, Maya scampered off through the curtain into
the next chamber. Rumiko called out in a hoarse whis-
per, "Maya! Oide!" ("Come!") Maya just giggled. Giving
chase, I scooped her up and on returning saw, to my astonishment, that Papa was sitting up, clear-eyed and
smiling.*

*"Maya-chan," he called in a papery voice, and beck-
oned to her. Grinning, she went over and mischievously
pointed a forefinger at him. His mind was clear, his body
evidently free of pain. It was one of those mysterious
remissions that cancer patients sometimes have. He sat
up and chatted pleasantly with everyone for a while,
then went back to sleep.*

A few days later, on September 30, 1990, he died.

YOU CAN'T GO HOME AGAIN

The early death of a family member is always hard to
bear. Still, it rarely has importance for those outside the
dead person's immediate circle of family, friends, and coworkers. That was the case with my father-in-law. Not
being a man of great prominence, he lies mostly unre-
membered save by his family and friends.

And yet, his death has great significance for Japan, I believe. For although Papa was in many ways an extraordinarily good, generous, and broad-minded man, the ordinariness of his demise should sound a warning to the nation. It must face grim facts and take difficult steps. The combination of tremendously long life for women and premature death for many men confronts Japan with a multihorned dilemma. Women want to work and will be needed in the workforce, particularly as Japan's population growth shifts into reverse. With so many expected to live for thirty or forty years beyond retirement, it is inconceivable that they will be cared for primarily by the younger women in their families. The extremely old often have complex medical, dietary, and therapeutic needs. They frequently require trained attendants. The trend away from family care is already clear. A few decades ago, more than 80 percent of elderly Japanese lived with their children; now the proportion has fallen below 60 percent and is ticking downward by about one percentage point a year.[95] As a result, slightly more than 10 percent of Japanese households are now composed of elderly people, many of them widows living alone.[96]

I do not mean to suggest that filial piety has altogether evaporated in Japan. My wife's grandmothers, for example, are both in their nineties and both are attended by Rumiko's aunts and assorted relatives. Still, an underground current of resentment flows between the generations in Japan.[97] Gerontologist Daisaku Maeda writes, "The Japanese tradition of family care for aged parents cannot avoid a considerable degree of weakening, if it is not to be totally lost."[98] Occasionally a mother-in-law, whose power has weakened with age and the withering of tradition, faces abuse at the hands of her vengeful daughter-in-law.[99] In the extreme, a few greedy children,

exasperated by the remarkable longevity of Japanese widows, have committed murder to get their hands on valuable property.

Not all the victims are women, of course. I came
across a particularly sad case when I went to interview
patients at a day-care facility for the elderly in Tokyo.
The Kosai Care Center was a cheerful sort of place with
an attentive staff and numerous activities. The patients
themselves appeared far from cheerful, however. I
watched them struggle through a round of mild calisthenics. They sat in chairs, raising one foot and then the
other, making a sound like the clopping of a tired milk-
wagon horse on a cobblestone street. Their bodies were
twisted, their skin spotted. Some appeared to have the
frost of death across their faces. No one smiled.

Yet they were pleased to be at the center; their sorrows
lay elsewhere. Demand was so great that services had to
be rationed. Old people could come only two or three
days a week. Shunichi Masami had a particularly com-
pelling need for the center's warmth. At seventy-five, he
seemed comparatively youthful and fit, though I soon
learned that he was suffering from diabetes. But his physical distress was nothing compared with the ache in his
soul.

Masami sat down and in a hoarse, flat voice told me
his story. It seemed that for many years he had operated
an inn with his wife. Five years earlier, she had died. It
was a devastating blow. He could not get over his grief.
His health suffered, and on his doctor's advice he went to
stay with a friend in a small town by the sea while he
recovered. He left the inn in the keeping of his only
daughter and her husband. After some months he returned, only to find that the inn had been converted into
a girl's dormitory and, worse, that his daughter had removed him from the family registry. In effect, she had

disowned him. He was brusquely turned away from his
own door. Alone, he took a small apartment near the care
center, which became his lifeline.

"If I didn't come here, I wouldn't have anyone to talk
to at all," he told me. "That's like being in solitary con-
finement in a prison."

But only two days a week at the drop-in center left him
an awful lot of time for private misery. He said he might
commit suicide if it were not for the thought of what
would follow his death.

"A person never comes into the world alone," he told
me. "So when someone dies, his passing should be hon-
ored by someone. But a person like me has no one to celebrate his life or to mourn his passing when he dies. It
will be like the death of a tree or a blade of grass."

If institutions are to take up the slack left by the loosening of family ties, there is enormous work to be done.
Only about 1.5 percent of Japan's elderly are accommodated in nursing homes, far below the U.S. proportion of
5 percent. However, three or four times as many Japanese
are bedded down in hospitals as in nursing homes.[100]
Taken together, the proportion of elderly Japanese in institutions is about the same as in the United States, but
their arrangement is quite different.[101] Some argue that
this disparity results from the shame that Japanese children feel in placing their parents in nursing homes.[102] A
hospital, by contrast, offers medical justification for giving over the care of one's parents to strangers. There are
other reasons why nursing homes are unpopular in Japan:
The admission fee to a private facility can swallow up life
savings (unlike hospitalization, which is largely covered
by insurance). Also, nursing home patients tend to be
bedded down or locked up. Thirty-four percent of the elderly in Japanese nursing homes are bedridden, compared

with just 6.5 percent in U.S. nursing homes.[103] Half of all senile patients are kept under lock and key.

In any event, hospitals clearly remain the first choice of the elderly who need care. Many of Japan's 9,500 hospitals and its 27,000 doctor-owned clinics with inpatient facilities are already performing the function of nursing homes: Nearly 85 percent of their beds are occupied.[104] And with bedridden Japanese expected to top a million before long, the number of geriatric hospitals in Japan leaped by nearly 40 percent between 1987 and 1991 to more than 1,100.[105]

The Japanese preference for hospitalization causes a far greater drain on national resources, both financial and medical. If the elderly are not to be abandoned, and society is not to be bankrupted, nursing homes and day-care centers will simply have to become a way of life in Japan. Children cannot or will not continue to care for them as they did in the past.

THAT GOOD NIGHT

Papa's funeral was a solemn, gorgeous, and even touching affair, but it kept emotion thoroughly muffled. My earlier exposure to the rather dry religion of Japan had led me to prepare in my own way. I was determined not to let the occasion pass without saying farewell.

I found my chance the night before the funeral, during the wake. It took place in a small chapel attached to the Buddhist temple where the service was to be conducted. Papa's body, encased in a simple wooden casket, lay out of sight behind a cascade of flowers. In the middle of the wreaths was a black-bordered photo of him. Shot in black-and-white, the photo formed a dark, dismal cloud amid the profusion of flowers. Papa appeared in it un-smiling, dignified, and purposeful.

Rumiko, her mother, her sister, and I sat on folding chairs on one side of the tiny chapel. I wore the black suit I had bought months earlier in anticipation of the occasion. The women were in black dresses. As family members, we had each been given an artificial flower, white with black ribbons, to wear as a badge of mourning. Before us, on a small wooden altar, an iron brazier burned. Next to it was a box of some sort of woody incense, like pencil shavings.

A Buddhist priest in fantastic robes of purple, white, and gold came in. He took a pinch of the incense, genuflected with it in the direction of the photo, and then sprinkled it over the brazier. Kneeling, he began to chant—a deep, melodious, and soothing chant. Beginning with Tatsuko, each of us in turn rose and placed a pinch of incense on the brazier.

Then came a long line of mourners: friends of ours, friends of Papa's, executives from his company, and laborers too, some still in their muddy, cleft-toed boots and pale-green uniforms. Each performed exactly the same ritual. Crossing the threshold, they would bow to us. From our seats, we would bow in return. Then the mourner would step forward, place a pinch of incense on the burner, and step out. The executives, however, stayed. Having a claim almost as great as that of the family, they sat opposite us in fold-up chairs along the far wall and bowed solemnly to each subsequent mourner.

I was pleased to see so many people come to honor my wife's father, but the ritual soon became tedious. There were no tears, no personal expressions of comfort or grief, no words at all except a few formal condolences.

At last, the line petered out. Rumiko and her family

*got up and went to stretch their legs. Peering around to
be sure I was alone, I rose and pulled from my leather
shoulder bag—a gift from Papa—the book I had bought
earlier that day. Taking a deep breath, I began to read
from a poem that had come drifting back to me months
before as I watched Papa grapple with death. It was
Dylan Thomas's ode to his own father: "Do Not Go Gentle into That Good Night." The words, sublime when
penned by Thomas just two years before his own death,
fell hoarsely from my lips. It didn't matter. I had not intended for anyone else to hear them. But when I finished, I saw Tatsuko standing there. Brimming with
tears, I impulsively pushed the book into her hands.*

*"Kore agemasu," I said hoarsely. ("I give this.") She
looked puzzled. God knows what she thought I was doing. Casting spells, for all she knew. I wanted to explain,
but I could not find any other words to speak at that
moment. I went out into the night alone and wandered
through the temple yard, among the huddled graves that
would soon have to make room for one more.*

*A few years later, Tatsuko published a memoir of the
months she had spent caring for her husband as he died.
Browsing through it, I was pleasantly surprised to find
she had reprinted Thomas's poem. It was, after all, a fitting elegy.*

COMING OF AGE

To care for its masses of aged and dying, Japan will need
to make a massive reallocation of its most precious re-
source: labor. Japan's economy has been gradually shifting
from manufacturing toward services for some years, but
the rapid change in population will require far greater

shifts. The Ministry of Health and Welfare's plan to triple the number of nursing aides to 100,000 by the end of the century hardly seems adequate. There are more than 16 million old people in Japan. Little more than half live with their children. Only about 5 percent reside in nursing homes or hospitals. That leaves about 5 million elderly on their own, and the number is rising swiftly every year. Can a nursing aide visit fifty people a day?

Moreover, the Japanese government, aware of the financial burdens it faces, wants to increase the numbers of elderly living on their own. The Golden Plan itself calls for shifting care from hospitals to homes. But the plan appears optimistic, to say the least. To treat those suffering from debilitating ailments such as Alzheimer's disease, round-the-clock emergency facilities are to be set up with *two nurses* for every 2,100 old people.[106] Recognizing the disproportion, the plan calls for eight "volunteers" to supplement the nurses' efforts to deal with this phenomenal patient load.

Self-reliance is a great thing, and the Japanese have an abiding faith in it, but it only works for the old while they are healthy. Even now, nearly 5 percent of the Japanese elderly are bedridden.[107] This proportion seems likely to grow. As we've seen, Japanese men are prone to degenerative disease, while women, though they may live longer, may become quite frail once they move beyond mere old age into superannuation. Most older Japanese shun dairy products, and their low-calcium diet makes them vulnerable to bone loss. Old women bent over like question marks are a sad but common sight in Japan.

The precise solution to these problems may be uncertain, but one thing is sure: Japan cannot forsake its old. Many cultural precepts have been manufactured for the Japanese by self-serving rulers. But if there's one genuine and strongly felt cultural belief in Japan, it is respect for the elderly. And however much private morality may stray from the ideal, public opinion remains a powerful ally of the elderly. A few official experiments in pragmatism have proven that.

The most infamous of these was the "Silver Colonies" program proposed by the Ministry of International Trade and Industry in 1986. Taking account of the high cost of land and personnel in Japan, and the superior climates available abroad in places like Spain and Australia, MITI proposed to export elderly Japanese to overseas retirement communities. Among the many advantages of this proposal, it said, was that doing so would help reduce Japan's pesky trade surplus.[108] What MITI failed to consider, of course, was that no matter how attractive some foreign climes might be, most people want to die on their native soil. Public outcry soon put a damper on the idea of shipping the elderly abroad.

Such callous behavior is to be expected of entrenched bureaucracies. But politicians know they can't afford to ignore the elderly, and scholars generally agree that on the whole the Japanese government has responded to the needs of the aging over the last two decades.[109] Henceforth, it is bound to be even more responsive. In a democracy, especially one grappling with the unaccustomed phenomenon of shifting parties in power, no politician can afford to slight what is potentially the largest single bloc of voters: the elderly. Indeed, in the historic election of 1993, with every candidate stumping on the issue of political reform, voters took a different view of the nation's priorities. Medical, welfare, and pension issues topped their list of concerns, outdistancing such pressing matters as economic policy, political change, and tax reductions.[110] Within half a year, the Hosokawa government proposed to more than double the national sales tax to 7 percent and rename it the "welfare tax." Before long, a government task force was recommending a 10 percent welfare tax.

In short, Japan has no choice but to radically alter course. Though it may blunt its industrial edge, Japan must become a social-welfare superpower. That is its self-constructed destiny.

6
OUT OF THE CAGE

In the months that followed Papa's death, we grew increasingly hungry for a change. I loved my work; the combination of reporting for UPI and NPR made me sizzle with excitement. (Mikhail Gorbachev came to town just as I was thinking of quitting.) But I was weary of the daily frustrations of life in Tokyo: the crowds, the smoke, the insincere declarations of sincerity, the mother-henning loudspeakers that pop up everywhere and blare at everyone. The strain was making me snarl at perfectly nice Japanese, like my wife. I wanted to get out before, as my friend Carl put it, I began to daydream about packing a .45 in my lunch pail.

Rumiko was at last approaching the end of her dissertation. She hoped to begin a new career in academics. But it had long since become apparent that Japan held no such opportunities for her. Not only was she a woman in a field dominated by men, not only was she earning a Ph.D. from a foreign institution, but she lacked the one indispensable achievement needed to gain entrée to the Japanese academic community: She had not completed a postdoctoral apprenticeship with a

Japanese professor. In the cloistered world of Japanese scholarship, earning a doctorate is a first step; earning a professorship requires years of bonding. So Rumiko, too, was eager to get out of Japan.

Then there was Maya. She was flourishing in the public nursery near our apartment. We had been extremely lucky, we knew, in getting her admitted to one so close to our home. Many of our friends had to travel miles to and from the day-care centers assigned by the city. We were even more fortunate that Maya, though plainly not of pure Japanese blood, hadn't been harassed by teachers or students the way so many foreign or mixed children in the Japanese school system were. In fact, Maya, a bright and cheerful child, if I say so myself, had become something of a favorite in the nursery. All the same, the head teacher warned us against placing her in public school: "We like her, but this is just a nursery. She's too independent, too questioning to get along in a regular school." We got the point. Public nurseries are governed by the Ministry of Health and Welfare, and as such have no curricula. They are expressly noneducational institutions. But the public schools fall under the jurisdiction of the arch-conservative Education Ministry. I had interviewed an Education Ministry bureaucrat who freely admitted that Japan's education system was designed to turn out good, compliant workers. We had seen the uniformed kindergartners in our neighborhood marching about the yard, shouting in unison like a squad of tiny soldiers. It was one more signal that we ought to be moving on.

But we worried about Rumiko's mother. Since the death of Papa, she had seemed frail, at times dazed. A temporary altar had been set up in the living room where we had spent so many cozy Sunday evenings together. That stark black-and-white portrait stared out at

us whenever we entered the room, softened only by a
flock of cotton angels Tatsuko had arranged about it.

She spent most of her time dealing with the practical
remnants of his death: the permanent tombstone to hold
his ashes, the settlement of his estate, inheritance taxes,
and a hundred other details great and small. There was
also money to be worried about. We had no idea how
she stood financially, but we feared the worst. The expenses of the last year must have been shattering. There
were the months that Papa spent in a private room at
the Seventh-Day Adventist hospital. At nearly $200 a
day, the bill must have been enormous. Then there was
the funeral. Like living, dying in Japan is a costly affair.
Funerals cost an average of 2.1 million yen (about
$20,000).[1] But that's just the beginning. The purchase of
a gravesite in crowded Tokyo ranges from $40,000 to
nearly $90,000. It might have been cheaper to place
Papa's cremated remains in one of the new multistory
bone lockers entrepreneurs have developed, but Tatsuko
didn't want that sort of thing. Though a modernist in
many ways, she was a traditionalist about death. After
a lengthy search, she bought a gravesite in a Buddhist
temple near her home and commissioned a large black-
granite tombstone to be erected. With its squared-off
obelisk, it stood nearly as tall as the man whose ashes
it contained. The boxlike base had a compartment into
which the urn containing Papa's remains was placed. In
the front were a chamber for incense-burning and two
holes that served as vases for flowers. We all attended a
ceremony at the temple in which an aged priest chanted
the sutras, punctuating his words by striking a bowl-
shaped gong that sat on a velvet cushion before him.
Then he formally announced the posthumous name
given to Papa.

This Buddhist custom, as incomprehensible to me as

the name itself, seemed to settle things for Tatsuko. Gradually, she began to live for herself again. She re- tired, a step we all welcomed, though we knew she would never give up work altogether. And she assured us that money would not be a problem for her; she had a pension of her own, as well as savings and other income.

So, in the spring of 1991, we decided to leave Japan. Rumiko got a job offer from the University of Michigan's College of Architecture and Urban Planning. For my part, I resolved to write the book I had been contemplat- ing for more than a year. We sold off everything we could not pack, and on July 8, 1991, flew back to the United States with a great sense of impending renewal. Rumiko was excited about embarking on her academic career. Maya, then two, burbled happily about seeing her Amer- ican grandparents again. And I? I daydreamed about seeing my book on bookstore shelves early the next year. We all suffer delusions of grandeur now and then.

THE POWER OF THE MAGI

Three years later, the signs of a grassroots revolution, of citizen power overcoming arbitrary authority, continue to sprout all over Japan. In Tokyo, some parents sued a pub- lic school in Tokyo for requiring boys to crop their hair like convicts. In 1993, they won. This prompted the school board in a neighboring province to reverse itself and abolish the haircut rule in all its schools. What began as public protest over the Kanemaru scandal has now shattered Japan's political structure into smithereens.

But before uncorking the champagne, we must ac- knowledge that the system remains deeply rooted. Since the arrival of Commodore Perry's Black Ships a century and a half ago, Japan's rulers have frequently seized on any formal ideology that would create an "us against them" mentality to bind the people together under their command. The central manifesto of Japan's militarist era was full of sentiments such as: "The Way of the subjects exists where the entire nation serves the Emperor united in mind," and "We subjects are intrinsically quite different from the so-called citizens of Occidental countries."[2]

Of course, racism was even more of a global plague then, and fascism was hardly confined to the East. But it is disturbing to find echoes of this ideology in the *nihonjin-ron*, or "theory of the Japanese people" of contemporary Japan. In search of "pure Japanese spirit," this body of thought has ranged over an enormous variety of topics, including the "Japanese" nose. In the view of sociologist Kosaku Yoshino, however, the central aim of *nihonjin-ron* was to revalidate the "family-nation" myth so important to prewar fascists.[3] Yoshino contends *nihonjin-ron* borrowed freely from the same Nazi racial theories that bolstered the prewar regime. The results are often just silly: No foreigner could write a really good Japanese poem, one such theory asserts, because foreigners lack "Japanese" blood. But true to its Nazi parentage, the rise of *nihonjin-ron* has been accompanied by a barrage of vicious anti-Jewish tracts, some of which have turned into best-sellers.[4] These diatribes receive tacit support from the establishment. Major newspapers carry ads for them without comment. Few if any Japanese historians publicly dispute their wild claims. The reason seems obvious: Such scapegoating deflects heat away from the system.

Policy, history, and the like may be debated, but the *nihonjin-ron* notion of the pure Japanese is demonstrably a myth. Examine the faces of any roomful of Japanese and you can see that they are compounded of many peoples. But that hasn't stopped Japanese politicians from making ample use of *nihonjin-ron* at home and abroad. Most infamously, Prime Minister Yasuhiro Nakasone told his countrymen that they were winning the fight for economic supremacy because unlike America, which was weighed down by "inferior" minorities, Japan was a pure-race nation.

So has the shadow of the Black Ships passed from Japanese consciousness? Not quite. Many Japanese still feel clannish, threatened, and ill at ease with foreigners, though to be sure this is far more true of the elderly than the young.[5] What's more, the brainwashing continues. In 1993, 140 years after Perry's arrival, Apple Corporation and other U.S. personal computer makers finally began to make inroads into the Japanese market. Responding to the "crisis," a Japanese computer magazine urged its readers to be "patriotic PC users" and buy from Japan's NEC, which still held about half the domestic PC market. To seal the argument, it likened the invading American computers to—what else?—the Black Ships.[6]

THE ROAD LESS TRAVELED BY

A widow's life does not bring to mind images of happiness.[7] But while Tatsuko continued to miss Ichio and to behave as if his spirit were hovering nearby (she set out a tiny bowl of rice for him at every meal), her life in some ways became more fulfilling than ever. After ten years of publishing her magazine, lecturing at universities, and leading social-change groups of various kinds, she suddenly found herself in the floodlights of public recognition. Every major newspaper ran a profile of her, and when we returned to Japan for a working visit the following summer, we found a television crew in her living room, conducting an interview.

Tatsuko continued to lecture, both at her regular post at the Japan Women's University and as a guest speaker at forums all across the country. However, work was not her only pursuit. She astonished us by announcing her intention to join in a camel caravan across the remote deserts of China to retrace the Silk Road that in centuries past had joined Asia and Europe. This was a woman well past her sixtieth birthday, a woman who, just a few years earlier, had been so afflicted by arthritis she could barely climb a staircase. The trek across arid and uninhabited badlands would take a month. We implored her to reconsider. China was unstable, we insisted, and the back roads were probably full of bandits. Besides, I told her, the camel is perhaps the world's most unpleasant form of transportation. Judging from my experience as a boy in Egypt, I said, a camel actually has a worse temper than a New York City cabbie, spits more, and gives a rougher ride. But she would not be dissuaded. Cured of her arthritis by acupuncture and injections of gold, she would not let any talk of danger or discomfort prevent her from seeing the Silk Road. When she began to train by climbing mountains, we gave up.

October of 1992 rolled around. By then, we had moved to the high plains of Texas. Rumiko had been made an assistant professor at Texas Tech University, while I obtained a sinecure as a research associate in the university's fledgling Asian studies program.[8] Fingers of frost had begun to cling to the rugged plains of Texas, and a spiteful, moaning wind kicked up vast clouds of dust. Just the kind of weather we imagined must be afflicting

*the outer reaches of China. We had no word from Tat-
suko; she was probably a thousand miles from any post
office. We feared we might not see her again. Coming
just two years after the death of Rumiko's father, it was
a dreadful thought.*

*After weeks of worry, a letter finally arrived. Tatsuko
had returned to Tokyo in triumph. The journey had been
a success in every way, as we later saw for ourselves. A
documentary filmmaker who accompanied them had recorded sights that must have been unchanged for centuries: villages where Islam had long ago made inroads
into China, causing the street signs to be written in Ara-
bic and the women to wear veils; Aladdin-like castles
carved into cliff sides; vast stretches of rocky desert,
where the wind whistled through the bones of animals
that had died on earlier crossings; and finally, rising out
of the desert floor with fearsome majesty, the snowy
mountains that divide China from Pakistan. It was a
stunning accomplishment. And far from bridling at the
discomfort of sleeping in tents, relying on nature's sani-
tary facilities, and spending most of her days topside on
a lurching desert cruiser, Tatsuko had reveled in it all.
She positively adored her camel.*

*In May, we returned once again to Japan. It was 1993. A
little more than a year before, President Bush attempted
his own Black Ships sortie, descending on Tokyo with a
phalanx of U.S. auto executives. But unlike Commodore
Perry, Bush could not make the Japanese quail. The victor of the Gulf war found himself on the most humiliat-
ing mission ever carried out by a chief executive of the
United States. Bush practically begged for business,
and compounding his misfortune, he vomited, then
swooned, into the lap of Prime Minister Miyazawa.*

About the same time, Rising Sun, *a best-selling novel*

by Michael Crichton, hit the bookstalls with a vivid por-
trayal of Japan the Juggernaut careering across Ameri-
ca's body, personified by a dead woman. In the ensuing
climate, no American publisher had been willing to
touch my book.

"The change you're talking about may be true, but it
will take years, maybe a generation," one publisher
explained as I silently strangled my telephone. "People
don't think that far ahead."

What a difference a year makes. By the time I re-
turned to Japan, Bush was gone and Bill Clinton was
president. I had secured a publisher. Japan had gone into
an economic seizure. Large companies were cutting bo-
nuses and, whether they admitted it or not, laying off
workers. Small companies, pressed beyond endurance
by their large partners, were hurtling into bankruptcy
like buttons popping off a fat man's vest. But all this
was nothing compared with the spasm of political
change that would convulse Japan over the summers
to come.

HOW SHARPER THAN A LAWYER'S TOOTH

Ideology is hardly Japan's sole instrument of control. Although the Japanese are frequently labeled apathetic and
passive, ideology alone has never been sufficient to keep
them in check. Before the war, the state used secret police, neighborhood control groups, and the military itself
to preserve "order." Despite all that, the Japanese people
at times pressed hard for real democracy. In 1913 they
demonstrated their will in what came to be known as the
"Taisho Political Crisis." When the Imperial Army tried
to assert control over the cabinet, thousands of angry citizens stormed the Diet building, set fire to police stations,

and so rattled the army-backed government that it fell. Eventually, of course, the army regrouped and, by assassination and intimidation, sealed its control of the nation in the thirties.

After the war, with the military disbanded and the Americans looking on, it was no longer possible for the authorities to rely on blatant oppression. What's more, Japan's leaders were stuck with constitutional guarantees of popular sovereignty and basic human rights. All the same, they were not prepared to relinquish control. Intimidation remained an important method of dealing with anyone who threatened the existing order.

Despite its much-ballyhooed "nuclear allergy," for example, Japan embarked on a nuclear power program that involves shipping plutonium, the world's most dangerous substance, across the high seas and using it for a breeder reactor—one that creates more nuclear fuel than it consumes.[9] This prompted a grassroots opposition campaign, backed, to be sure, by the Socialists, but conducted for the most part by ordinary citizens. How the establishment responded is instructive. In 1991 Yui Kimura, a thirty-eight-year-old housewife, and a handful of her antinuclear friends bought shares in the Tokyo Electric Power Company, Japan's largest electric utility and the company that stands to benefit most from the government's breeder reactor. They attended TEPCO's annual shareholders' meeting with the intention of asking many awkward questions and filing a motion to end the company's reliance on nuclear power. Instead, they found themselves set upon by fifty fellow "shareholders"— goons, in reality—who beat the living daylights out of them under management's approving eyes. One victim needed stitches afterward. Mrs. Kimura got away with bruises. When I later interviewed her, she told me she was convinced that the thugs had been hired by management. TEPCO denied this, of course, and nothing can be proved against it. However, it is rather difficult to believe that ordinary shareholders would have been so outraged by the antinuclear group as to beat them up. In any event, the practice of either paying off gangster shareholders or employing them to silence opponents has become quite commonplace in Japanese business.[10]

In a country that boasts of having just one lawyer for every 9,000 citizens (compared with one for every 321 Americans), the job of preserving *wa* often falls to gangsters. They settle traffic disputes, shareholder complaints, and a whole lot more. In the years that I lived in Japan, hardly a day went by when gangsters and right-wing thugs did not engage in some sort of intimidation. The police, eager to maintain the appearance of a crime-free society, all but licensed the *yakuza* to conduct such activities within "acceptable" bounds. Mob influence was felt everywhere from politics to the movie industry, which did its bit by perpetuating the mystique of the *yakuza* as a sort of modern-day knight-errant bent on upholding the traditional honor of Japan. In truth, the *yakuza* enslaved women, trafficked in drugs, and preyed on elderly homeowners and shopkeepers. When the celebrated director Jyuzo Itami produced a film critical of the *yakuza*, a gangster showed what mob honor was all about by slashing Itami's face with a straight razor.

The mob's political front, the ultraright, made the radical left's occasional rocket attacks look tame. Shortly before I began working at the *Japan Times*, a thug walked into a regional bureau of the *Asahi Shimbun*, a newspaper the right-wing despises. He calmly fired off a shotgun, killing a young reporter.

At last, however, a prolonged gang war seems to have pushed the mob beyond the pale. Police have begun cracking down in earnest on the vast underworld syndicates. *Yakuza* movies have fallen out of favor with the public.

What's more, despite all intimidation, the grassroots campaign against nuclear power has made headway. The Japanese government has begun to scale down its plutonium-reactor plans and may be backing away from nuclear power altogether.

Still, whenever I hear some naive American repeating the cant about how Japanese have so few lawyers because they are able to settle their differences harmoniously through informal mediation, I think of those swaggering remants of Japan's fanatical past. It's enough to make me appreciate lawyers.

WHAT THE WORLD NEEDS NOW

I had long been convinced that Japan was undergoing fundamental changes: In the summer of 1993, I began to see the results before my eyes. I had returned, with my family, for a season of work, research, and fun. One Saturday, an old salaryman friend of mine called to invite me for a drink. Slightly embarrassed, I explained that I was looking after my daughter. (This had been a point of tension between us in the past.) No problem, he said, he would bring his kids, too. Half an hour later, we found ourselves in a Denny's, our children noisily demolishing a stack of pancakes while we attempted to have a conversation over the hubbub. My friend looked after his kids pretty much every weekend now, he told me, while he wife went off on forays to support the small merchandising business she was running out of their home. "I even cook on Sundays," he added with a grin. Over the summer, it became clear that my friend had all the best instincts of fathering, and had only been de-

layed in the fulfillment of the role by his career and the male culture that went with it.

He was not alone. We reenrolled Maya at her old neighborhood nursery. At first glance, nothing had changed. Now four, she encountered many of the same children she had known as toddlers. Most of her teachers were still there. The time-consuming obligations the nursery placed on parents—putting a towel here, a towel there, placing extra clothing just so, fitting covers over the mattresses—hadn't changed a whit. But as I dropped Maya off on my way to work, I noticed one huge difference. In the past, whenever I took my daughter to the nursery, it caused an uproar among the children. This was partly because I was a foreigner, but also because the sight of a father taking his child to the nursery was so rare. That was women's work. Now, however, the place was crawling with fathers. They went about their chores with the same quiet efficiency the Japanese display in nearly all tasks. Yet this was truly revolutionary. Somehow, in the last three years, they had come to accept their responsibilities as fathers, even if that meant going to work at the ripe old hour of nine o'clock.

Small changes prefigured large ones. At a campaign rally in the city of Omiya, about an hour north of Tokyo, I watched with fascination as Morihiro Hosokawa climbed onto the roof of his green and white Japan New Party bus to address a crowd that had gathered in a square outside the train station.

I had met Hosokawa a couple of years earlier on a reporting trip to Kumamoto, where he was governor at the time. That meeting had confirmed what I'd heard from a Japanese colleague.[11] Governor Hosokawa was a bright, self-confident politician with a maverick streak and a brewing distaste for the status quo. Since then,

those traits had matured to make him the boldest Japanese political leader of his day.

The rally took place at dusk. A light rain thinned the
crowd. But Hosokawa, who had acted in films once or
twice, captivated those who remained with a thundering
rhetoric. He told them that after thirty-eight years of
LDP rule, the time had come to take Japan out of the
hands of bureaucrats and transform it into a more open,
liberalized society. The citizens I interviewed afterwards
had not fully overcome their cynicism about politics,
but like those who flocked to Bill Clinton in the 1992
American presidential election, they were ready for the
politics of change.

Later, Hosokawa gave a press conference in which he
spelled out his strategy. He and his tiny party would remain aloof from the selection of the next prime minister,
he said, because all the alternatives were tainted by
their pasts. "Frankly, I don't see any fit candidate among
the choices," he remarked coolly. Instead, the Japan New
Party would allow a weakened LDP to rule while it built
up its forces to take power in a subsequent election,
which Hosokawa anticipated might come within a few
years. He seemed utterly confident that, if he refused un-
principled compromise and relied on patience, he would
eventually become his nation's leader.

After the press conference, I filed a story that began
"Japan is a country at ease with paradox, but even here
the sight of a man campaigning for election by promising to stay out of government is a bit startling. . . . But
Hosokawa would rather take power than taste it." [12]

However, even Morihiro Hosokawa, who had been
farsighted enough to anticipate the splintering of the ruling party, misjudged the speed of change. A few weeks
later, to his undoubted surprise, he found himself
elected prime minister.

Of course, his administration didn't last long, and at the end of it he appeared anything but bold. But during his eight-month tenure, Hosokawa succeeded in putting Japan on the record as a wartime aggressor, pushing political reform through the Japanese parliament, and placing deregulation squarely on the public agenda. Though largely symbolic, these accomplishments will turn out, I believe, to have been historic.

THE GOLDEN ROAD TO REVOLUTION

During four decades of one-party rule, Japan had been largely a shamocracy. Bureaucrats ran the nation; politicians shook it down for contributions.

This wealth was not directly distributed to the people. Nevertheless, corporations accumulated more money than they could manage. During the first big round of *endaka*, the rise of the yen against the dollar, wholesale prices in Japan plunged by more than 10 percent in 1987 alone. Companies were buying cheaper products overseas and trading them among themselves (especially within their corporate groups) at proportionally lower prices. But during the same period, consumer prices showed a momentary dip of a couple of percentage points, then ticked steadily if slowly upward, ending the decade about 5 percent higher than when *endaka* began.[13] Housing costs skyrocketed as corporations plunged excess cash into land. In plain language, the Japanese public had been cheated out of every yen that corporate Japan gained by the doubling of its purchasing power abroad.

This was not merely a consumerist issue: When Matsushita Electric Corporation bought its own chunk of Hollywood in the form of MCA, it paid a breathtaking $6.6 billion. But that was little more than half the $12 billion in cash that Matsushita had stockpiled. This mountain of cash, equivalent to one-third of the company's annual income from sales, was left over after investments in new factories and equipment. Other big Japanese companies had similar war chests. Whose money was that? If Japanese companies were truly the workers' cooperatives that propagandists have claimed, then surely most of that excess cash should have been distributed to the workers. They could have used it. By 1990, Japan's per capita wealth exceeded America's by $3,640, but its household purchasing power lagged by $5,514.[14] The difference, it may be argued, was the cash denied to workers plus the artificially high prices charged them.

On the other hand, if Japanese companies were, as some American economists argued, just longer-sighted versions of Western corporations, then surely those billions in what the bankers delicately called "excess liquidity" must have gone to shareholders. In truth, however, Japanese companies could accumulate vast amounts of cash without claimants. This seems to me the crowning evidence that the Japanese economy was structured neither to benefit the Japanese worker nor to profit the owners of capital. It was simply meant to extend the dominion of the bureau-industrial complex.

With Japanese politics in a shambles, that complex has never looked more powerful. Indeed, some people see the entire political reform movement as a setup contrived by the elite to get the political leeches off their backs.

Some have argued that bureaucrats, led by the Bank of Japan governor, Yasushi Mieno, engineered Japan's slump to restore "Japanese" values to the populace. There is some plausibility to this claim. I myself attended a meeting at which Mieno said he would be glad to see land prices fall by a third if it would rein in the overheated economy. So are the changes of the last few years entirely phony? If only the people who ask such questions would lower their eyes to the level of ordinary folk, the answer would be clear. No, Japan's ministries aren't going to yield to U.S. pressure, and its gigantic companies aren't going to dry up and blow away. But that doesn't mean they won't be dramatically transformed from within.

The real question is whether a recession, or the return to power of the old guard in the guise of a new party—or any other force—can reverse the trends in place. I think not. The problems created by Japan's postwar system require nothing less than transformation.[15] Ultimately, that system has produced a bizarre and insupportable social structure: a nation in which there are too few children and too many elderly. A nation so hungry for personal identity that its popular culture revolves with the speed and force of a typhoon, but also a nation so steeped in racial identity that it cannot readily accept the immigrants it needs to survive its aging.

The course of political revolution never runs straight, and only a fool would dare make specific predictions. But I believe the imperatives of social revolution will drive Japan's political processes along a fairly foreseeable path. There may be political instability for a time, there may even be a stronger bureaucracy for a time, but sooner or later, politicians will begin—perhaps are beginning now—to coalesce around shared ideas. As they do, the people will come to see that they have to choose which political solutions to the nation's problems they really want.

In the resulting competition among political parties, the old constituencies of farmers and shopkeepers will inevitably lose ground to new constituencies of women, consumers, and the elderly. Indeed, if the Japanese public had its way now, there would be massive deregulation, lower taxes, more imports, less corruption, and considerably more attention to social welfare needs.

When a government eventually gains a clear mandate, it will be able to direct the bureaucracy toward its policy goals. Politicians have always had power bureaucrats in Japan, if only because they have the power to block promotions and budgets, but they have almost never tried to use it to shape policy. When they do, the revolution will be complete.

INCENSE AND ALTAR

At home, there were other harbingers of change. Tatsuko had by now fully reconstituted her life. Papa was still a part of her daily world—she regularly burned incense to him in a cabinet-sized altar that stood in what used to be their bedroom. But she herself had moved to a room downstairs. The garden that he used to tend with such care had been altered to her taste by some hired hands. And once again Tatsuko was on the move. Following her triumphant journey across China by camel, she had become the living embodiment of vitality. Most weekends she went mountain climbing, pausing at the ridges to sketch. She took us on an overnight trip to a mountain resort. Fortunately, owing to Maya's tender years, we were not obliged to actually climb the mountains, but we did accompany Tatsuko on a six-mile hike through a steep and spectacular gorge along Japan's own Silk River.

Rumiko, I now had occasion to notice, had also gone through a spectacular change. She was no longer anybody's employee but a fully fledged professor of architecture. Crackling with intellectual energy, she clambered all over Japan conducting research for papers she would write in the academic year to come. Meanwhile, Nippon Steel, her former employer, had come to grief. Having found that the business of leisure could not soak up the company's excess workers, it had begun to let them go. In 1993, with its workforce already shrunk by more than half to 37,000, Nippon Steel announced plans to trim roughly 20 percent of its remaining employees from the rolls.[16] And, ironically for a company that had worked at least one man to death, it began giving workers an extra two days' leave a month—not out of benevolence, but out of the need to save money.

Megumi, too, was in action, having made a decisive break with her childhood. She moved out of her mother's home and set up household for herself with a man she had fallen in love with. In her independent way, she was still not prepared to marry him, at least not then, but she had no qualms about living with him. This choice, so commonplace in America—indeed, the very one Rumiko and I had made three years before we married—remained highly unconventional in modern Japan. Eventually, though, Megumi and her boyfriend married in a quiet civil registration.

I have no doubt that Megumi, like her parents, will simply prove to have been ahead of her time. With all the demands imposed by Japanese marriage and the uncertainties that attend it in an age of dual careers, living together on a trial basis seems a highly sensible choice for many young people.

Late in the summer of 1993, on one of the few days when the rains let up, we all went to visit Papa's grave. It stood as upright as he once had. Its black-granite edifice had been sullied by rain and dust, but we soon set that to rights. Picking up a wooden bucket and some ladles

*at the entrance, we took turns pouring fresh water over
Papa's tombstone and gently restoring its gleam. Tatsuko
and her daughters and granddaughter placed flowers in
the vases and lit a fat bundle of incense while I stood
respectfully by. Then we all prayed.*

*I'm not much of one for prayer as such. I simply don't
believe in supernatural intervention in this world. But
having attended a Quaker school in my youth, I find in
silent meditation a calm, clear peace. At that moment,
as I emptied my mind of deliberate thought, a sudden
realization struck me. This small family about me had
been not only the embodiment of the changes sweeping
Japan, but actual agents of that change. Warmed by the
spark of Tatsuko and Ichio's idealism, they had oriented
their lives away from sacrifice on the altar of economic
growth toward equality, individual dignity, and a willingness to look on humankind as their brethren. This
last, I was vividly aware, took shape with their acceptance of me. Tatsuko, by her tireless work as a publisher
and speaker, had helped to popularize these ideas, and
Ichio, by his unflagging support, had made her work possible. At last, their virtues were emerging as necessities.
For all his stoicism, his dedication, his sense of duty and
routine, Papa, I felt sure, would approve of a Japan
set free.*

A NEW BIRTH OF FREEDOM

Half a century after General MacArthur strode into Japan, the seeds of true democracy have begun to sprout
from its soil. We must acknowledge, however, that it is
the Japanese people themselves who, by hard tilling, have
brought them to life. In their best moments, the Japanese
appear on the verge of achieving the ancient Greek ideal

of democracy as freedom exercised in self-imposed moderation.

Of course, things may still go spectacularly wrong. Japanese democracy remains a frail plant in shallow soil. Economic gloom, a military threat from North Korea, or even China, or a deepening sense that America is an insatiable bully: Any of these could swiftly put Japan into a dangerous nationalistic fever.

If the United States wants to advance liberalization in Japan, it should ally itself with the Japanese people. America can help simply by respecting Japan's political process. It can quit making fruitless deals with the bureaucracy. To a remarkable degree, America still sets the agenda for public debate in Japan. The more the United States is seen to be advocating a freeing up of Japanese society in general, rather than just trying to pry loose a little business for itself, the swifter change in that direction is apt to be.

We should recollect that at another time in our recent history, Japan was in the process of democratizing under U.S. influence. It was 1947 and the Japanese people had just elected a moderate Socialist government. But the Occupation authorities, in the midst of a cold-war spasm, refused to authorize even the tamest of the new government's bills. Whether a freewheeling Socialist government would have made a hash of things is beside the point. The Katayama government died on the vine, and with it died meaningful democracy in Japan.

In less than a year, the archconservative Shigeru Yoshida, a former bureaucrat and friend of leading businessmen, was back in the premiership. That was the beginning of the system that has so troubled the United States in recent decades. Political leadership would remain in conservative hands for another forty-five years. And we put it there.

We owe it to the Japanese people to help them gain the sovereignty over their nation that their constitution promises. After all, we wrote that constitution. If we fail now, if we try to sabotage their economy, or if we cynically bypass their elected representatives in favor of the bureaucrats or business community, we run a great risk. The Japanese people could, like the Russians, become so disgusted that they decide to place their faith in "strong" leaders. Japan, we should remember, has its own neofascists, on both the right and the left, lurking in the halls of power.

And yet, for the most part, I am confident that Japan has failed to make its system stick. This is cause for great joy. Not selfish gloating, but joy for all of humankind. The grassroots revolution in Japan strikes me as the most important political development since the collapse of communism. Much of the world, including virtually all of Asia, had looked to Japan as a model. It was Japan that gave Vietnam's communist regime the means to enjoy economic growth without the awkward baggage of human rights and freedom. It was Japan that, by its success, inspired the strong-arm regimes of Singapore, Malaysia, and other fast-developing capitalist countries to snub the human rights pleas of the West. Most important, it was Japan that actively persuaded China's leaders after the Tienanmen Square massacre that they could pursue capitalism without democracy. Asian oligarchs began to speak with open contempt of the decadent West and its "alien" views of human rights. Japan made them believe they could export their cake and eat it, too.

To further deflect criticism of their human rights violations, Asian leaders, particularly Malaysia's President Mahathir Mohamed, have sought to cast the East-West economic conflict in racial terms. "Asia for Asians" is the new slogan, one that Japan has been pleased to quietly echo.[17] In short, Japan's success in becoming an economic giant without playing by Western rules of economics or democracy persuaded some Asian leaders to accept a new version of Imperial Japan's concept of a Greater Asian Coprosperity Sphere.[18] Japan today is no fascist state, but had it been able to make its system stick, it might have lent permanent justification to neofascism abroad: the suppression of individual rights and liberties in favor of national growth and state power.[19] Fortunately, in the end, Japan's experience suggests that even the most powerful motivational ideology and sophisticated machinery of control operating under ideal conditions of economic growth cannot suppress people's natural yearning for freedom indefinitely.

The psychotherapist Rollo May once wrote a parable about a king who cages a man like a beast in the zoo to see what will happen. He brings in a psychologist to supervise the experiment. At first the caged man is angry. Every day, however, the king reminds him that he is being fed and sheltered and cared for, so why should he complain? The man in the cage enters a long period of apparent acceptance. He even tries to please his captors. Eventually, he seems to lose all sense of self. Then the psychologist has a dream in which the man suddenly summons the people around him with an impassioned appeal to the cause of individual freedom. Stirred, the people break apart the cage and use the iron bars to storm the palace.

The psychologist wakes and hears an inner voice say that it is merely a wish-fulfillment dream.

"The hell it is!" said the psychologist as he climbed out of bed. "Maybe some dreams are made to be acted on."[20]

The Japanese people have unquestionably broken out of their cages. Prying open the palace has only just begun. But it is my dream—no, not just my dream but my reasoned expectation—that in years to come, the Japanese people will be a shining example of something more than economic achievement. They will show the world real democracy in action and hard-won prosperity enjoyed. Some dreams are made to be acted on.

NOTES

1. HAPPY NEW YEAR, MICKEY MOUSE

1. The Japanese normally wait until New Year's Day to feast, but I suppose in our case the schedule was moved up a bit because we were guests. The traditional New Year's Eve dish is *toshi-koshi soba*, "passing-the-end-of-the-year buckwheat noodles."
2. *New York Times*, 2 Dec. 1991, A13.
3. E.g., Brian Reading, *Japan: The Coming Collapse* (London: Orion Books, 1992).
4. *Washington Post*, 22 Aug. 1993, C5. In this article, correspondent T. R. Reid argues, as I do, that the Japanese are far more pluralistic than is generally imagined.
5. William J. Holstein, *The Japanese Power Game: What It Means for America* (New York: Plume, 1990), 15.
6. Tokyo trembles incessantly and has many palpable earthquakes a year. In 1923 the city was leveled by a monstrous quake; a similar one is forecast to strike before the end of the century.
7. Van Wolferen, James Fallows, and Clyde Prestowitz, vanguard of the so-called revisionists, tower over most others.
8. Boye Lafayette de Mente, *Japan's Secret Weapon: The Kata Factor* (Phoenix: Phoenix Books, 1990). De Mente is no fool. The book itself contains many sound observations, but the author cannot escape responsibility for the sensationalistic framework in which it is posed.

9. "Teijin President Orders Workers to Air Gripes," *Nikkei Weekly,* 12 July 1993, 11.
10. Edwin O. Reischauer, *The Japanese* (Cambridge, Mass.: Belknap Press, 1977), 64–68.
11. Richard Storry, *A History of Modern Japan* (Middlesex, England: Penguin, 1969), 64–65.
12. Reischauer, 81.
13. Clyde V. Prestowitz Jr., *Trading Places: How America Allowed Japan to Take the Lead* (Tokyo: Tuttle, 1988), 8.
14. Karel van Wolferen, *The Enigma of Japanese Power* (New York: Vintage Books, 1989), 260.
15. This, like many other names in this book, is a pseudonym. It is meant not to deceive but to offer cover to members of her family who may desire it.
16. Editorial, *Yomiuri Shimbun,* 30 Oct. 1989, as translated in the *Daily Yomiuri* of the same date.
17. I mean no disrespect: The fact is most Japanese now declare themselves nonbelievers who participate in religion simply because it's expected of them. See, for example, "Poll Shows Japanese Losing Faith in Religion," *Daily Yomiuri,* 3 July 1994, 2.
18. Kojin Karatani, as quoted in *Postmodernism and Japan,* eds. Masao Miyoshi and H. D. Harootounian (Durham, N.C.: Duke University Press, 1989), xv.
19. From a study by the Dentsu Institute for Human Studies, as reported in the *Japan Times,* 13 June 1991, 2.
20. Prime Minister's Office, *Public Opinion Survey on the Life of the Nation,* translated and summarized by the Foreign Press Center, Tokyo (October 1993).

2. ANYBODY HOME?

1. Michael Shapiro, *Japan: In the Land of the Brokenhearted* (New York: Henry Holt & Co., 1989), 74–75.
2. Robert O. Blood, Jr., *Love Match and Arranged Marriage* (New York: The Free Press, 1967), 17.
3. "The Family and Character Formation," in *The Japanese Family* (Tokyo: The Foreign Press Center, 1981), 7.
4. G. B. Sansom, *Japan: A Short Cultural History* (Stanford, Calif.: Stanford University Press, 1978), 114–117.
5. Janet E. Hunter, *The Emergence of Modern Japan* (New York: Longman, 1989), 70. Here and throughout my book, I use the

term *state* loosely, to encompass the mesh of business, politics, and bureaucracy that constitutes authority in Japan. The bureau-industrial complex is the part that dominates the whole.

6. Conrad Totman, *Japan Before Perry* (Berkeley: University of California Press, 1981), 151.
7. Reischauer, 72.
8. Tadashi Fukutake, *The Japanese Social Structure*, trans. Ronald P. Dore (Tokyo: University of Tokyo Press, 1982), 33.
9. Ibid., 41–42.
10. The Tokugawas made one important contribution to the eventual weakening of family ties: In their eagerness to remove all possibility of divided loyalties, they refashioned the leading families into *ie* whose members were not necessarily blood relations and whose corporate loyalties lay with the central authorities. See van Wolferen, 165–166.
11. Hunter, 66.
12. Fukutake, 37.
13. Ibid., 27.
14. With apologies to Garrison Keillor, the Thurber of our generation, who wrote a book of stories by this title.
15. Fukutake, 30.
16. Sansom, 520.
17. Tadashi Fukutake, *Japanese Society Today*, 2nd ed. (Tokyo: University of Tokyo Press, 1981), 36.
18. Joy Hendry, *Marriage in Changing Japan* (New York: St. Martin's Press, 1981), 16.
19. Hendry, 21.
20. Vogel, 256.
21. Katsutoshi Yamashita, "Divorce, Japanese Style," *Japan Quarterly* 33 (1986): 417.
22. Hendry, 22.
23. Alice Mabel Bacon, *Japanese Women and Girls* (Cambridge, Mass.: The Riverside Press, 1902), 102.
24. Bacon, 101.
25. See Richard H. Mitchell, *Thought Control in Prewar Japan* (Ithaca, N.Y.: Cornell University Press, 1976).
26. Anne E. Imamura, "The Japanese Urban Housewife: Traditional and Modern Social Participation," *The Social Science Journal* 24, no. 2 (1987): 139–156.
27. Ezra Vogel, *Japan's New Middle Class* (Berkeley: University of California Press, 1963), 37.

28. Coleman, 141–147.
29. Ibid., 162.
30. Ibid., 175.
31. Takeyoshi, Kawashima, cited in Hendry, 24.
32. Coleman, 173.
33. Hendry, 25.
34. Vogel, 108.
35. Etsuko Yamashita, "Three Women and a Baby," *Japan Views* (March 1993): 13.
36. E. Yamashita, 14.
37. Yomiuri Poll, cited in the *Daily Yomiuri*, 13 June 1993, 3.
38. "Firebrand Lawyer Fights Domestic Violence Issues," *Nikkei Weekly*, 24 May 1993, 25.
39. Sumiko Iwao, *The Japanese Woman: Traditional Image and Changing Reality* (New York: The Free Press, 1993), 95.
40. Published in the *Daily Yomiuri*, 5 June 1991, 8.
41. Economic Planning Agency, *1991 White Paper on the Life of the Nation* (Tokyo: Foreign Press Center), 10.
42. The 1991 Management and Coordination Agency study found that 70 percent of women with children between six and eighteen years old held jobs, and many of them had done so since the children were in infancy, according to a report in the *Daily Yomiuri*, 12 May 1991, 2.
43. *The Japanese Family*, 20.
44. Mark O'Neill, "Japanese Marriages Now Stop at Grave," Reuters article in the *Dallas Morning News*, 26 Sept. 1992.
45. *The Japanese Family*, 22.
46. Coleman, 131.
47. *Japan Times*, 18 May 1992, 2.
48. As Shakespeare so aptly said. The full quote, lest I be misunderstood, is from Sonnet 116 and runs: "Love alters not with his brief hours and weeks/ But bears it out even to the edge of doom."
49. Hendry, 170–171.
50. *Nikkei Weekly*, 26 July 1993, 22.
51. Estimate obtained from the Japan Institute for Social and Economic Affairs. It is also possible to have a Buddhist wedding or, as in the case Rumiko recalled from her childhood, a civil one.
52. Indeed, researchers found that a distrust of love matches continued well into the postwar era, and the *nakōdo* continues to provide formalistic cover of the approval of elders. Hendry, 24, 30.
53. "Tailor-made Weddings Buck Traditions," *Nikkei Weekly*, 31 Jan.

1994, 26. It says that 10 percent of the callers to a marriage hot line in Tokyo inquire about "witnessed weddings."

54. Coleman, 34.

55. "*Kaisha ningen,*" in *PressGuide* (November 1990): 2.

56. Anne E. Imamura, "The Japanese Urban Housewife: Traditional and Modern Social Participation," *Social Science Journal* 24, no 2 (1987): 148.

57. Collected in *Ellery Queen's Japanese Golden Dozen: The Dectective Story World in Japan* (Rutland, Vt.: Tuttle, 1978), 287.

58. Mariko Fujita, "It's All Mother's Fault: Childcare Choices in Japan," *Journal of Japanese Studies* 15 (Winter 1989): 90.

59. *Changing Japan Seen Through the Camera* (Tokyo: Asahi Shimbunsha, 1933), 36. The book is somewhat propagandistic, but as sexism was not an issue of the day, there appears to be no conscious intent to mislead about gender roles.

60. "Health Problems Among Children Are Increasing," *Japan Times,* 18 Oct. 1990, 3.

61. Editorial, *Daily Yomiuri,* 22 April 1991, 6.

62. Hiroshi Ishida, *Social Mobility in Contemporary Japan* (Stanford, Calif.: Stanford University Press, 1993), 247.

63. Kyoko Kubota, "Alcoholism and the Housewife," *Japan Quarterly* 33 (Winter 1986): 54.

64. Yasuko Muramatsu, "For Wives on Friday: Women's Roles in TV Dramas," *Japan Quarterly* 33 (Winter 1986): 160.

65. "Education Expenses Double in Ten Years," *Mainichi Daily News,* 25 April 1991, 12.

66. Management and Coordination Agency, 1991.

67. Katsuyoshi Iwabuchi, "Baby Boom or Social Security Bust," *Sankei Shimbun,* 28 Jan. 1993, trans. in *Japan Views* (March 1993): 15. This would be about half the U.S. divorce rate.

68. K. Yamashita, 416–419.

69. From an interview conducted by the author in June 1992 for a public radio documentary.

70. Figures from Ministry of Health and Welfare, obtained in interview. See also *Japan Labor Bulletin* 33 (March 1994):1

71. NHK television report, 1 Oct. 1993.

72. Ministry of Health and Welfare, *White Paper on Health and Welfare, 1989* (Tokyo: Foreign Press Center, March 1990), 6.

73. "30-Something Japanese Men Say It Is Difficult to Marry," Asahi News Service, 2 July 1991.

74. *Economist,* 9 Sept. 1989, 25.

75. Merry White, "Home Truths: Women and Social Change in Japan," *Daedalus* 121, no. 4 (Fall 1992): 71.
76. Possibly, this was an echo of Shintaro Ishihara's *The Japan That Can Say No.* Though they stand at opposite ends of the political spectrum, especially on military issues, Doi and Ishihara share a political antipathy for the United States.
77. This story was related to me in a 1991 interview with Koji Kakizawa, then the LDP's parliamentary secretary of defense.
78. "Young Women Turn to Plastic Surgery," *Nikkei Weekly*, 4 Jan. 1993, 21.
79. Kim Slote, "The Current Japanese Women's Movement," *ISIS Women in Action*, no. 3 (1991): 17–20.
80. *Japanese Women Yesterday and Today* (Tokyo: Foreign Press Center, 1991), 11.
81. Brenda Bankhart, "Japanese Perceptions of Motherhood," *Psychology of Women Quarterly* 13 (1989): 64–65.
82. *Japan Times Weekly*, international ed., 13 Dec. 1993, 2.
83. NHK television report, 1 Oct. 1993.
84. E.g., "Women Want Large Families, Poll Finds," *Japan Times*, 13 March 1992, 3.
85. Masako Amano, "Non-family Women Are on the Increase," *NWEC Newsletter*, no. 8 (May 1991): 7–11.
86. "More Households Have Elderly," *Japan Times*, 3 May 1992, 2.

3. OF HUMAN CAPITALISM AND ITS CORPSES

1. Paraphrased from a quotation in Lou Cannon, *Reporting: An Inside View* (Berkeley: California Journal Press, 1977), 16.
2. T. R. Reid, "The Company Wedding: Bowing into a Japanese Firm Is for Life," *Washington Post*, 2 April 1992, 1.
3. Arthur M. White Jr. and Shinichi Takezawa, *The Other Worker: A Comparative Study of Industrial Relations in the United States and Japan* (Honolulu: East-West Center Press, 1968), 111.
4. "How Japan Puts the 'Human' in Human Capital," *Business Week*, 11 Nov. 1991, 22.
5. Organization for International Cooperation and Devleopment, *Purchasing Power Parities and Real Expenditures*, 1990 (Paris: OECD, 1992), 27.
6. For example, Kazuo Ara, author of a book on his experience as a bank executive, refers to the "feudal management style" of banks in an article titled "Blowing the Corporate Whistle Can Pay," *Nikkei Weekly*, 16 Aug. 1993, 18.

7. Ministry of Labor figures obtained during interview, Aug. 1993.
8. Ministry of Labor figures.
9. "'Non-Paid Overtime' Should be Reduced, Says Metropolitan Labor Standards Bureau," *Japan Labor Bulletin*, 1 April 1992, 2.
10. "Dealing with the Labor Shortage," *Japan Report* (Sept. 1991): 2.
11. *Daily Yomiuri*, 4 May 1991, 2.
12. *New York Times*, 29 Nov. 1990, C13.
13. Letter to *Asahi Shimbun* reproduced in "Vernacular Views," *Japan Times*, 12 April 1992, 20.
14. Miyamoto Musashi, *A Book of Five Rings*, trans. Victor Harris (Woodstock, N.Y.: Overlook Press, 1974), 47.
15. I owe an intellectual debt to Karel van Wolferen for so forcefully drawing a vital distinction in chapter 10 of *The Enigma of Japanese Power*, aptly titled, "Power in the Guise of Culture."
16. Ichiro Kawasaki, *Japan Unmasked* (Rutland, Vt.: Tuttle, 1969), 151.
17. Quoted in Andrew Gordon, *Labor and Imperial Democracy in Prewar Japan* (Berkeley: University of California Press, 1991), 17.
18. Gordon, 133.
19. Quoted in Gordon, 134.
20. Quoted in Joe Moore, *Japanese Workers and the Struggle for Power, 1945–1947* Madison: University of Wisconsin Press, 1983), 11.
21. Koji Taira, *Economic Development and the Labor Market in Japan* (New York: Columbia University Press, 1970), 97–99.
22. *See* Robert S. Ozaki, *Human Capitalism* (New York: Kodansha America, 1991), 97. MITI has used the same defining characteristics.
23. Ministry of Labor figures.
24. Moore, 47–61.
25. William J. Coughlin, *Conquered Press: The MacArthur Era in Japanese Journalism* (Palo Alto, Calif.: Pacific Books, 1952), 74–92.
26. Moore, 240.
27. Takie Sugiyama Lebra, *Japanese Patterns of Behavior* (Honolulu: The University of Hawaii Press, 1976), 158.
28. See, for example, "The Ironies That Built Japan Inc.," *Washington Post*, 18 July 1993, H1. It reports, in part, that well into the fifties, Washington, still fearful of communist influence in Japan, propped up Japanese business by "deciding trade complaints in favor of Japan on political rather than economic grounds; failing

to force Japan to follow its own laws and allow U.S. companies
to invest, steering military contracts to Japan," etc.

29. From an interview with Muto conducted in March 1992 by Carol
    A. Kates of Ithaca College. Published in *Labor Notes* (June 1992):
    J-2.

30. I am not suggesting that long strikes are a good thing. But the
    inability of unions to bargain for workers across company lines
    was obviously an important factor in the overworking of the Jap-
    anese.

31. *Japan 1991: An International Comparison* (Tokyo: Keizai Koho
    Center, 1991), 71.

32. *Japan Labor Bulletin* 31, no. 4 (April 1992): 2.

33. Satoshi Kamata, *Japan in the Passing Lane,* trans. Tatsuru Aki-
    moto (New York: Pantheon, 1982), 53–55.

34. In his book *The Revolt of a Man Who Was Killing Time by the
    Window,* Yasuhiko Ushiba tells of how after disagreeing with his
    superior over how to manage an athletic club the company
    owned, he was transferred to a ghetto of outcasts—all highly paid
    executives with virtually nothing to do. To kill time, he wrote
    his book. See "Blowing the Corporate Whistle Can Pay," *Nikkei
    Weekly,* 16 Aug. 1993, 18.

35. During the lengthy terminal illness of Emperor Hirohito, hun-
    dreds of Japanese reporters camped out in bitter weather for
    months outside the Imperial Palace. Three died of heart attacks
    apparently brought on by stress and exposure.

36. The *Japan Times,* I am pleased to say, had cosponsored Bloomberg's
    application. On a retry, three months later, the club relented.

37. Taira, 109; Gordon, 75–76; and Mary Saso, *Women in the Japa-
    nese Workplace* (London: Hilary Shipman, 1990), 24. Women's
    wages were a third less than those of men doing the same job,
    and less than half those of men doing comparable work in other
    industries, according to Gordon. Of course, the West has had its
    share of satanic mills, too.

38. Saso, 25.

39. Quoted in Mikiso Hane, *Reflections on the Way to the Gallows*
    (Berkeley: University of California Press, 1988), 12.

40. Gordon, 36.

41. Ibid., 76.

42. Ibid., 75.

43. Saso, 17.

44. The Japanese actually use the term "O.L.," pronouncing it "oh-ehru."
45. Jeannie Lo, *Office Ladies/Factory Women* (Armonk, N.Y.: M. E. Sharpe, 1990), 42–43.
46. Iwao, 18.
47. In her tart-tongued novel *Northanger Abbey.*
48. *Japanese Salarymen at the Crossroads* (Tokyo: Hakuhodo Institute of Life and Living, 1991), 152.
49. "Agency Says Protective Rules Hurt Working Women," Kyodo News Service report, 13 June 1991.
50. "Number of Female Company Chiefs Is Up 8 Percent from Last Year in Survey," *Japan Times*, 25 May 1991, 7.
51. "More Married Women Study for Entry to Top Professions," *Nikkei Weekly*, 31 May 1993, 26.
52. "Women Find Not-So-Equal Employment Opportunities," *Nikkei Weekly*, 19 April 1993, 21.
53. "Women Face Stiff Competition for Promotion," *Nikkei Weekly*, 15 March 1993, 21.
54. "Still a Man's World in Japan," *Mainichi Daily News*, 14 Jan. 1991, 1.
55. "Working Women Put in More Hours Than Men," *Asahi Evening News*, 9 June 1992, 2.
56. "Japan's Working Women 'the Most Dissatisfied,'" *Japan Economic Journal*, 23 Feb. 1991: 13. In a multinational survey, 33 percent of Japanese women expressed dissatisfaction with their jobs, compared with 14 to 16 percent in the Untied States, Germany, Australia, and Brazil.
57. Ozaki, 11.
58. Steven R. Weisman, "More Japanese Workers Demanding Shorter Hours and Less Hectic Work," *New York Times*, 3 March 1992, A6.
59. See, for example, "Firms Skeptical About Reaching Work-Hour Target by 1996," *Nikkei Weekly*, 30 Nov. 1992, 8.
60. "Working Hours Mark First Fall Below 2,000," *Japan Times*, 1 May 1993, 3.
61. "Gradual Switch to 40-Hour Workweek at Smaller Firms Urged," *Nikkei English News* wire report, 8 July 1993.
62. "Firms Accused of Sly Tactics to Force Managers to Quit," *Japan Times*, 10 April 1993, 3.
63. Robert E. Cole, *Work, Mobility, and Participation: A Compara-*

tive Study of American and Japanese Industry (Berkeley: University of California Press, 1979), 120.

64. "Number of Workers over 55 Is Rising," *Asahi Evening News*, 3 Aug. 1993, 4.
65. "Labor Letter," *Wall Street Journal*, 2 March 1993, 1.
66. "Japanese Starting to Link Pay to Performance, Not Tenure," *New York Times*, 2 Oct. 1993, 1.
67. "Labor Takes First Bonus Cut in Eighteen Years," *Nikkei Weekly*, 21 Dec. 1992.
68. "Unions Squeezed in Corporate Restructuring," *Nikkei Weekly*, 12 July 1993, 11.
69. "Japan's New Generation of Adults Has Less Loyalty to Employers," *Nikkei Weekly*, 7 Dec. 1992.
70. "Isolation and Job-Related Stress Hit Japan's Women Executives," *Nikkei Weekly*, 27 Sept. 1993, 26.
71. "Young Women Flock to Public Job Agency," *Nikkei Weekly*, 4 Jan. 1993, 20.
72. "Working Wives Want Their Own Money," *Nikkei Weekly*, 5 July 1993, 22.
73. Figures cited in "Women Want Large Families, Poll Finds," *Japan Times*, 13 March 1992, 2.
74. Katherine Graven, "Sex Harassment at the Office Stirs Up Japan," *Wall Street Journal*, 21 March 1990, B1.
75. Ibid.
76. "Suit Puts Face on Sex Harassment," *Japan Times*, 19 May 1993, 3.
77. "Women Take Harassment into Their Own Hands," *Japan Times*, 25 March 1993, 16.
78. "Defendants Accept Ruling in Landmark Sexual Harassment Case," United Press International, 1 May 1992.
79. "Women Speaking Out Against Unequal Pay," *Nikkei Weekly*, 1 March 1993, 24.
80. "Women Turn to Courts for Discrimination Relief," *Nikkei Weekly*, 23 May 1992.
81. That is the view of the Labor Ministry, as related to me in an interview with three ministry officials in August 1993.
82. Iwao, 15–16.
83. Hakuhodo, 154.
84. Ibid., 63.
85. Known in Japanese as 3-K work—for *kitanai, kikeni, kitsu,* which translate as "dirty, dangerous, or difficult."

86. *Daily Yomiuri*, 28 June 1991.
87. Solomon B. Levine, "Careers and Mobility in Japan's Labor Markets," in *Work and Lifecourse in Japan*, ed. David W. Plath (Albany: State University of New York Press, 1983), 27.
88. Hakuhodo, 71.
89. "'Tanshin Funinsha' in Tokyo Form Self-Help Group," Asahi News Service, 28 June 1991.
90. "Not All Men Want to Work Away from Home," *Asahi Evening News*, 26 May 1991.
91. "Poll Finds 30% Would Reject Transfer," *Japan Times*, 12 April 1992, 2.
92. "Honda Sued by Family for Overwork Death," *Japan Times*, 28 Dec. 1991.
93. "Fewer Burning Late-Night Oil," *Japan Times*, 30 April 1992, 3.
94. "Employees, Be Ambitious," *Nikkei Weekly*, 11 Jan. 1993, 9.
95. "Honda Personnel Policy Stresses Youth Over Experience," *Nikkei Weekly*, 28 March 1994, 13.
96. Haruo Shimada, "The Challenge to Japanese Management," in *The Japanese Economy in the 1990s: Problems and Prognoses* (Tokyo: Foreign Press Center, 1993), 88.

4. FOLLOW THE FLOATING WORLD

1. In Japan, the Sunday paper is thinner, not thicker, than the weekday version, so only a skeleton crew is required to assemble it.
2. A shortcoming first pointed out to me in a column by Scott McDonald, then of the *Japan Times*.
3. Sansom, 477.
4. Ibid., 477.
5. Storry, 79.
6. From a radio documentary "Barbarians Within the Gates," produced by the author for WUOM-FM, Michigan Public Radio, July 1992.
7. "Lifestyles," *Kodansha Encyclopedia of Japan*, vol. 5, 7.
8. Kazunori Higashino, "Theme Parks in Japan," *Journal of Japanese Trade and Industry* 10, no. 5 (1 Sept. 1991): 22.
9. These trips could be heavy-handed. One old Japan hand tells of a time when his boss at a Japanese company overruled the plans he'd made and ordered everyone to visit a sister factory on their vacation so they could improve output. Some holiday!
10. *Leisure and Recreational Activities* (Tokyo: Foreign Press Center, 1990), 27.

11. Ann McCreedy, "The Japanese Punk Invasion," *The Study of Current English* (Oct. 1991): 57.
12. "Employees Kept 'Out of Trouble' on Weekends," *Nikkei Weekly*, 11 Jan. 1993, 21.
13. Figure based on 4.55 trillion yen in entertainment expense deductions reported in 1989 by the National Tax Administration.
14. I obtained this estimate from Kazutaka Nakamura, a Japanese accountant who assisted me in a story I wrote for the AP on business entertainment.
15. Ian Buruma, "Americainerie," *New York Review of Books* 40, no. 6 (25 March 1993): 27.
16. Sam Jameson, "Need Excuse to Drink? In Japan There's Always Cherry Blossoms," *Los Angeles Times*, 16 April 1991, H-5.
17. Ibid.
18. Ibid.
19. Takeo Doi, *The Anatomy of Dependence* (Tokyo: Kodansha International, 1973).
20. Ibid., 92.
21. Ibid.
22. Ibid., 175.
23. *"Shinda"* literally means "Dead," while *"Onakunari ni narimashita, ne!"* means "Became dead, eh?" One of the charms of Japanese is that different levels of politeness and formality produce totally unrelated expressions.
24. Sōseki Natsume, *Botchan*, trans. Umeji Sasaki (Tokyo: Charles Tuttle Co., 1968), 30–31.
25. Ibid., 37.
26. Quoted in Jack Seward, *The Japanese*, rev. ed. (Tokyo: Yohan, 1988), 113.
27. Keiichi Yanagawa, "Religious Views of the Japanese and Their Characteristics," *Religion in Japan Today* (Tokyo: Foreign Press Center, 1992), 11.
28. Having recently come across a *karaoke* machine in Rosa and Carmen's Mexican Restaurant, near Detroit, I suspect there can hardly be an American left who does not know what one is. However, for the benefit of those recently rescued from desert isles: The *karaoke* machine is a mutant jukebox that displays the words to its song on a television screen, usually against some gauzy background video that looks like an old Clairol commercial. The selections have been stripped of their lyrics to tempt drunken patrons to get up and make fools of themselves by singing.

29. Keiko Nakamura, Atsuko Tanaka, and Takehito Takano, "The Social Cost of Alcohol Abuse in Japan," *Journal of Studies on Alcohol* 54, no. 5 (Sept. 1993): 620.

30. Except where otherwise noted, these and other figures on alcohol consumption were gathered from various official and industry sources by Associated Press researchers for a story I wrote while working for the AP in 1990.

31. Algernon Bertram Freeman-Mitford, Baron Redesdale, *Mitford's Japan: The Memoirs and Recollections, 1866–1906,* ed. Hugh Cortazzi (London and Dover, N.H.: Athlone Press, 1985), 68.

32. Jameson. With all the liquor-vending machines around, they doubtless had no trouble obtaining alcoholic drinks.

33. Nakamura, Tanaka, and Takano, 624. The social cost in the United States is even greater—3.5 percent of GNP, according to the authors. However, this is largely due to Americans' low reliance on public transport, which translates into many more auto deaths and injuries caused by drunk drivers.

34. Reprinted in the *Japan Economic Journal,* 16 Feb. 1991, 13.

35. Gavan McCormack, "The Price of Affluence: The Political Economy of Japanese Leisure," *New Left Review,* no. 188 (1 July 1991): 123.

36. David Lazarus, my friend and fellow journalist, drank one once and found the effect startling: "I became peppy, full of life, downright hyper," he writes in his book *Japan, Seriously* (Tokyo: The Japan Times Press, 1992), 106–107. "My coworkers watched me bounce off the walls for the remainder of the day and generally be a pain in the neck with all my supercharged behavior." Intrigued, he decided to investigate, and found that the Ministry of Health and Welfare, which is so scrupulous about foreign pharmaceuticals that few make it onto the Japanese market, was blithely unconcerned about these stimulants. "Energy drinks are becoming a part of people's lifestyles," an MHW official told Lazarus. "They are replacing food as a vitamin source." Coffee and cigarettes, too, evidently.

37. Higashino, 22.

38. Unless, that is, the event has been specially designed for family participation, such as an intracompany athletic meet on National Sports Day.

39. George Fields, the business consultant, quotes an irate Japanese woman telling an audience of skeptical foreign correspondents in Tokyo: "We Japanese women don't particularly feel that men

are doing us a favor when wives are invited to acompany their husbands to a business function. . . . It is an imposition rather than a favor." George Fields, *From Bonsai to Levi's* (New York: Penguin Books, 1983), 64.

40. Lately, anyway. In 1984, Natsume replaced Hirobumi Ito, the brilliant Meiji era oligarch who crafted a government that could appear democratic without having to be so and who was at least partly responsible for setting Japan on the expansionist path that led to its fatal spasm of militarism.

41. Hakuhodo, 122.

42. Ibid., 125.

43. Research tends to confirm my impressions. HILL's study found that even in workplaces that do require the singing of the company song, less than half of young workers knew the words at all, and only 11 percent could sing the entire song. Hakuhodo, 111.

44. Ibid., 67.

45. *Leisure and Recreational Activities*, 11–12.

46. Yoko Sano, "Japanese Work Hours," *Japan Economic Studies* 18, no. 2 (Winter 1989–90): 58.

47. NHK television report, 14 March 1993.

48. "Girl of Summer Undaunted by Ban," *Daily Yomiuri*, 13 July 1993, 2.

49. According to Tsuneaki Iki of the *Japan National Tourist Organization* (interview).

50. Robert E. Cole, "Work and Leisure in Japan," *California Management Review* 34, no. 3 (Spring 1992): 52–63.

51. "Bureaucrat Rocks the Ministry Boat by Denouncing Code of Conformity," *Japan Times*, 4 Aug. 1993, 3.

52. Ishihara's unvarying technique is to play Perry Mason knocking over the straw man. There is, for example, this preposterous exchange in his book: "'U.S.-Soviet ties have dramatically improved and it's quite possible that the partnership between Washington and Tokyo might even be dissolved,' he [an unnamed congressman] said gravely. 'The United States may even abandon Japan.' Laughingly, I replied, 'Do you mean that Americans and Russians have rediscovered their mutual identity as Caucasians?' He nodded in agreement." From Shintaro Ishihara, *The Japan That Can Say No* (New York: Simon & Schuster, 1991), 77–78. Interestingly, in the same book Ishihara traces what he calls his

"provocative" attitude to an incident in his youth, when a white GI threw a "water ice" (slush cone) in his face.

53. Letter, *Japan Times*, 1 March 1992.
54. *White Paper on Tourism, FY 1991 (Summary)* (Tokyo: Foreign Press Center, 1992), 7.
55. "Record Drug Seizures Reported," *Asahi Evening News*, 5 Aug. 1993, 4.
56. "Activists Fight Plan to Ban Pornography," *Japan Times*, 31 March 1992, 4.
57. "Porno Comics Read by 60% of Students," *Daily Yomiuri*, 27 June 1993, 2.
58. "Police Break High School Porno Ring," *Daily Yomiuri*, 12 Aug. 1993, 2.
59. See K. A. Adams, "Protest and Rebellion in Japanese Comics," *Journal of Popular Culture* 25, no. 1 (Spring 1989): 99.
60. See, for example, Seiichi Kitayama, "Kissing Up a Storm," *Japan Views*, April 1993; or see any park in Tokyo on a sunny weekend. Look in the bushes and you will see that kissing is not all they are up to.
61. *Nikkei Weekly*, 15 Feb. 1992.
62. *Mainichi Daily News*, 30 April 1992.
63. See, for example, "Muscular Look Gets Big Billing," *Nikkei Weekly*, 1 Feb. 1993, 21.
64. *Nikkei Weekly*, 11 Jan 1992. Izaak Walton (1593–1683), an English ironmonger with a literary flair, is best remembered for *The Compleat Angler*.
65. Leslie Helm, "Debts Put Squeeze on Japanese," *Los Angles Times*, 21 Nov. 1992, 1.
66. Paul Bluestein, "The New Asceticism: Japan's National Mood Shift," *Washington Post National Weekly Edition*, 8–14 March 1992, 16.
67. See, for example, "Edo Renaissance Seen in Heisei Era," *Nikkei Weekly*, 29 March 1993, 21.
68. Colin Nickerson, "Tokyo Getting Beaned Big Time," *Boston Globe*, reprinted in *Dallas Morning News*, 14 March 1993.
69. NHK television report, 1 Oct. 1993.
70. Ibid.
71. Mike Pall, "Seven Wonders of Japan," *Mainichi Daily News*, 10 March 1991, 17.
72. I am obligated to Robert Whiting and his marvelous book, *You*

Gotta Have Wa (New York: Vintage Books, 1989), for some of these obsrevations.

73. The usual chant is *"Katobase, Kono-san,"* or whoever-san happens to be batting. It means, roughly, "Make the ball fly."

74. "J-League Venture Scores Runaway Victory," *Nikkei Weekly,* 26 July 1993, 20.

5. THE DEAD TREE GIVES NO SHELTER

1. This phrase, taken from T. S. Eliot's poem "The Waste Land," echoes Ecclesiastes 12 and its bleak picture of desolation.

2. We weren't quite courageous enough to go for natural childbirth through a traditional Japanese midwife, and as it turned out, this was a lucky thing. It bears noting that while Japan's rate of infant mortality is low, its rate of maternal death is comparatively high.

3. *Japanese Women Yesterday and Today* (Tokyo: Foreign Press, 1991), 28.

4. There is a loophole in this regulation, but it permits only a high-dose pill to be taken as a means of regulating the menstrual cycle. Consequently, most Japanese women fear its side effects and rely on condoms instead.

5. Naohiro Ogawa and Robert D. Retherford, "Prospects for Increased Contraceptive Pill Use in Japan," *Studies in Family Planning* 22, no. 6 (Nov./Dec. 1991): 378–383.

6. Robert W. Hodge and Naohiro Ogawa, *Fertility Change in Contemporary Japan* (Chicago: Chicago University Press, 1991), 325.

7. Management and Coordination Agency figures as reported by the Associated Press, 4 May 1993.

8. Douglas McConatha et al., "Japan's Coming Crisis: Problems for the Honorable Elders," *Journal of Applied Gerontology* 10, no. 2 (June 1991): 225.

9. Ministry of Health and Welfare figures.

10. Linda G. Martin, "The Graying of Japan," *Population Bulletin* 44, no. 2 (July 1989): 5.

11. From an interview with Makoto Atoh, Ministry of Health and Welfare, June 1992. The latest available figures show Japan's elderly constitute 13.1 percent of the population.

12. *Statistical Abstract of the United States 1993* (table), 113th ed. (Washington, D.C.: U.S. Government Printing Office, 1993), 17.

13. *Health and Pension Reform in Japan,* Labor Market and Social Policy Occasional Papers no. 2 (Paris: OECD, 1990), x–xi.

14. "Japan's Declining Fertility: '1.53 Shock,'" *Population Today* 20, no. 4 (April 1992): 3–4.
15. Prime Minister's Office, *Public Opinion Survey on the Aging Society* (summary) (Tokyo: Foreign Press Center of Japan, May 1992), 1.
16. Ministry of Health and Welfare figures, as reported by the Associated Press, 8 Sept. 1993.
17. "Super-old" being defined as seventy-five or older, "merely aged" as sixty-five through seventy-four. Martin, 7.
18. Public schools are, of course, free, but the ancillary costs of education—the uniforms, the kits, and, above all, the after-hours cram schools for entrance exam preparation—soaked up 12 percent of household spending in Japan by 1990. See "Education Expenses Double in 10 Years," *Mainichi Daily News*, 25 April 1991, 12.
19. See, for example, "Women Want Large Families, Poll Finds," *Japan Times*, 13 March 1992, 2. A government poll found more than half of women wanted three or more children, but 70 percent felt unable to do so because of the financial burden as well as a lack of space and other concerns. A 1993 poll by NHK television news found young women in Tokyo reluctant to settle down and raise children because of the loss of freedom entailed.
20. Quoted in "Housework Burden Shifts from Elderly," *Nikkei Weekly*, 9 Nov. 1992, 21.
21. Working women in the fifty-five to sixty-four age bracket jumped 12 percent in 1991. See editorial, "Social Reform Needed to Cope with Aging Population," *Nikkei Weekly*, 23 Nov. 1992, 6.
22. A "dead-cat bounce" is a false recovery in stock prices, brought on by technical buying after a rapid drop in prices. "Even a dead cat will bounce if you drop him from high enough," explained a gleeful young trader. The trick, she explained, is to make your money on the fall, not the bounce.
23. Martha Ozawa, "Child Welfare Programs in Japan," *Social Service Review* 61, no. 1 (March 1991): 22–42.
24. John Creighton Campbell, *How Policies Change: The Japanese Government and the Aging Society* (Princeton: Princeton University Press, 1992), 106.
25. James H. Schulz, Allan Borowski, and William H. Crown, *Economics of Population Aging* (New York: Auburn House, 1991), 42.
26. Campbell, 8.

27. Kiyoshi Murakami, "Severance and Retirement Benefits in Japan" in *Pension Policy: An International Perspective*, eds. John A. Turner and Lorna M. Dailey (Washington, D.C.: U.S. Department of Labor, 1990), 118.
28. Erdman B. Palmore and Daisaku Maeda, *The Honorable Elders Revisited* (Durham, N.C.: Duke University Press, 1985), 79.
29. Campbell, 9.
30. Murakami, 130.
31. Schulz et al., 191.
32. About 38 percent of Japanese workers are covered under private pension plans (up from just 20 percent in 1970), compared with 46 percent of U.S. workers. *Pension Policy*, 11. The benefits are roughly comparable in terms of wage-replacement ratio, according to various scholars. See, for example, Palmore and Maeda, 78.
33. Palmore and Maeda, 76–77.
34. *Pension Policy*, 22. The comparative figures for the West were: Canada, 32 percent; France, 70 percent; Germany, 33 percent; and the United States, 29 percent.
35. OECD, 38.
36. Ibid., 47.
37. "The New Challenge: Aging Gracefully," *Focus Japan* 18, no. 1 (Jan. 1991): 2.
38. Alice Wade, *Social Security Area Population Projections 1991* (table), Actuarial Study No. 106 (Washington, D.C.: U.S. Department of Health and Human Services, Feb. 1992) (microfiche), 47.
39. Campbell, 9–10. The 1986 figures he cites are: Japan, 14.6 percent of national income devoted to social security; Germany, France, and Great Britain, in the 25–36 percent range; Sweden, 40.7 percent; the United States, 16.2 percent.
40. Daisaku Maeda, "Aging in Japan," in Manfred Bergener et al., *Aging and Mental Disorders: International Perspectives* (New York: Springer Publishing Co., 1992), 5.
41. *Facts and Figures of Japan* (Tokyo: Foreign Press Center, 1991), 80.
42. "Cutting Health Care Costs: Experiences in France, Germany, and Japan" (table), Joint Hearing Before the Committee on Governmental Affairs, United States Senate, and Special Committee on Aging, United States Senate, 102d Congress, 1st sess., 19 Nov. 1991 (Serial 102-15), 175.
43. "Cutting Health Care Costs" (table), 175.
44. The Japanese government has attempted to curb this habit by

instituting copayments for elderly patients, who previously received entirely free medical care. But the copayments are quite modest and seem to have had little effect on the frequency of patient visits. See OECD, 14.
45. Ikegami, 614.
46. Stephen J. Anderson, *Welfare Policy and Politics in Japan: Beyond the Development State* (New York: Paragon House, 1993), 143.
47. Editorial, "Health Care: A Bitter Pill," *Daily Yomiuri*, 18 Feb. 1991, 6.
48. National Medical Council finding, reported by NHK television on 31 May 1991.
49. Sachiko Sakamaki, "Your Money . . . and Your Life," *Far Eastern Economic Review* (26 Aug. 1993): 34.
50. "Ministry to Boost Warnings on Drugs Given to Elderly," *Daily Yomiuri*, 3 Feb. 1991, 2.
51. NHK news, 25 Nov. 1993.
52. *Japan Labor Bulletin* 30, no. 4 (April 1991): 1.
53. Ibid.
54. John E. Woodruff, "Japanese Nurses Organize as Job Pressures Increase," *Baltimore Sun*, published in the *Daily Yomiuri*, 29 May 1991, 3.
55. According to figures supplied by the Japan Federation of Medical Workers' Unions (Nihon Iroren) in a letter dated 24 April 1991.
56. "Japanese Least Satisfied with Health Care, Survey Shows," Kyodo News Service, 4 March 1991.
57. Anderson, 144.
58. Ikegami, 617. He notes that to see a specialist often requires a substantial bribe. The entry-by-bribery I have on the authority of sources who have worked in Japanese medical and dental schools.
59. OECD figures cited in Ikegami, 614.
60. "Aging Japan Faces Higher Health Costs," *Daily Yomiuri*, 18 Feb. 1991, 2. The national health-care cost for that year was 21.72 trillion yen, or about $16 billion at then-prevailing exchange rates. U.S. per capita cost was double, according to U.S. Health Care Financing Administration estimates. See testimony in "Cutting Health Care Costs," 45.
61. "Cutting Health Care Costs" (table), 172.
62. See OECD report, 11–12.
63. Martin, 30.

64. Ibid.
65. The Japanese government itself makes this reckoning. See "Japanese People Smoke the Most in Industrial World," *Mainichi Daily News*, 29 May 1993, 21.
66. "Japanese Doctors Smoke Too Much: WHO Chief," *Japan Times*, 31 May 1993, 2. The actual percentage is 44.
67. "More Tokyo Restaurants Adopt Nonsmoking Policies," *Daily Yomiuri*, 23 Feb 1993, 3.
68. Private antismoking groups in Japan are gaining momentum and influence. One 100,000-strong *ken-en-ken* ("smoke-free rights") group has succeeded in persuading train companies to increase the number of smoke-free platforms and cars on long-distance routes.
69. See editorial, "Lighting Up More Than Ever," *Japan Times*, 27 April 1992, 20.
70. "Smoking Population Declines," *Nikkei Weekly*, 14 Dec. 1992, 21.
71. Martin, 10.
72. Ministry of Health and Welfare figures. In 1990 cancer killed 130,395 men and 87,018 women in Japan. Overall, cancer accounted for 50,000 more deaths than heart disease, the second leading killer.
73. "Lung, Colon Cancer Deaths on Rise," *Japan Times*, 23 March 1992, 2. Massive ingestion of salt seems to have been one cause of common stomach cancers in Japan. Though a Westernized diet threatens more heart disease, it contains less salt than the traditional Japanese one.
74. Ministry of Health and Welfare figures, as reported in "Japanese Continue to Live Longer," *Daily Yomiuri*, 11 Aug. 1993, 3.
75. Ibid.
76. Bruce D. Long and Susan O. Long, "Curable Cancers and Fatal Ulcers: Attitudes Toward Cancer in Japan," *Social Science and Medicine* 16, no. 24 (1982): 2101–2108. A small example of the taboo on death: *Shi*, which means "death," can also mean "four"; therefore, one does not give as a gift any set containing four. If you're sending a wedding present of wineglasses to a Japanese friend, better make it a set of five.
77. Long and Long.
78. "Most Prefer to Know the Worst When It Comes to Deadly Cancer," *Daily Yomiuri*, 28 March 1991, 2. Other surveys I've seen show similar results.

79. "Cancer Victims Want Real Info, Survey Says," *Japan Times*, 14 Jan. 1991, 3.
80. Shusaku Endo, "A Forty-Year-Old Man," in *Stained Glass Elegies*, trans. Van C. Gessel (Tokyo: Charles C. Tuttle, 1984).
81. As Lord Tennyson put it in the most famous of all retirement poems.
82. Schulz et al., 146–147.
83. Murakami in *Private Pensions*, 119.
84. *Japan Labor Bulletin* 30, no. 4 (April 1991): 5.
85. Ibid.
86. See, for example, "Downturn Strains Securities Keiretsu," *Nikkei Weekly*, 3 May 1993, 12.
87. "The Elderly Seek Answers to Life After Retirement," *Nikkei Weekly*, 2 Nov. 1992.
88. See Martin, 20.
89. *Japan Labor Bulletin*, 7.
90. "As Japan Ages, Support Groups Help Elderly Gild Golden Years," *Nikkei Weekly*, 24 May 1993, 26.
91. Palmore and Maeda, 104.
92. Susumu Matsumoto, "Elderly Could Help Solve Labor Shortage" (in column), *Daily Yomiuri*, 11 March 1991.
93. Okuma Corporation, a major machine-tool maker, dropped its retirement age from sixty to fifty-six in early 1994 in order to cut the jobs of 150 highly paid midlevel managers, according to an Associated Press report of 10 Jan. 1994.
94. "Most Elderly Pass Away in Hospitals," *Japan Times*, 23 March 1992, 2.
95. McConatha et al., 231; Martin, 14; and Anderson (table), 27.
96. "Elderly Households Hit Record," *Daily Yomiuri*, 3 July 1993, 2.
97. McConatha et al., 231.
98. Maeda, 10.
99. See Y. Kaneko and Y. Yamada, "Wives and Mothers-in-law: Potential for Family Conflict in Postwar Japan," *Journal of Elder Abuse and Neglect* 2(1/2) (1990): 87–99.
100. Campbell, 17.
101. Martin, 14.
102. Ibid., 30.
103. "Bedridden Elderly Are Many Times the Western Average," *Japan Free Press*, 21 Aug. 1989, 126.
104. See, for example, "Cutting Health Care Costs" (testimony), 50 and 175 (table).

105. "Hospitals for the Elderly on the Rise," *Japan Times*, 19 Dec. 1991, 2.
106. Robert N. Butler and Kenzo Kikuni, eds., *Who Is Responsible for My Old Age?* (New York: Springer Publishing Co., 1993), 199.
107. Ibid., 197.
108. Campbell, 239.
109. For a good summary of scholarly views, see Anderson, 5–13.
110. "Welfare Top Poll Issue," *Daily Yomiuri*, 15 July 1993, 2.

6. OUT OF THE CAGE

1. According to figures compiled by the Japan Funeral Directors Association, cited in "Aging Population Boon for Funeral Trade," *Nikkei Weekly*, 16 Aug. 1993, 16.
2. *Kokutai no Hongi* ("Cardinal Principles of Our National Essence"), trans. John Owen Gauntlett, ed. Robert King Hall (Cambridge, Mass.: Harvard University Press, 1949).
3. Kosaku Yoshino, *Cultural Nationalism in Contemporary Japan* (London: Routledge, 1992).
4. Titles in the genre include: *Understand the Jews and Japan Comes into View, Now Japan Is In Danger!* and *The Revenge of Hitler*.
5. One poll of Tokyo residents, for example, found 60 percent were reluctant to get to know foreigners living in their neighborhoods. The percentage was highest among elderly women, and descended with age (*Japan Times*, 19 May 1992, 3). Polls continue to show that Japanese believe their country experiences trade friction mainly because it is "misunderstood" by foreigners. Japan is misunderstood, but that is not a cause of trade friction.
6. Quoted in "Computer Makers Look Abroad for Parts," *Nikkei Weekly*, 20 Sept. 1993, 8.
7. Or does it? Some in Japan say that married women envy their friends who are widows because they are rich but free. Reality often differs, but such comments are another reflection of the sorry state of marriage in Japan.
8. I had held a similar post the year before at the University of Michigan's Center for Japanese Studies. I shall always be grateful that it sheltered me from the Michigan winter while I began this book.
9. The "allergy" refers to the Japanese people's horror of things nuclear in the aftermath of the atomic bombings they suffered during the war. The government responded by pledging not to build

or harbor nuclear weapons, but this pledge was soon violated. The Japanese government for decades tolerated the presence of nuclear-armed U.S. warships in its waters.

10. The *sōkaiya*—the "professional shareholder"—began as a simple extortion racket. Gangsters would buy a few shares in a company whose dirty dealings they were familiar with, then attend the meeting to raise embarrassing questions—unless they were paid off first. The scheme was highly successful. But managers at quite a few companies soon found ways to turn *sōkaiya* to good use in suppressing other shareholders. The roll of executives indicted for bribing gangsters is quite impressive. Most recently, top executives of Kirin, Japan's largest brewery, joined the list.

11. This was Hanabusa Midori, now of Bloomberg Business News, one of the brightest, wittiest, and most dedicated young Japanese journalists I know.

12. Clayton F. Naff, "A Japanese Power Broker Washington Might Love," Bloomberg Business News, 16 July 1993.

13. *LTCB Economic Bulletin* (April 1991): 3.

14. Ibid., World Bank and OECD figures.

15. Just to recap: By making women entirely responsible for the household, Japan eventually alienated men from their homes; by bottlenecking the paths to success through a handful of universities, Japan fomented an absurd level of competition in an already rigid school system; and by an exploitative sexism, Japan's companies used women as cheap and disposable labor while binding men to their employers for life or age fifty-five, whichever came first.

16. "Nippon Steel to Cut 7,000 from Payroll," *Nikkei Weekly*, 1 Nov. 1993, 1.

17. See, for example, a column by the astute *Nikkei* editorial writer Masahiko Ishizuka, "Mahathir's Criticism of U.S. Strikes a Chord in Asia," *Nikkei Weekly*, 13 Dec. 1993, 7. Other Japanese editorialists have attempted to frame the argument in terms of language and culture (Anglo vs. Asian), but in view of Asia's staggering diversity of race, religion, and culture, this can only be regarded as racism clothed in a neat suit.

18. Not that anyone wants Japan to be a dictator, or even a strong political leader. But there is a powerful "bloc" mentality taking hold in Asia, partly in response to perceptions of European and North American moves in the same direction.

19. These were precisely the "non-Western ethics" championed by Third World dictators and Asian oligarchies at the 1993 United Nations Conference on Human Rights in Vienna.

20. Rollo May, "The Man Who Was Put in a Cage," *The Conscious Reader*, 4th ed., eds. Caroline Shrodes, Harry Finestone, and Michael Shugrue (New York: Macmillan, 1985), 1042.

INDEX

Abe, Shintaro, 117
abortion, 83, 234
academia, 285–86
activism, 84–85
aerobics, 223
affluence, 29, 176, 239, 258, 300
aging of population, 152–53, 234–37, 239–42; government policy, 245–48, 269–70, 278–81; *see also* elderly
AIDS, 234
Ainu, 14
air conditioners, 176
aircraft carriers, 109
alcohol, 173, 176, 183–84, 189–90, 222
alcoholism, 88, 195–99
All Japan High School Baseball League, 211
All Japan Hula Association, 222
Alzheimer's disease, 279
amae ("dependence"), 184–85, 205
amakudari ("descent from heaven"), 268
Amaterasu, 46
American Banker, 105, 120
American lifestyles, 33, 238
amusement parks, 139–40, 147, 202
angling, 223
antibiotics, 253
anti-Semitism, 289
antisocial behavior, 224
Apple Corporation, 290

Ara, Kazuo, 314
Army, Imperial, 120, 293–94
artisans, 45
arubaito ("guest workers"), 163
Asahi News Service, 91
Asahi Shimbun, 30, 59, 86, 127, 295
asceticism, 223
Asia, 7, 19, 21, 165, 202, 305–307, 331, 332
assembly-line workers, 114, 135
Associated Press, 160, 164, 242–43
Atoh, Makoto, 236–37
Austen, Jane, 144
automobile industry, 292
automobiles, 103, 158, 176, 249

Bacon, Alice, 52
Bank of Japan, 224, 300
bankers, 78, 134
Bankhart, Brenda, 97
bankruptcy: company, 293; personal, 223
banks, 114–15, 150, 314
bars, 258; *see also* Ginza bars
baseball, 210–11, 225–28, 324
basketball, 227–28
baths, 54, 82, 170, 193
beer, 25, 195
belly talk. *See haragei.*
birth control, 83, 324
birthrate, 83, 97, 145, 234–35, 237, 239–40

Black Ships, 14–15, 288, 290
Blinder, Alan, 112
Bloomberg Business News, 138–39, 316
"bodi-con girls," 93, 223
Book of Five Rings, 122–23
Botchan, 186–87
bōsōzoku ("wild tribes"), 222
Brazil, 94, 175
breweries, 25
bribery scandals, 31–32, 123, 137, 288
brides, 73–75, 90
Britain, 46, 150, 235, 247, 255
Brother Industries, 144
brothers, role of, 51
Buddhism: alcohol, 189; in first constitution, 12; funerals, 276–277; New Year's
   festival, 4; posthumous naming ceremony, 287; and World War II, 19–20
bureaucrats: and closed bidding system,
   123; development of system, 14–15; hierarchy and, 150; motives in recession,
   300–302; work hours of, 212–13
burikko, 144, 211
Buruma, Ian, 183
Bush, George, 292–93
business cards, 207
Business Week, 7, 112
Butts, David, 138–39, 161

cabdrivers, 145, 268
Cambodia, 161
Canada, 30, 255
cancer, 110, 255, 257–62, 328
cartoons, 59, 65, 221
Catledge, Turner, 108
celebrities, 73
censorship, 220
Chicago Bulls, 227
chichi naki shakai ("fatherless society"),
   58
childbirth, 65–66, 149, 231–34, 324
children: atomic bomb and, 20; competition for schools and, 30, 41, 58, 86–90;
   divorce and, 57; drugs and, 219; exposure
   to pornography, 220–22; feelings toward
   fathers, 64–65; foreign, 286; love and, 40;
   mothers' role in raising, 86–90, 157; role
   in family, 51–52; teaching saving to, 224
Chile, 30
China, 6, 19, 305–306

chōkai ("neighborhood governing associations"), 53, 84
Christianity, 54
Christians, 13, 55, 73
Christmas, 10
cigarettes. *See* smoking.
"Cinderella surgery," 93
class, 45; in Meiji Restoration, 46–47
clients, 182–83
Clinton, Bill, 293, 298
closed bidding system, 123
CNN, 139, 162
Cole, Robert, 152
Coleman, Samuel, 54
college. *See* educational system.
Collins, Robert, 183
comfort women, 19
comic books, 220
communism: U.S. fears of, 18, 132, 315;
   women and, 84
companies: business culture, 176; family
   metaphor of, 112–13; government protection of, 19; hiring of midcareer men,
   68; investment in American properties,
   26–27; labor relations and, 132–35,
   165–66; leisure time and, 205–207; lifetime employment and, 150–53; paternalism, 126, 207; profits, 299–300; public
   opinion toward, 30; retirement policy of,
   266–70; small, 134, 151, 293; socializing
   in, 183–84; vacation policy of, 212;
   women in, 145–46; *yarikata*, 123–24
company songs, 206
company sports teams, 178
company trips, 172, 176, 188–89,194, 206–
   207, 319
computer industry, 290
condoms, 234, 324
conformism, 11–12
Confucianism, 88, 123; constitution, 12;
   notions of family, 41, 52
constitution: and Gulf war, 92; human
   rights and, 294; *ie* in, 47, 53; sovereignty,
   306; *wa* and, 12; women and, 143, 146
construction, 182
consumer groups, 84, 224
consumerism, 223–24
consumers, 91, 165, 224, 299; as constituency, 301
contraception. *See* birth control.

contracts, 153
cosmetic surgery, 93
counseling, 59
courts, 158–60, 164
cram schools, 30, 88–89, 325
credit cards, 223
Crichton, Michael, 293
crime rates, 236, 295
culture, 123–25, 133, 135, 267; respect for elderly, 279–80
cycling, 222–23
Czechoslovakia, 30

daimyō, 45
dance, 223
daughters, role of, 51
daughters-in-law, 51–53, 142, 273
day care, 59, 286
de Mente, Boye Lafayette, 11, 309
dead-cat bounce, 325
death, 260–61, 264, 270–73, 275, 286, 328
Death File, 222
Defense Academy, 145
defense spending, 235
democracy, 304–308; economic, 132; during Occupation, 18–19, 305; during Taisho crisis, 16, 293
department stores, 224
deregulation, 302
descent from heaven. See amakudari.
dialysis, 255
diet, 239, 260, 328
DINK lifestyle, 97
discipline, 88
discos, 93, 194
discount stores, 224
Disneyland (Tokyo), 28, 33, 208, 237
division of labor, 83
divorce, 52, 57, 64, 89–90
doctors, 83, 232, 236, 251–53, 257–58, 327
Doi, Takako, 91–92
Doi, Takeo, 184–85, 205, 314
Drug Abuse Prevention Center, 219
drugs, 202; illegal, 218–19, 295; prescription, 252–53, 255
Dutch, 13

earthquakes, 309
economic democracy. See democracy.

economic development. See industrialization.
economic miracle, 122–23, 235
Economist, 91
Edmonton, Canada, 147
Edo, 9, 14, 24, 54, 174–75, 223
educational system, 15, 20, 41, 80, 85–89, 241, 286, 325; colleges, 88, 95–96
Education Ministry, 19, 80, 87–88, 107, 286
elder statesmen. See genrō.
elderly: benefits, 234–35, 245–48; as constituency, 301; family care of, 241–42, 273–75, 279; health care of, 251–56, 273, 275–79, 327; percentage of population, 235, 324; respect for, 279–80; in workforce, 268–69; and yakuza, 295; see also aging of population
elections, 91, 160, 280
Elvis impersonators, 222
endaka, 299
Endo, Shusaku, 262
English language, 89
enryo (self-restraint), 196
entrance exams, 20, 85, 96, 325
equal opportunity law, 145–46
erotic art, 221
exchange rates, 21, 43, 161, 211, 224, 299
expense accounts, 182, 184, 320

factory work, 142
Fallows, James, 309
family: budgeting, 84; care of elderly, 273–74; changes in, 30, 58, 100; love in, 39–40; in Meiji Restoration, 46–47, 51–53; in militarist period, 53; policy toward, 83–84; in Tokugawa period, 41, 311
farmers, 18, 29, 45, 174, 301
fascism, 16; see also neofascism
fatherhood: "fatherless society," 58; during Meiji Restoration, 86; family's negative views of, 63–66; in nurseries, 297
feasts, 75–76
feminism, 16, 84, 91, 93
festivals, 174
feudalism, 41, 45, 113
Fields, George, 321
Finance Ministry, 247
"Floating World," 174–75
food, 82, 191; prices of, 24
footwear, 190

Foreign Ministry, 92, 119–20
Foreign Correspondents' Club, 97, 119, 131
foreigners, 7, 23, 44, 208, 289–90; 301, 330;
    children of, 286, 297; employment, 116–
    17, 156; and marriage, 99; relations with
    Japanese women, 214; during Tokugawa
    period, 13
France, 247, 260
freedom, 185, 305, 307
friendship, 124
fujinkai (housewives' associations), 84–85
Fujita, Mariko, 86
Fukoku Life Insurance Company, 115
Fukui, Atsushi, 99
Fukutake, Tadashi, 41, 46–47
funerals, 51, 64, 276–78, 286
Fuyo, 22–23

gambling, 208
gangsters. See yakuza.
Genroku Age, 175
genrō ("elder statesmen"), 16
Germany, 163, 247, 255
Gin-san, 240
Ginza bars, 182–83
giri man, 54
Golden Plan, 247, 279
Golden Week, 176
golf, 176, 182, 202, 223, 228
Gorbachev, Mikhail, 285
government: and aging population, 245–48,
    269–70, 278–81; change in, 32; and fam-
    ily policy, 57–58; Meiji Restoration, 41,
    46–47; policy on work hours, 151; policy
    toward marriage, 98; promotion of
    amusement industry, 139–40; promotion
    of leisure, 202; and sexual harassment
    suits, 158
grandmothers, 241–42
grassroots movements, 294–96, 306
Greater Asian Coprosperity Sphere, 307
Greenpeace, 126–27
grooms, 75, 91
ground-breaking ceremony, 189
. Guam, 213
Gyoba, Yukiko, 210–11

haircuts, 288
Hakodate, 15

Hakuhodo Institute of Life and Living,
    175, 206
handicapped, 245, 248
haragei ("belly talk"), 141
harmony. See wa.
Harvard Community Health Plan, 254
Hayashi, Razan, 45
headhunters, 140, 163
health drinks, 202
health-care system, 159, 199, 252, 254–
    256; and elections, 280; see also doctors,
    government, nurses
Hearn, Lafcadio, 40
help-wanted ads, 143
Hibiya Park, 125
Hideyoshi, 12
hierarchy, 124, 133, 151
Higashi Fuchu Byoin, 232
Higuchi, Keiko, 59, 64
Hirano, Takashi, 164
Hirohito, Emperor, 20, 127–28, 316
Hiroshima, 20
hiroen, ("announcement feasts"), 75–76
historians, 289
Hitachi Corporation, 159
Holstein, William J., 7
Honda Motor Company, 164–65
honeymoons, 90
Hong Kong, 6
Hosokawa, Morihiro, 21, 96, 297–99
hospitals, 232–33, 236, 248–49, 251, 253,
    275–76
hotels, 73–74, 181, 188, 190
housekeeping, 59, 100, 146
housewives, 11, 58, 63, 84–85
housing prices, 22–23, 66, 241, 299
hula hoop, 222
human rights, 164, 294, 306–307
human capitalism, 150
Hunter, Janet, 47
husbands: divorce after death, 64; infidel-
    ity, 56; in Meiji Restoration, 52–53,
    56
hygiene, 239
Hyogo Prefecture, 202

identity, 33, 99–100, 112, 177, 228
ideology, 86, 289, 293
ie ("household"), 58, 112; in Meiji Restora-
    tion, 46–47, 51; nostalgia for, 59; during

Occupation, 53; in Tokugawa period, 311
Ieyasu, 14
Iki, Tsuneaki, 90
Imamura, Anne, 84
immersion tanks, 201
immunizations, 245
Imperial Army. *See* Army, Imperial.
Imperial Household Agency, 138
Imperial Palace, 125
Imperial Rescript on Education, 16
India, 94
individualism, 33, 53, 98, 207–208
industrialization, 18, 21, 41, 124
infant mortality rate, 232, 239, 255, 324
infanticide. *See mabiki.*
infidelity, 54–56, 89, 176
inheritance, 47, 53
Institute of Public Health, 115
insurers, 252, 275
International Whaling Convention, 126
introductions, 62–63
investments, 27, 165, 300
Ishihara, Shintaro, 213–14, 314
Itami, Jyuzo, 295
Ito, Hirobumi, 322
Iwao, Sumiko, 160
Izu Peninsula, 170

Japan Institute for Social and Economic Affairs, 312
Japan Labor Bulletin, 269
Japan National Tourist Organization, 90
Japan New Party, 297–98
Japan Railways, 164
Japan's New Middle Class, 53–54
Japan's Secret Weapon: The Kata Factor, 11
Japan That Can Say No, The, 213, 314
Japan Times, 103–104, 116, 118–20, 127–28, 136–37, 153, 155–156, 160, 197, 213–14, 316
Japan Tobacco, 259
Japan Women's University, 81, 291
Japan-bashing, 214, 293
Japanese language, 33, 43, 82, 84, 107, 124, 219–20, 320
jet skiing, 222
job-hopping, 163–64, 263
Jordan, Michael, 227
journalists, 6; Western, 112

kabuki, 39–40, 174, 223
Kabuki-cho, 208
Kaibara, Ekken, 142
Kaifu, Toshiki, 92
kaisha ningen ("company men"), 83
Kamata, Satoshi, 135
kamikaze, 15
Kanemaru, Shin, 32, 123, 137–38, 288
Kanematsu Corporation, 159
kankeisha ("connected people"), 104
kanri yakyū. *See* baseball.
karaoke, 184, 191, 320
karōshi ("death by overwork"), 147, 150
Kashima, 226
kata. *See yarikata*.
kata-tataki ("shoulder tapping"), 152
Katayama government, 305
katei-nai-rikon, ("divorce within household"), 57
Kawabata, Yasunari, 61
Kawasaki, Ichiro, 124
Keio University, 207
keiretsu corporate groups, 268
kendō ("fencing"), 122, 225
ki ("spirit"), 261
Kikuchi, Kiyomi, 158–59
Kim Il Sung, 137
Kimura, Yui, 294–95
Kin-san, 240
Kirin, 331
kisha clubs, 137–39
kissing, 222, 323
Kitakyushu, 139
Kobe beef, 62
Koito Corporation, 268
Komei party, 92
Kono, Hiroaki, 184
Konoe, Fumimaro, 21
Koreans, 96, 120
Kosai Care Center, 274
Kublai Khan, 15
Kubota, Kyoto, 88
Kumagai, Naohiko, 164–65
Kumamoto province, 96, 297
Kyoto, 4–5
kyōiku mama ("education mother"), 85–89
Kyushu, 13, 150

L. L. Bean, 224
labor law, 143, 145

Labor Ministry, 115, 146, 163
labor movement. *See* unions.
labor shortage, 6, 89, 114, 142, 145, 149, 159, 269
Labor Standards Law, 143
land sharks, 29
Law for the Development of Comprehensive Resort Areas, 202
lawyers, 145, 295–96
layoffs, 152, 293, 303
Lazarus, David, 321
leisure, 176–77; of elderly, 269–70; government promotion of, 140–41; and women, 84; work hours, 113; and young people, 207
Leisure Development Center, 184, 207
Liberal Democratic Party (LDP), 19, 21, 91–92, 123, 133, 137–38, 298
life expectancy, 239–40, 255, 260
lifetime employment, 116, 126, 134, 152, 156, 165, 267
liquor stores, 25
Little League, 210–11
Lo, Jeannie, 144
local organizations, 84
Los Angeles Times, 184, 223
love, 39–40, 57
love match. *See* ren'ai.

mabiki ("infanticide"), 51
MacArthur, Douglas, 18, 53, 131–32
madogiwa zoku ("windowside tribe"), 107, 135
Maeda, Daisaku, 247–48, 273
Mainichi newspaper, 127, 222
makeup, 222
Malaysia, 306
Management and Coordination Period, 312
management system, 133–34, 150–51, 153
managerial positions, women in, 146
managers, 114, 132
Mandela, Nelson, 155
manufacturing sector, 114, 159, 278
marriage, 37, 39, 238, 330; infidelity, 54–57; and love, 39–41; women and, 51, 90, 142, 241
Maruyama, Makoto, 112
Matsumoto, 218–19

Matsushita Electric Corporation, 206, 299–300
May, Rollo, 307
May Day, 125
MCA, 299
McCormack, Gavan, 201
media, 93
medical schools, 255
Meiji, 15–16
Meiji Restoration, 15–16, 41, 46, 51–52, 55, 72
meishi. *See* business cards.
men: avoidance of home, 66; leisure of, 178; life expectancy, 260; relations with mother, 56–57; and sex, 54–55; single, 163; and smoking, 258; and women's freedom, 91; *see also* husbands, fatherhood, salarymen
menstruation, 143, 324
mental health, 158
merchants, 24, 29, 45, 174–75, 301
Metropolitan Labor Standards Bureau, 134
Mexico, 30
Mickey Mouse, 28, 33
Midori, 177
Mieno, Yasushi, 300
mikudarihan (divorce custom), 52
militarism, 131
militarist era, 16–17, 125, 293–94; family in, 53, 55; "us-against-them" ideology, 289
military: creation of, 15–16, 46; in Meiji Restoration, 47; Occupation era, 18; Persian Gulf war, 92
Ministry of Health and Welfare, 89, 97, 195, 213, 234, 236, 247, 255, 260, 279, 286, 321
Ministry of International Trade and Industry, 19, 280
Ministry of Labor, 113
missionaries, 13, 55
Mitford, Algernon, 196–97
Mitsubishi Bank, 114
Mitsubishi Corporation, 164
Mitsui & Company, 164
Miyamoto, Masao, 212–13
Miyamoto Musashi, 122–23
Miyazawa, Kiichi, 292
Mohamed, Mahathir, 306

moral relativism, 219, 221
motherhood, 96, 100; ideology, 86; relation to sons, 56–57; see also kyōku mama, women
mothers-in-law, 51–53
Motoshima, Hitoshi, 20
Mount Fuji, 190
mountain climbing, 222
movie industry, 29, 295–96
mura, 46; see also village
Muramatsu, Yasuko, 88
music: classical, 177; traditional, 223
Muto, Ichiyo, 133
Mutsuhito. See Meiji, Emperor.

Nagasaki, 13, 20
Nagoya, 144, 240
Nakasone, Yasuhiro, 290
nakodo, ("marriage go-betweens"), 76, 312
narikin ("newly rich"), 29
"Narita divorce," 90
Naruhito, Prince, 138
National Cancer Center, 261
National Institute on Alcoholism, 184
nationalism, 15–16, 124–25
National Public Radio, 206, 236
National Sports Day, 321
National Tax Administration, 320
national teachers' union, 80
Natsume, Soseki, 186, 204, 322
Nazi racial theories, 289
NEC, 112, 290
neighborhood control groups, 293
neighborhood governing associations. See chōkai.
neofascism, 306–307; see also fascism
New Year's festival, 3–5, 28, 237, 309
New York, 214
New York Times, 5, 151
newspapers, 30, 107, 119–20, 127, 136–37, 289, 319
NHK, 27, 237
Nigeria, 30
Nihon-bashi, 17
nihon-jin-ron ("theory of the Japanese people"), 12, 289–90
Nihon Keizai Shimbun, 199
Nikkei Weekly, 165, 178, 268
Nippon Steel, 139–40, 147, 163, 303

Noh plays, 174
nomiya ("drinking house"), 184
North Korea, 137–38, 305
nuclear power, 85, 294–96
nuclear weapons, 330–31
nurses, 247, 254, 279
nursing homes, 236, 247, 274–76

O.L.'s. See office ladies.
o-miai ("formal introduction"), 40
obligation, 40
Occupation, 18–19, 33, 53, 84, 131–32, 143, 305; and redistribution of land, 47
office ladies, 74, 93, 143, 159, 317
Ohmae, Kenichi, 6
Okamoto, Ayako, 211
Okifuji, Noriko, 242
Okochi, Kazuo, 125
Okuma Corporation, 329
Olympic Games, 19, 94, 122
Omiya, 297
Organization for Economic Cooperation and Development, 236, 246
Osaka, 175, 202
Oshima Island, 171
outreach offices, 247
overpopulation, 83, 241
overtime, 114–15, 134
overwork, 201–202, 316
Owada, Masako, 138
oyaji gal, 211
Oyakusho no okite, 213
Ozaki, "Jumbo," 211
Ozaki, Robert, 150
Ozawa, Seiji, 177

pachinko, 208
pacifism, 85, 92
parent-teacher associations, 84
part-timers, 115
patriotism, 30
Peace Park, 20
Peace Preservation Law, 53
Pearl Harbor, 5, 19
pension benefits, 234–35, 245–46, 269–70, 280, 326
Perry, Matthew, 14, 21, 41, 288
Persian Gulf war, 92, 161, 292
personality, 99

pharmaceutical industry, 202
Philosophy of Honest Poverty, The, 223
Pickens, T. Boone, 268
Pioneer Electric Corporation, 152
Plaza Accord, 21
Poland, 30
police, 124, 220, 293, 295
political parties, 301
politics, 18, 91, 93, 301; and elderly, 280–81; press coverage of, 137–38; scandals in, 31–32; women in, 91–93, 143, 301; *yakuza* involvement in, 295
poor, 245
popular culture, 88, 301
population pyramid. *See* aging of population.
populism, 7
pornography, 55, 219–22
Portuguese, 13
"posh boys," 223
press clubs. *See kisha* clubs.
Prestowitz, Clyde, 309
price-fixing cartels, 123
private schools, 88; *see also* educational system
productivity. *See* work hours.
promotion, 68, 164–65, 183
prosperity. *See* affluence.
prostitution, 51, 54, 202
Public Order Police Law, 125
public transportation system, 248
punk rock, 177
purchasing power, 113

racism, 289–90, 301, 306–307, 331
rakugo ("storytelling"), 210
Reagan administration, 21
recession, 146, 151–52, 158–59, 164, 183, 223–24, 270, 293, 300–301
Redesdale, Lord. *See* Mitford, Algernon.
Reid, T. R., 138, 309
ren'ai, 73, 312
resorts, 202
restaurants, 182–83, 258
restructuring, 139, 150, 153
retirement, 237, 245–46, 266–70, 273
Reuters, 139
Revolt of a Man Who Was Killing Time by the Window, The, 316
Rhea, Joe, 177

ringi, 136
riots, 125
Rising Sun, 292
rote learning, 123
rotenburo ("volcanic baths"), 170, 180
rural areas, 55
Russia, 14, 16, 306
ryosai kenbo ("good wife, wise mother"), 52–53
Ryukyu kimgdom, 14

sake, 72, 189, 195
salarymen, 104, 144; change in culture of, 162–66; drinking culture of, 197–99, 204; leisure of, 176, 182–85; relations with family, 63–66; *tanshin funin,* 46, 66; women as, 146–47; work hours of, 114
salt, 328
samurai, 14, 45–46, 174–75, 196
Sano, Yoko, 207
Sanpo (Patriotic Industrial Association), 125
Sanryū temple, 4
Sansom, G. B., 174–75
Sanyo Electric, 153
satori, 27
savings, 224, 246, 270; household, 84
"Sazae-san," 59
scholars, 7
school system. *See* educational system.
sei-sha-in. See lifetime employees.
Sekiguchi, Reiko, 98–99
Sekizawa, Hidehiko, 175
sekuhara. See sexual harassment.
seniority, 126, 153, 270
senpūki (electric fan), 176
sentakki (washing machine), 176
service industries, 139, 159
settai (client entertainment), 182–83
sex, 54–55, 213–15, 221
sex industry, 55, 208–209
sex objects, 93
sex tours, 202
sexual harassment, 144–45, 158–59
shabu shabu, 62
Shakespeare, William, 312
Shapiro, Michael, 40
shareholders, 112, 165, 294–95, 300, 331
shigo rikon ("divorce after death"), 64
Shimada, Haruo, 165

Shimoda, 15
shinjinrui ("new species"), 95
Shinjuku district, 208
Shintoism, 4, 16, 72, 75
shogun, 12–15, 45
shopkeepers. *See* merchants.
Shotoku, Prince, 12
shōtengai, 23–26
sick days, 134
Silk River, 302
Silver Colonies program, 280
Singapore, 306
smoking, 258–60, 328
soccer, 226–27
social security, 161, 234–35, 245–47, 269
social workers, 245
socialism, 16
Socialist party, 92, 137–38, 145, 305
songenshi. *See* death.
sons, 47, 51–53
South Korea, 30
Soviet Union, 132
Space World, 139, 147, 202
Spain, 30
speculators, 26, 29
sports, 225–28
steel industry, 139
stock market, 242–43; crash, 32
Storry, Richard, 175
stress, 87, 115, 201; in women, 158
strikes, 125, 132, 134, 254, 316
suihanki ("rice cooker"), 176
Sumitomo Life Insurance Company, 159
sumo, 225, 228
support groups, 164
Supreme Court, 145
Sweden, 90, 235, 255, 260

taiko drums, 174
Taira, Koji, 125
Taisho Democracy, 16
Taisho Political Crisis, 293
Taiwan, 6
Takahashi, Tom, 17–18
Takeshita government, 247
Tanabe, Makoto, 137
tanshin funin, 66, 163–64
tax, 302; cigarette, 259; sales, 91, 247, 280–81
teachers, 30, 254

telephone cards, 240
television, 29–30, 59, 65, 73, 88, 155, 176, 214, 259
temples, 4, 28
Tetsuji Sagawa, 164
textile mills, 142–43
theory of the Japanese people. *See nihon-jin-ron*.
Thorson, Larry, 160
Time, 122
tipping, 187
Tokugawas, 12–15, 45–46, 174, 311
Tokyo, 14, 22, 196; description of, 8–10, 17; earthquakes, 309; marriage statistics, 90; Olympics, 19, 94, 122; riots in, 125; sex industry in, 208; smoking bans in, 258
Tokyo Chamber of Commerce, 152
Tokyo Electric Power Company, 294–95
Tokyo Lawyers Association, 164
Tokyo Rose, 119
toshi-koshi-soba, 309
tourism, 4, 211
Toyota, 135, 165, 268
trade: complaints, 315; exports, 21; friction, 7, 139–140, 330; imports, 224, 302; negotiations, 21–22, 123, 224; surplus, 280; in Tokugawa era, 13–15; *see also* United States
tradition, 30, 47
training, 117, 123
traveling, 269
tsukiai ("socializing with bosses"), 182–84
Tsunoda, Yukiko, 57
tsunokakushi, 75
Tsutsui, Yasutaka, 85
tuberculosis, 143, 255

uchi ("inside"), 124
Ueno Park, 17, 125
ultraright, 295
Umigahara, 178, 180
U.N. Decade of the Woman, 145
unemployment, 146
unions: during Occupation, 131–32; in Taisho democracy, 16, 125–126; weakness of, 132–34, 151, 153, 316; and women, 160
United Press International, 138, 161
United States, 6, 165; aging of population, 235–36; as ally, 92, 305; health care in,

United States (cont'd)
251, 255, 275–76; introduction of trade
with Japan, 14–15; Japan-bashing, 293;
Occupation, 18–19, 33, 53, 84, 131–32,
143, 305; patriotism, 30; products,
21–22; social security, 247; strikes, 134;
support of Liberal Democratic Party, 133;
trade complaint settlement, 315; trade
frictions, 139, 290; work hours, 114,
122–23; World War II, 19
universities. See educational system.
University of Tokyo, 95
Uno, Sousuke, 91, 99, 117
urbanization, 241
Ushiba, Yasuhiko, 316

vacation, 113, 134, 136, 212, 319
van Wolferen, Karel, 5, 309
Varcoe, Fred, 227
vending machines, 173, 320
videos, 220–21
Vietnam, 306
villages, 30
Vogel, Ezra, 53–54, 56
Vonnegut, Kurt, 99
voting rights, 16

wa ("harmony"), 12, 19, 24, 124, 295
wagamama ("selfishness"), 212
wage discrimination, 159
wages, 91, 126, 134–35, 142, 152–53, 267,
270; of women, 316
Wall Street Journal, 6
Washington Post, 6, 33, 112, 138, 162
We magazine, 79–81
wealth. See affluence.
wealth indicators, 114
weddings, 72–78, 98, 312, 313
weight training, 223
whaling, 126–27
wife battering, 57
wives, 31, 52–53, 64, 184; see also
housewives
women: activism, 84, 91–93; and alcohol,
88, 196, 222; and childrearing, 58–59; as
constituency, 301; in creative arts, 177;
dissatisfaction with jobs, 317; effect on

salaryman culture, 162–63; family role
of, 51–54; and feudalism, 41; leisure activities, 210–12; life expectancy of, 260,
273–274; and marriage, 89–91, 96–100;
size of family, 241, 325; and smoking,
259; stress, 157–58; travel, 211–12; wages
of, 159, 316; and work, 142–47, 242, 312;
yellow cabs, 213–215; see also motherhood, sexual harassment, wives
women's groups, 145
women's rights. See feminism.
work hours, 113–15, 134, 148, 151, 164,
201, 212
workforce. See labor shortage, layoffs, recession.
World Health Organization, 258
World War II, 5, 19–21, 92, 120

yakuza ("gangsters"), 14, 29, 32, 137, 197,
208–209, 295–96, 331
Yamada, Takaharu, 153
Yamaguchi, Takehiko, 183
Yamanote Line, 104–105
Yamashita, Etsuko, 57
Yamashita, Koji, 222
Yanagawa, Keiichi, 189
yarikata ("way of doing"), 11, 124
Yedo. See Edo.
Yellow Cab rumor, 213–15
yen. See exchange rates.
Yokohama, 213
yome, 51
Yomiuri Hochi, 132
Yomiuri Shimbun, 27, 58, 127
Yoshida, Shigeru, 132, 305
Yoshino, Kosaku, 289
young people, 25, 31, 33; and antisocial be-
havior, 224; attitudes toward family and
marriage, 78, 89–91, 96–97; Disneyland
and, 28–29; drinking culture of, 199; leisure interests, 205–207, 228; and pornography, 220–21; work and, 152, 154, 163,
165
yoma, 49

Za Shocks!, 221
Zimmerman, Bill, 120